Legal and Legislative INFORMATION PROCESSING

Legal and Legislative INFORMATION PROCESSING

edited by
Beth Krevitt Eres

GREENWOOD
PRESS
Westport, Connecticut • London, England

Library of Congress Cataloging in Publication Data
Main entry under title:

Legal and legislative information processing.

Includes bibliographical references and index.
1. Legislation—United States—Data processing—Addresses, essays, lectures. 2. Legal research—United States—Data processing—Addresses, essays, lectures. 3. Information storage and retrieval systems—Law—United States—Addresses, essays, lectures. 4. Information storage and retrieval systems—Court administration—United States—Addresses, essays, lectures. I. Eres, Beth Krevitt.
KF242.A1L37 340'.028'5 79-7063
ISBN 0-313-21343-7 lib. bdg.

Library of Congress Catalog Card Number: 79-7063
ISBN: 0-313-21343-7

First published in 1980

Greenwood Press
A division of Congressional Information Service, Inc.
88 Post Road West, Westport, Connecticut 06881

Printed in the United States of America

10 9 8 7 6 5 4 3 2 1

This book is dedicated to
the memory of my father, Irving A. Krevitt,
a man of goodness, love, and pride

Contents

Illustrations

Tables

Preface

The field of textual information processing has exploded in the 1970s as a result of the overwhelming flow of paper information and the increased sophistication of and economies of scale for online computer storage and retrieval network capabilities. Not the least affected by these dramatic developments has been the legal profession. Both lawyers and legislators have been confronted with the need to keep abreast of current events, with the depth of research required to acquire comprehensive topic- or case-related knowledge, with the amount of text processing (such as indexing and editing) necessary to access available information, and, finally, with the speed in which the work must be done.

Concurrently the computer profession has developed the ability to provide online access to millions of bytes of information via international communications networks. The more effective indexing and greater manipulation of natural language text resulting from research conducted in the 1960s has extended these networks to the textual and bibliographic information-processing field. The needs of the legal profession and computer and information-processing abilities combined has resulted in the emergence of legal and legislative computer information processing. In some areas, the effect has been that a greater quantity of work can be done and at greater speeds. In all areas, the qualitative results have been impressive.

This book presents a broad picture of existing and future endeavors. It has been designed to appeal to a wide audience of readers—among them, practicing lawyers, legislators, librarians, information specialists, and computer scientists. Accordingly the contributors to the book were chosen to represent a broad spectrum of professionals, each viewing the field from his or her own vantage point.

Each of the five parts of the book are introduced with a headnote that briefly describes the material to be found in the chapters therein. The chapter authors have provided a brief history of the topic of their chapter, described current activities and procedures, discussed future possibilities, and drawn conclusions, along with appropriate references.

This book is not intended to be an exhaustive treatment of this expanding field; it could not be. Readers interested in particular areas are urged to delve into the references listed in each chapter for further information.

Acknowledgments

My greatest debt is to the twenty-six men and women who unsparingly contributed their time and expertise in order to produce the chapters for this book. I greatly appreciate their assistance in reviewing the initial outline, contacting other potential contributors, and providing general moral support. Particular thanks go to Robert L. Chartrand for his willingness to undertake a second, and most difficult, chapter (with Jane Bortnick), and to Lawrence H. Berul, whose guidance to me many years ago was so important. I am also indebted to Charles H. Davis for his teaching efforts in my graduate school years as well as for his personal recommendation to Greenwood Press. I am grateful to those who have helped me in many technical and editorial matters, particularly Phyllis Safer.

To my husband, Michael, who overwhelmingly gave his time, advice, and support so that I could accomplish each requisite task, I can never fully express my gratitude. To my father, Irving Krevitt, in whose memory this book is dedicated, there is no longer anything that can be said. Knowing how proud he would have been is enough.

Part I

FEDERAL LEGISLATIVE INFORMATION PROCESSING

Each of the three chapters in this part presents both general and specific discussions of the history, needs, current status, and future plans of the U.S. Congress with regard to information technology. Congress's relationship to supportive information agencies (such as the Congressional Research Service, Government Accounting Office, Office of Technology Assessment and Congressional Budget Office) is presented by Bruce Norton and Robert Chartrand along with their observations regarding the use of other federal government and nongovernment data bases and information retrieval systems. Norton shows that relations between the Congress and the executive branch have altered, and continue to do so, as a result of Congress's increased use of information technology. Chartrand further cites the subtle changes that have taken place within Congress itself as a result of the introduction of new methods of voting, determining bill status, analyzing fiscal matters, and so on.

Neal Gregory enumerates the similarities and differences between the two houses with regard to history, committee activities, budget, size, and seniority. The chapters also stress the manifold character of congressmen as legislators, representatives of their constituency, party members, and overseers of government policy.

Norton describes how the distribution of influence is affected as new members of Congress arrive and are immediately afforded access to information with the aid of the computer to the same extent as more senior members.

According to Gregory, it is often these same new members who are introducing the information technology acumen they have acquired in business and academia.

The chapters conclude by envisaging the future of the Congress as one of greater centralization, improved quality of legislation, broader focus on long-range problems, and more sophisticated use of audiovisual computer-related communications systems.

1

BRUCE F. NORTON

The Quiet Revolution of Information Technology in Congress

Several revolutions were staged on Capitol Hill in the 1970s. Some produced reforms dealing with Congress's internal operations, and others, with bolstering its position vis-à-vis the executive. But just as noteworthy, and certainly just as significant, was a quieter revolution that ushered in the development of a sophisticated information-support capability that has become the envy of nearly every other legislature in the world.

Although it is a genre of reform not commonly referred to in discussions about strengthening Congress, the introduction of information technology on Capitol Hill signals new directions in the legislature that have the potential of producing as profound an effect on the way it goes about its business as reforms intended to improve its internal organization or enhancing its powers vis-à-vis the executive. In fact, the objectives of reform represented in these latter, more publicized reform efforts ultimately required Congress to come to grips with the frustrations of dealing with an inferior information capability. Had it ignored the many benefits that can flow from an advanced information-support system, it would have neglected one of the means by which it could revitalize and maintain itself as a legislative institution.

The fundamental premise thus is that Congress needs information, so that it can act as an effective decision-making body of government. This does not mean, however, that it should or can duplicate the vast reservoirs of data held by the executive branch. Nor does Congress's possession of an adequate supply of information guarantee that it will produce rational decisions, for rationality lies in the eye of the beholder. Moreover, some legislators ignore the facts on some issues. The second premise is that information used in the political arena is rarely neutral. Whether information is of a policy substance or a political nature, advantages can be derived from misinterpreting it, distorting it, or ignoring it. The likelihood that information will occasionally be misused, however, should not be construed as an argument against yet a third premise: the Congress requires information that is objective, accurate, comprehensive, timely, and relevant. How legislators act on information makes the Congress a political institution, but how they use it does not detract from the imperative that it be useful.

Before exploring the strides that have been made in the wake of the quiet revolution of information technology on Capitol Hill, it is useful to ponder Congress's information problems from two perspectives—the constitutional and the institutional—and then to examine the development of an information-support infrastructure in the Congress. Both areas of inquiry will help put Congress's gains in information technology in the proper context.

Information Problems: Constitutional and Institutional

From one perspective, Congress's information problems are not unlike those of almost any other institution. But complicating the ordinary problems it experiences are a host of additional ones that are peculiar to it from both a constitutional and an institutional standpoint.

Constitutional Problems

Although the founders forged a partnership between the Congress and the executive, history shows that this partnership has been an uneasy one. Quite apart from the advantages that accrue from the assignment of different powers to two different branches of government, the principle of separate institutions sharing related functions and responsibilities has produced tension, rivalry, and suspicion between the two federal partners. The result was to create the conditions for what Arthur M. Schlesinger, Jr., has called a "permanent guerrilla warfare" between the two branches.[1] And precipitating some of the warfare has been the refusal by presidents and other major officials in the executive branch to share with Congress information that Congress feels it has a right to possess in order to make informed judgments in fulfilling its lawmaking and oversight responsibilities. The most dramatic and attention-getting instances of the outright denial of information is denial based on the use of executive privilege, a doctrine of constitutional controversy invoked by some presidents who contend that its release would jeopardize national security or in some way detract from the independence and integrity of their office. In fact, however, only a few presidents have resorted to this use and only in the rarest of instances.

A more serious threat to Congress's ability to obtain information from the executive branch has been the withholding of information based on acts of commission and acts of omission. Acts of commission occur when the president or other principal officers in the executive deny requests from congressional committees or individual members of Congress to examine data or review findings of studies relating to Congress's job as a legislative body. In the period from 1964 through 1973, the Senate Judiciary Committee's Subcommittee on Separation of Powers documented more than three hundred instances when the executive employed, in the words of Chairman Sam Ervin, "a full range of devices, subterfuges, preposterous extensions and assumptions of authority, and outright evasiveness . . . to thwart the Congress and its legitimate legislative inquiries."[2]

Perhaps just as serious a threat are acts of omission, whereby the executive fails, wittingly or not, to keep Congress informed of certain developments that are critical to Congress's legislative and oversight responsibilities. Dramatic as they are, occasional clashes between the executive and the Congress resulting from the latter's unmet requests for information represent only a small fraction of Congress's information problems with the executive. The legislature has little or no knowledge of countless numbers of decisions made in the bureaucracy each day. And it has little reason and even less time to question whether certain activities are being carried out or are even being contemplated.

Institutional Problems

Most would agree that the separation-of-powers arrangement makes many of Congress's information problems with the executive inevitable. But whereas information problems of this nature are constitutional, many others that Congress experiences are institutional.

Considering Congress as a whole, a salient characteristic bearing on the legislature's information problems is its bicameral organization and orientation. Going beyond the obvious fact that there are two houses of Congress, it is important to stress that there are two different houses of Congress—different with respect to their size, their organization, the constituents they represent, and, to a degree, the powers they possess. Each house has its own lore and traditions, the members of each house speak sometimes in religious tones of its accomplishments past and present, and there is ample evidence of the cordial disdain that one house has for the other. With this phenomenon of bicameralism triumphant, the only regular formal links between the two houses occur when one reports to the other that it has passed legislation and when there is a conference committee, which brings selected members of the two bodies together, out of necessity, to negotiate the differences in House- and Senate-passed legislation. The only other time when members of the two houses—and, again, selected members—meet is when a state delegation assembles for the purpose of discussing ways of generating support for federal projects in their state. In fact, only rarely do party leaders of the two houses gather to exchange information and ideas or to plot intercameral strategy on legislation.

Each of the two houses is highly decentralized, largely along committee and subcommittee lines. Over time, both houses have divided their labor by committee and, increasingly, by subcommittee. It is at these levels that specialization has developed, fostered in large part by the seniority rule, which encourages committee membership stability. As the complexity of legislation has become more pronounced, members of Congress have come to rely increasingly on the committees and subcommittees to collect and synthesize information of a specialized nature that others in the system have little or no time to obtain on their own. As one member put it once, Congress is "a collection of committees that come together . . . to approve one another's actions."[3]

Although decentralization of the work of Congress offers many advantages, it also poses a few problems, the most profound of which is the artificial fragmentation of large policy problems that occurs when bills are divided up and referred to a variety of committees having the relevant jurisdictions. Because committees generally do not pay much attention to what other units having similar legislative responsibilities are doing, the committee system gives little opportunity to members of Congress to examine the relationship between the essential elements of a large policy question.

An interesting departure from the norm is illustrated in the creation of the Ad Hoc Committee on Energy in 1977. This committee was made up of selected members drawn primarily from the half-dozen standing committees having jurisdiction over various aspects of energy. After President Carter sent his energy package to Congress, the Speaker of the House broke the recommendations down into several parts, referred them to the standing committees with the relevant jurisdictions, and instructed them to report their bills to the Ad Hoc Committee. After receiving all of the bills, the committee studied the recommendations reported and then developed an omnibus bill for consideration by the House. Although the committee could not alter the bills reported by the various standing committees, members of the committee were permitted to offer amendments and even propose a substitute bill after the bill was called up for debate on the floor. Through the mechanism of the Ad Hoc Committee, a large, significant measure was able to receive the benefit of a comprehensive, integrated study, something that probably would not have taken place had the various separate measures been considered in the piecemeal fashion that characterizes the processing of almost all other legislation.

Of approximately twenty-five thousand bills and resolutions introduced each Congress, about 3 percent are enacted. Each bill must proceed through the appropriate committee before reaching the floor. Once the proposed legislation is on the floor, debate is regulated by the rules of the chamber, which do not generally facilitate the full exchange of information and ideas, especially in the House. Three different rules of the House illustrate the restraints imposed on the flow of information. First, debate on amendments is confined to a brief period called *general debate* (usually one hour) when the overall thrust and intent of legislation is discussed. Further restraints are imposed at the next juncture when the bill is read for amendment under the five-minute rule: five minutes are permitted to those favoring and another five minutes to those opposing each amendment offered. The general unavailability of copies of amendments is another restraint on information exchange. Although copies of amendments are required to be circulated on the floor, they are frequently too few in number for general circulation, and they do not give those who read them an opportunity to determine the intent of those who propose them and how the language may relate to and affect other aspects of the legislation. Added to these rules-inspired restraints on information are those imposed by time. Members of Congress have little opportunity to understand the meaning and implications of every amendment introduced on the floor and, for that reason, cues provided by the voting patterns of certain committee members and key party leaders may serve as a substitute for informed judgment on how they should vote.

Infrastructure for Congress's Information Support

All members of Congress require information for every aspect of their job. As representatives, they need information to handle constituent casework, develop newsletters, assist in obtaining federal projects for the district or the state, and give speeches to local organizations. As legislators, they require information dealing with issues before their committees and subcommittees, legislation they would like to propose, the status of legislation, and bills on the floor of the chamber. As overseers, they need information to help in evaluating the management of federal programs, in assessing the impact of these programs, and in judging the economic implications of federal spending.

The traditional solution to members' needs for information has been to press more staff into the struggle. This response has led to rather dramatic increases in the number of staff personnel in the last several years. In 1947, more than two thousand people were employed on the personal staffs of members of Congress. This number jumped to more than five thousand in 1967, and to more than eighty-seven hundred in 1975. An even greater escalation has occurred in the number of staff members employed on the standing committees and subcommittees. In 1947, there were more than four hundred committee and subcommittee staff members—a number that rose to nearly a thousand in 1965 and to more than two thousand in 1975.[4] The total increase in personal and committee and subcommittee staff thus went from twenty-five hundred in 1947 to nearly eleven thousand in 1975 (which excludes the more than twenty thousand employees who in 1975 worked for Congress's four major support agencies: the Library of Congress's Congressional Research Service, the General Accounting Office, the Office of Technology Assessment, and the Congressional Budget Office).

These four agencies reflect still another response to Congress's information needs. Two of them—the Congressional Research Service and the General Accounting Office—were created early in the century. At first, their roles in assisting the Congress with its information needs were narrowly defined. It is only since the Legislative Reorganization Act of 1970 that their responsibilities have been expanded to help Congress cope with the increased complexity of its information needs. The other two agencies are more recent. The Office of Technology Assessment, created in 1972, is mandated to assess the technological implications of certain public policies. The Congressional Budget Office, which came into being after passage of the Congressional Budget and Impoundment Control Act of 1974, has the responsibility of providing information on various aspects of the budget and evaluating the impact of certain programs and the effects of alternative budget decisions on the economy.

The Congressional Research Service (CRS) began in 1914 with a small staff who provided rapid responses to members requiring literary citations and almanac types of queries. It grew to a bustling think tank of more than seven hundred by the mid-1970s. The volume of information and research requests, which ranges across a broad spectrum of topics requiring anywhere from a few minutes to a year to fill, has more than doubled every ten years since the late 1940s. In fiscal year 1947, there were twenty-three requests; in fiscal year 1965, there were a hundred thousand; and in fiscal year 1975, nearly two hundred and fifty thousand. In a recent year, the greatest percentage—86 percent—were initiated by individual members: 58 percent dealt with legislative matters and 28 percent were transmitted to CRS to help members respond to constituent inquiries. The remaining 14 percent were initiated by committees, which have turned increasingly to CRS since 1971 in response to the mandate in the Legislative Reorganization Act of 1970 that CRS give more emphasis to in-depth analytical research on issues of concern to committees.[5]

The General Accounting Office (GAO), in addition to performing many of the responsibilities assigned to it when it was created in 1921, has in recent years been charged by Congress to undertake additional tasks vital to meet the legislature's information requirements. The Legislative Reorganization Act of 1970 mandated the GAO to review the impact of federal programs, assist committees in conducting cost-benefit studies, and develop a standardized information- and data-processing system for budgetary and fiscal data. It has also been called upon increasingly to advise members and committees on proposed legislation, including the contract, fiscal, and administrative provisions of the law. With the passage of the Congressional Budget and Impoundment Control Act of 1974, the GAO was given responsibilities to work with the Congressional Budget Office in developing central data files to meet Congress's requirements for fiscal, budgetary, and program-related information; to assist committees in identifying their information needs; to help them acquire such information; and to work with them in developing legislative objectives and devising methods of determining whether these objectives have been achieved. In the area of presidential proposals to rescind or defer budget authority, the GAO was authorized to evaluate the validity of such proposals.

The Office of Technology Assessment (OTA), which was established in 1972, has as difficult a mandate as any of the four legislative support agencies. In fact, it has experienced some difficulties in attaining the level of assessment capability expected at the time it was created, in large part because of the complexities of public policy research dealing with technology and its orientation to the future. The Technology Assessment Act mandates the OTA to project the existing or probable impact of technology; to isolate alternative programs for achieving goals, develop methods by which to achieve them, and determine comparative estimates of their impact; and to identify areas where additional research and data collection are nececessary. The program areas organized under OTA indicate the breadth of its concerns: oceans, transportation, energy, materials, food, and health. Despite a number of shortcomings, OTA has developed "an in-house staff and access to outside experts which have enabled it, at least on occasion, to deliver useful information in a timely fashion to congressional committees."[6]

The fourth legislative branch support agency is the Congressional Budget Office (CBO), established in 1975. One of three units created by the Congressional Budget and Impoundment Control Act of 1974 (the other two are the House and Senate Committees on the Budget), the CBO was given substantial responsibilities to assist Congress in its efforts to play a more informed role in making budget decisions, analyzing the condition of the economy, and assessing the impact of budget decisions on the economy. It assumes these responsibilities by generating budget and fiscal data and preparing in-depth analyses primarily for the House and Senate Budget Committees. Specifically it furnished these committees with annual reports on fiscal policy for the following year that discuss alternative levels of revenue, budget authority, and outlays, as well as alternative allocations of funds among major programs and functional categories of spending, keeping in mind the need to meet national goals and achieve balanced economic growth. Developing long-term forecasts of revenue and spending is another function it performs. Recognizing that current decisions frequently imply long-term fiscal commitments, Congress charged the CBO with the task of making five-year projections of requirements for new budget authority, outlays, and tax expenditures for measures reported by the various authorizing committees. To help Congress assess the impact of its current legislative actions, CBO periodically calculates the results of Congress's budget decisions in relation to the most recently adopted concurrent resolution specifying ceilings on the budget, outlays, tax revenue, and the deficit. Information derived from this effort is vital to Congress because only when it keeps abreast of the results of its day-to-day decisions and compares these with the ceilings it has previously established can it make more informed judgments in developing priorities among programs and functional categories of the budget. Finally CBO works with the GAO in standardizing fiscal terminology and in developing an inventory of fiscal information sources, provides assistance to Congress in obtaining information from these sources, and assists in analyzing such information.

Committees themselves, of course, are basic to the information infrastructure of Congress. They draw information of a specialized nature from the four legislative support agencies. In addition, informal groups in Congress—political party groups such as the Democratic Study Group and the Senate Republican Policy Committee, and bipartisan groups such as the New England Congressional Caucus and Members of Congress for Peace through Law—are useful sources of information. They produce analytical studies on issues and thus constitute another part of this infrastructure.

The development of Congress's information infrastructure in the 1970s appears to symbolize the legislature's commitment to involve itself more intensely in the decisions of government. But the strides Congress had made in bolstering this infrastructure and the subsequent growth in volume and availability of information generated by it have given rise to another problem: information processing.

The Rise of Information Technology

The House Commission on Information and Facilities succinctly identified Congress's information problems in the 1970s when it asserted in 1976 that they "result from the massive volume of information, in print and online, generated by thousands of individuals and organizations, public and private, in and around Congress." The commission concluded that Congress needs "not *more* information but *better* information, better in terms of organization, coordination, accessibility, delivery, and usability."[7]

The first significant initiatives to achieve a measure of sophisticated information technology were made in the House of Representatives, under the auspices of the Committee on House Administration in 1969. The House sought to work with the Senate in a collaborative venture, but after its overtures met with no success, it endeavored to go forward alone. A major result of its efforts was the creation of the House Information Systems (HIS) in 1971. There is still no Congress-wide computer information system; progress in the development of information technology has proceeded separately and unevenly in both houses, with the House having achieved a higher level of internally based technology than the Senate has. In the House, leadership in the development of automated systems is exercised by the Committee on House Administration and its Ad Hoc Subcommittee on Computers; the committee oversees the work of HIS, which is responsible for the design and operation of computer applications. In the Senate, responsibility for systems development is vested primarily in the Committee on Rules and Administration and its Subcommittee on Computer Services. Progress in enhancing Congress's information technology capability has not been confined to the two houses, however, for the legislature's support agencies—the CRS in particular—have also made contributions in this area.

Progress in the development of computer information systems for Congress has been incremental. The first development efforts were undoubtedly the most difficult because of the costs and the perceptions that members of Congress had concerning the benefits of information systems. Members had to take into account not only the costs required to study their computer needs but also the expenditures required to install and staff the systems. Incremental development probably helped to temper the concerns of those opposed to mounting increases in the costs of congressional operations. It was also undoubtedly the best strategy of introducing members of Congress to the benefits that could be derived from computers. Some members were predisposed to exaggerate their benefits, and others were inclined to think of them as gadgets that would do more to fascinate than to serve. The hope was that as benefits were made manifest, the skepticism and exaggeration would be dispelled.

In examining Congress's information systems, it is useful to consider them in relation to the needs they serve. Two of the most important are those of the members and those of the committees.

Serving the Members' Needs

Before the advent of the Bill Status System in 1973, members and staff personnel had to resort to a number of sources to obtain information on the status of pending legislation. These sources were not always accurate, current, or even responsive. Which members have introduced bills dealing with national health insurance? To which committees have they been referred? Have hearings been scheduled by a subcommittee? If so, which one? What action, if any, has been taken by the other body? These and other questions are asked every minute of every working day on Capitol Hill. It is not surprising that an information system that would respond to this need was identified by so many members of the House who were interviewed by the House Administration Committee's Working Group on Automatic Data Processing in 1970. The Bill Status System, staffed by HIS and the Senate Library, was installed as a result of this need. In the early stages of development, HIS and the Senate Library maintained terminals exclusively, but after the system's benefits were demonstrated in a pilot project, increasing numbers of members of both houses have made system terminals part of their office equipment. Bill status data provide information on the bill number, the names of the sponsor and cosponsors, the date it was introduced, the committee and subcommittee it was referred to, the title of the bill, and a bill digest. A printed copy of the data can be produced and delivered to the member, data in the system are updated continuously, and the data can be manipulated to respond to different kinds of inquiries (for example, it can provide a list of all bills a member has introduced or a list of all bills introduced on a particular subject). In 1975, HIS responded to 235,000 telephone inquiries.

A further frustration congressmen expressed to members of the working group in 1970 was the lack of concise, timely, and accurate summaries of information drawn from public and private documents. A partial response to this problem was CRS's SCORPIO (Subject-Content Oriented Retriever for Processing Information Online) program, which contains data for the bill digest file, the major issues file, and a bibliographic citation file; access can be provided to each on typewriter terminals or cathode ray tubes available in the three CRS reference centers in the House and the Senate, as well as in CRS. The bill digest file contains data on legislative histories in abstract form of all public bills, resolutions, and public laws back to 1973, is kept up to date within thirty-six hours of introduction, and can be retrieved by bill number, public law number, subject, or committee to which they have been referred. The major issues file contains briefs on as many as two hundred public issues. Each brief provides background on the issue, cites current legislation before the Congress relevant to the issue, identifies a chronology of events that brought the issue to public attention, and lists references to literature on the subject. A catalog of the issues treated in the system is made available to all congressional offices every two weeks, and a busy member in need of basic information on an issue before giving a speech can obtain a hard copy of the issue brief the day the request is made. SCORPIO also contains a data base for CRS's bibliographic citation file. This file contains citations to CRS studies and to major publications of Congress, the executive branch, state and local governments, universities, and international organizations. Also included are the publications of approximately fifteen hundred interest groups and major articles drawn from about 150 law journals and six thousand magazines and scholarly journals. Some three thousand citations are added to the data base every month, and the file is updated weekly. From this base CRS draws Selective Dissemination of Information (SDI) profiles, which are sent to CRS research analysts and members of Congress who subscribe. A computer searches and selects annotated citations dealing with subjects that members have identified as being of special interest. The citations are then entered on SDI cards and transmitted each week to the subscriber. A member who wishes to obtain one or more of the materials cited alerts the CRS, and the materials are sent.

Available to a selected number of House members' offices and the news media galleries in the House is a pilot project operated by HIS that provides summaries of the action that is taking place on the House floor. Every five minutes a House debate reporter leaves the floor to transcribe the debates; the debates are then summarized, typed, and transmitted to a computer in the Rayburn House Office Building. A member in his or her office can turn to a video terminal to learn what business has been transacted on the floor only minutes before. After the bells have signaled a vote on the floor, the member can refer to the terminal again to determine the reason for the vote and can choose to receive a printout of a digest on the bill to review while proceedings to the floor to vote. From the same terminal, the member can receive information on the remainder of that day's schedule on the floor, as well as the schedule for the balance of the week. If successful, this summary of proceeding and debate could be made available in the future to all interested offices to help members divide their time between their offices and the floor.

Serving the Committees' Needs

The services provided by the Bill Status System, the bill digest file, the major issues system, and the bibliographic citation file benefit committees as well. Probably of greater value to them than to the individual members are the committee calendar preparation system and several other systems related to the federal budget: the comparative statement of new budget authority system, the federal budget analysis system, the fiscal data base system, and the prototype budget control systems.

The committee calendar preparation system was created to provide each user committee with data on bills that have been referred to that committee, their sponsors, and the status of legislation. Partly because of the heavy volume of legislation referred to them, the House Committee on Banking, Finance and Urban Affairs and the House Committee on the Judiciary were the first two users of the calendar preparation system. Through committee-based terminals, changes in calendar data can be made on a daily basis. Committee staffs are able to store and manipulate the data so that calendars can be edited, corrected, and displayed in a variety of ways. The system extracts, reformats, and provides typesetting instructions so that the calendar can be produced on electronic photocomposition equipment at the Government Printing Office.

In 1970, members of the Working Group on Automatic Data Processing learned from its interviews with selected congressmen that budget and economic data would be especially useful in making judgments about federal programs. A year later, the GAO picked up where the working group had left off to explore Congress's information needs in this realm in much greater depth. Largely as a result of the GAO surveys and the new responsibilities Congress assumed with passage of the Congressional Budget and Impoundment Control Act of 1974, several information systems have been developed and are currently operated by HIS. The Comparative Statement of New Budget Authority System (CSBA), used extensively by the subcommittees of the House Appropriations Committee, can manipulate budget data in such a way as to examine alternative budget considerations. The system, which organizes Office of Management and Budget (OMB) master tape data by subcommittee jurisdiction, updates information based on action taken in committee and on the floor of the House and Senate.

Replacing the slow and time-consuming manual calculations employed in analyzing the federal budget is the federal budget analysis system. It correlates the jurisdictions of the thirteen appropriations subcommittees with budget accounts established by the executive branch and permits detailed analyses of budget data by function, account, bureau, and department. Moreover it facilitates comparisons between these data and outlays, current budget authority, new budget authority, receipts, and spending authority. In addition to the House Appropriations Committee, primary users are the House Budget Committee and the Congressional Budget Office. The fiscal data base system organizes budget and fiscal information from OMB into the proper form for use by both CSBA and the federal budget analysis system. The prototype budget control systems aggregate budget data, apply algorithms suitable to the requirements of both the House Appropriations Committee and the House Budget Committee, and produce reports required by the Congressional Budget and Impoundment Control Act.

In addition to automated systems for the preparation of committee calendars and for budget and fiscal decisions, several miscellaneous systems provide services to committees generally through CRS. The Department of Justice has made available its Justice Retrieval and Inquiry System (JURIS). This system contains the full texts of the U.S. Constitution and the U.S. Code, and its data base is being expanded to include all public laws enacted since 1975, Supreme Court decisions since 1950, and various briefs submitted by the U.S. solicitor general to the Supreme Court. Data can be searched by specific word or subject from cathode ray tube terminals or computer-driven typewriters. Also available through CRS is the New York Times' information bank, which contains abstracts of *New York Times* articles from 1969 to date, as well as selected data from more than sixty journals. The Administrative Terminal System (ATS) is used by several committees to prepare their calendars and to list grant programs and dates when executive programs terminate, but a number of committees have relied on it for other purposes as well. One committee used it to analyze presidential appointments by region, political party, and profession; another analyzed several thousand research and development grants according to amount, recipient institution, region, and purpose; and a third committee conducted a study of interlocking directorates based on data generated through ATS.

Because of the specialized nature of CRS's data bases, other automated systems have been called upon through CRS to assist committees in their analyses. Data Resources, Inc. (DRI) offers a computer-based, large-scale econometric model of the U.S. economy, which contains forecasts of consumer spending and housing starts, among other information. This system's assumptions can be used, but other assumptions can also be entered at the terminal. Applied Urbanetics, Inc. is capable of analyzing the distributional effects of proposed federal aid-to-education formulas, assistance programs for the aged and children, and for crime prevention. EDSTAT and ERIC offer data bases on education. Through EDSTAT (Educational Statistics, from the U.S. Office of Education's National Center for Educational Statistics), the CRS can extract data by institution on student enrollments, expenditure and revenue statistics, and degrees awarded. ERIC (Educational Resources Information Center) distributes abstracts of approximately twelve hundred publications every month. And MEDLINE, which is available through the National Library of Medicine, contains approximately four hundred thousand citations to materials in twelve hundred journals in the fields of medical research and public health.

HIS has also developed data bases to respond to the specialized needs of several committees. It has provided economic forecasting and modeling services to the CBO and selected House committees—Agriculture; Banking, Finance and Urban Affairs; and Budget—and two joint committees, the Joint Committee on Internal Revenue Taxation and the Joint Economic Committee. Through HIS, the Joint Committee on Internal Revenue Taxation has direct access to the U.S. Department of the Treasury's individual tax revenue estimation system, which it uses to make estimates of the effects of changes in the income tax laws. Further assistance that has been provided by HIS includes data analyses of astronomy grants for the House Committee on Science and Technology, pension plans for the House Committee on Education and Labor, and welfare figures for the Joint Economic Committee.

Conclusion

The quiet revolution of information technology on Capitol Hill is in full swing. As difficult as it is to prove that information technology has helped Congress perform its job better, it is clear that the legislature has at least begun to equip itself with the tools that can assist it in its duties.

Initial efforts to introduce in Congress a technology that for years has proved useful to the private sector and other parts of the public sector proceeded with deliberation and caution. Members of Congress, on the whole, are tradition bound; they generally share an aversion to change because the effects of it in an institution as complex as Congress are so hard to predict. But as membership turnover has increased since 1971, especially in the House—coincidental with the first efforts to introduce a new information technology—and as a new generation of legislators have displaced their elders, it has become increasingly evident that they have been willing to accept the introduction of a technology they grew up with and that they have been less apprehensive about changes that it is likely to produce.

The effects of bolstering Congress's information-support system can have an appreciable effect upon its position vis-à-vis the executive and upon the distribution of influence in Congress. With respect to the former, the Congress is finding that it need not be so dependent upon data drawn from the executive and that it is in fact now capable of generating certain data from sources other than the executive. Moreover data that until recently lay in the exclusive domain of the executive today are increasingly being shared with Congress; and Congress, through its own manipulation capability, has given itself opportunities to analyze dimensions of public policy that it previously thought impossible to analyze on its own.

The introduction of a sophisticated information system is also likely to have an impact on the distribution of influence in Congress. Several factors have promoted an increasing tendency toward the decentralization of authority and influence in Congress—particularly in the House—in recent years, and providing all members with greater opportunities to gain access to data encourages even further decentralization. The net effect of increased decentralization is increased complexity in the decision-making process. Complexity itself is not to be decried; it is inescapably a hallmark of our times. Thus those who assume that expanding information technology on Capitol Hill will accelerate the decision-making process will probably be disappointed, for as Congress avails itself of greater access to more information, the legislative process is likely to be slowed. But what is most important is the quality of the decisions that Congress makes—at least that is the assumption—and the hope—of the leaders of this quiet revolution on Capitol Hill.

Notes

1. Arthur M. Schlesinger, Jr., and Alfred de Grazia, *Congress and the Presidency: Their Role in Modern Times* (Washington, D.C.: American Enterprise Institute for Public Policy Research, 1967), p. 3.

2. Quoted in U.S. House of Representatives, Commission on Information and Facilities, *Final Report of the House Commission on Information and Facilities,* 95th Cong., 1st sess., House Document No. 95-22, 1977, p. 78.

3. Clem Miller, *Member of the House* (New York: Charles Scribner's Sons, 1962), p. 110.

4. Harrison W. Fox, Jr., and Susan W. Hammond, "The Growth of Congressional Staffs," in Harvey C. Mansfield, Sr., *Congress Against the President* (New York: Praeger Publishers, 1975), p. 115.

5. Communication from the chairman, U.S. House of Representatives, Commission on Information and Facilities, *Information Resources and Services Available from the Library of Congress and the Congressional Research Service,* 94th Cong., 2d sess., House Document No. 94-527, 1976, pp. 76-77.

6. House, *Final Report,* p. 12.

7. Ibid., pp. 2, 3.

2

ROBERT LEE CHARTRAND

Information Technology for Congress: A Proven Potential

If Congress may be characterized as a mirror, or perhaps more accurately a kaleidoscope, of our society, then its imagery must at times contain both blemishes and distortions. The sheer complexity of the United States today, affecting mores and long-revered political practices, has led to the obsolescence of many institutions. During the past decade, Congress has repeatedly initiated actions that would enhance its flexibility, realizing that the maintenance of a responsive posture would depend on adopting and adapting those procedures, tools, and techniques that would allow it to cope with time pressures. In noting the pressures placed on government by a pluralistic society, veteran observer Hugh Sidey correctly opined "We run too fast . . . we pause too little."[1]

The inclination of contemporary congressmen, more than half of whom have been in office fewer than six years, is to take full advantage of technical innovations that allow them to communicate more effectively with their constituencies and other key groups. This new breed of legislator tends to agree with the statement in *Technology, Society, and Man* that "technology is already tilting the fundamental relationships of government. . . . A new and heavy factor has entered the old system of checks and balances."[2]

The views expressed in this chapter are those of the author and are not necessarily those of the Congressional Research Service or the Library of Congress.

High on the priority lists of many in Congress who seek more effective legislative functioning is the acquisition of those man-machine capabilities that would facilitate member performance, whether in the chamber, during committee sessions, or related to constituent services. The incredible advances in computer and communications technology during the past quarter century offer a wide spectrum of opportunities for senators and representatives who want to work and communicate more effectively.

Much is said in these times about accomplishing better two-way communication. Both the Congress and the general public have come to understand that virtually all legislative actions may have to be modified as the result of changing conditions in society. An informed people, with access to key information and a better understanding of governmental deliberations through such mechanisms as the Freedom of Information Act and the more recent sunshine legislation, can comprehend the need for new public laws and become more integrally involved in the managing of our country.

The ways in which the general public learns about congressional doings is haphazard and fragmentary; they rely on selective television, radio, and press coverage. Congressional newsletters are of some help, and dedicated citizens may read the *Congressional Record* and hearings documentation. Taken as a whole, however, the reality of citizen awareness is fragile at best.

In an age where a broad base of popular support often is a prerequisite to successful governmental programs, ways must be found to span the chasm between those in power and those who are governed. A trenchant encapsulation of the loss of attunement to grass-roots' needs is found in a *New Yorker* cartoon wherein a man in a conservative business suit, espying a muttering Walt Whitman-like figure at the other end of the bar, asks: "Why does he keep saying 'I can't hear America singing'?"

And so Congress appears to be moving toward a rendezvous with the inevitable: optimizing the use of information technology to meet the challenges inherent in governing an advanced society.

Congress as a Responsive Entity

In the hurly-burly of everyday activities, some officials in government could stand accused of forgetting that the federal bureaucracy and elected officials are accountable mechanisms. But the Congress seldom is allowed to be anything less than socially responsive. In fact, it has survived as an institution—and its members reelected as essential elements—because of an ear-to-the-ground proclivity.

With a revival of interest in the importance of information support engendered by the Legislative Reorganization Act of 1970 (PL 91-510), the two chambers have moved to reexamine the organization, jurisdictions, and procedures comprising the fabric of the institution through the creation of such groups as the House Select Committee on Committees, the Temporary Commission on the Operation of the Senate, and the Temporary Select Committee to Study the Senate Committee System. An even more penetrating focus on information-related matters has been undertaken by the House Commission on Information and Facilities and the House Commission on Administrative Review. In all instances, the need for information support emerged as a key factor in congressional responsiveness.

With the advent of computer and microform technology, special efforts to overcome the lack of synchronization between traditional tenets and procedures and modern approaches have been undertaken. Representative John Brademas, a leader in the use of information technology, reminded his colleagues of their responsibility: "Because the effective use of computers requires disciplined human thought, in order to program the computer policy makers must undertake a more exacting analysis of issues than they might otherwise do."[3]

Another critical aspect of employing such technology is its impact upon the measured-response capability of the Congress—that is not to be impelled into precipitous reaction simply because modern technology (such as television) communicates a series of cascading events—often countering one another—which can accelerate into a crisis. In the recent past, yet another adjustment was enacted after the House of Representatives installed its electronic voting system, which allows less roll-call time for members to consult with each other concerning party or faction strategy and tactics relevant to the issues at hand.

These time constraints, real and imagined, when added to the unceasing flood of visitors, telephone calls, and letters, often prevent Hill personnel from developing more than just basic knowledge about many of the problems within their purview. But there are ways in which the institution can assist individuals in selectively obtaining and applying requisite narrative, graphic, and statistical information. Examples range from the House bill status office or the Senate record of voting statistics to the range of services provided by the Congressional Research Service: consultations, "pro and con" evaluations, translations, major research reports, computerized files on issues, new key writings, and data on pending legislation.

Technology is making many things possible or easier to accomplish. Much as the telephone and elevator allowed skyscrapers to be functional, computer terminal networks are providing varied access to distant and diverse data bases. The computer should not be deemed a magician's wand, but it does embody the capability to mesh and manipulate information in a variety of useful ways. And much of the once-restricted data, which were so hard to obtain, are now more accessible either through direct entrée to electronic files or by referral to master indexes, which confirm their existence.

The Congress reports on its activities and responds to the myriad demands for information through bills and resolutions, hearings and reports, debate proceedings, conference reports, amendment data, and voting statistics. When meeting the wide-ranging, voluminous constituent needs it also uses casework responses, newsletters, speeches, district or state forums, sessions with visitors, telephone discussions, television appearances, and radio programs.

Sometimes the Congress in its collective spirit must ask whether the public needs and cares to know about what it is doing and saying. It must also ask whether current communications modes are adequate, discriminatory, and useful in providing an insight into congressional functioning.

One innovation, whose use is on the rise, is computer-supported modeling. Several econometric models are effectively employed to help cope with fiscal-budgetary matters. The potential for utilizing the results of scenarios that treat such problems as pollution, population growth and mobility, and the use of natural resources is great. Furthermore the results can be made understandable to members and constituents alike.

Information Needs of Congress

Information could be aptly defined as "a credible overlay of human senses." In no other environment are all of the senses more exhaustively and adroitly called upon than in the Congress of the United States. Consider the threefold nature of the congressman's role:

1. As legislator responsible for analyzing and making decisions on issues of regional, national, and international significance.
2. As representative of a district or state, charged with the responsibility for its welfare and all requisite related legislative actions.
3. As an ombudsman of sorts, accessible to each constituent and responsible for attempting to provide assistance on any problem.[4]

These requirements place an imposing burden on the people and systems who will furnish any necessary data. Among the criteria that these seekers of information apply are speed and flexibility of access, nonambiguity of responses, accurate and comprehensive coverage of key topics, and convenience in asking for and acquiring the desired information. Representative Richard Bolling, whose perception of congressional strengths and shortcomings is legendary, aptly remarks that "information will always be partial, often imprecise and difficult to interpret. . . . A great deal of what Congress receives falls far short of the ideal."[5]

One often overlooked but nonetheless essential consideration in any discussion of congressional information needs is the ability of the member or committee office to utilize the data it receives. A number of offices, including those of Senators Philip Hart and Charles Percy, have had management studies conducted to determine how well staff are being used, information flows are monitored and utilized, and the member's needs served. If reading and understanding are the key to a useful existence (or operation), then many offices will not receive high ratings because of time pressures, work volumes, or misallocation of resources.

To decipher the dilemma facing many offices, these questions must be considered:

1. Is it possible to distinguish between what Congress wants to know and needs to know?
2. Who determines the questions to be asked, and within what framework?
3. Who legitimizes the answers, according to what context?
4. What changes in existing information-handling systems are needed and can be tolerated?

Many members have become convinced that they can be served better by taking advantage of innovative technology. Often it is simply a matter of organizing and bringing to bear a critical mass of knowledge on a task. Or it may require the imposition of self-discipline while a new routine is mastered.

If a better understanding of the process of change can be imparted, as reflected in the following four key elements, then the risk of a planned transition is minimized: condition of things at the point of origin, character of the primary agents of change, nature of the resistance to change, and means to facilitate general accommodation to the changes introduced.

Members attach much importance to information indicating what their constituents and colleagues think of their actions. Although the need for reelection can scarcely be ignored, and many conduits are maintained to ensure reactions from the citizenry, astute members also must know how to function effectively within their chamber.

A popular device for obtaining the views of constituents is the survey. Sometimes questionnaires are enclosed with newsletters, or, increasingly, they may take the form of punched cards for registering opinions on selected issues. Depending on the wording, it is possible to acquire both factual and attitudinal information. Members may be seeking guidance for their stand on a vital issue or may be interested in how constituents will react if some legislative initiative is required. An analysis of a constituent survey may, in turn, generate new requirements for information so that the members can take appropriate corrective action. They may seek help from universities, corporations, trade associations, and state and local governments that can supply the needed information.

The Congress always has opportunities to take imaginative action for its charter is broad and its resources immense, and the record reveals that quite often the best response to a public predicament stemmed from properly supplied information.

As the oversight responsibilities of the Congress continue to expand and intensify, with dozens of key issues to be faced concurrently and then resolved, reliance on information technology will grow apace. Already members and committees are trying to identify problems that might be tackled better through legislative initiative rather than crisis-choked reaction. Also, as the result of the Congressional Budget and Impoundment Control Act of 1974 (PL 93-344), authorization and appropriations activities are being interleaved into a coordinated, more responsible cycle of review and approval.

The age of information has arrived, creating dependencies perhaps unlike any yet encountered. Unlike earlier inventions in information handling, printing, and telecommunications, computers actually have the capacity to derive new information from source data. And so, gradually, separate and complicated spheres of interest and activity are being joined and, in some instances, simplified and made more workable through the systematics of technology. The continued mastery of information and its technology has become a major responsibility of those who govern.

Information Resources for Congress

Now that Congress as an institution is focusing on the techniques, procedures, and devices that ensure more effective information transfer and utilization, there is an accompanying realization that such a resource must be managed. All too often, busy members and senior staff may delegate—either consciously or by default—the handling of information to less experienced personnel. Corrective action now is being undertaken in many offices to restore control over the acquisition, storage, and retrieval of all forms of information to those most involved in its utilization.

The information resources available to the Congress are remarkably diverse, and because of the prestige of the customer, they are often packaged carefully and delivered with a flourish. Even the most cursory look at the array of information support elements will include:

1. The member's own staff, often rich in the knowledge of the Hill operations and those committee and subcommittee personnel dedicated to furthering the member's effectiveness.
2. The quartet of legislative organizations—General Accounting Office (GAO), Congressional Research Service (CRS), Office of Technology Assessment (OTA), and Congressional Budget Office (CBO)—that offer numerous information resources and services.
3. The federal executive branch departments, agencies, and special entities, such as commissions, plus the Office of Management and Budget (OMB).

4. The thousands of state, county, and municipal governmental units and certain regional government organizations.
5. The party-oriented support groups such as the Democratic and Republican National Committees, the Senate campaign and policy committees for each party, the House Republican Conference, and the House Democratic Caucus.
6. The private-sector institutions: universities, foundations, trade associations, professional societies, nonprofit corporations, and the varied for-profit institutions (business, industrial, commercial, trade).
7. The consumer or citizens' rights groups (such as Ralph Nader's organizations, Common Cause).
8. The media: press, television, and radio.

In most instances, congressional offices have found that their information needs are responded to by those resource organizations that understand Capitol Hill machinations. Two-way communication has become more mandatory than a nicety. Illustrative of the active interplay between Congress and its producers-consumers are several articles appearing in a special "Congress in the Information Age" issue of the American Society for Information Science *Bulletin.* [6] They show that Congress must determine to whom it listens and whose materials are used apropos of policy analysis and options determination, budgetary alternatives, prioritizing of issues, and preparing new legislation.

Differing information requirements—based on parameters of time response, quality of data, and completeness of coverage demanded—often dictate source selection. The *Washington Post* cited a GAO survey of 238 House members revealing that up to 80 percent depended upon the news media for crisis information.[7] In the same article, dissatisfaction with executive branch information under emergency conditions was expressed, along with a desire for the establishment of a "congressional watch center to monitor emerging or cataclysmic crises."

Information technology in its several forms clearly has penetrated congressional consciousness. Thoughtful observers of the innovative trend, however, are beginning to echo Dr. Jerome Wiesner's admonition in "Society as a Learning Machine": "the computer, with its promise of a million-fold increase in man's capacity to handle information, will undoubtedly have the most far-reaching consequences of any contemporary technical development. The potential for good in the computer, and the danger inherent in its misuse, exceed our ability to imagine."[8]

Sharing the responsibility for how computers and other technology are used is the fast-growing cadre of several hundred information specialists within the legislative branch. As these groups—typified by the House Information Systems organization—continue to expand their service role, it becomes imperative that chamber management and legislative oversight mechanisms understand the emerging complex pattern of changed behavior. For example, there is an identifiable need:

1. To ensure that these new experts are properly qualified and understand the Hill environment.
2. To update the training of these professionals regularly and to ensure continued orientation of the broader community of users among the office staffers.
4. To revise the priority lists of information needs periodically to ensure that answers are provided to the right questions.
4. To reevaluate continually whether the information going to congressional clients is properly packaged.
5. To understand and redefine, where necessary, the ethical implications of information handling and technology.
6. To establish a coordinating (management) mechanism to oversee information-systems development.

The advent of technology has only served to point up these considerations. But Congress is now starting to share with its support elements the responsibility for deciphering those influences, barriers, and stimulants that affect lawmaking and legislative-executive communication.

Another aspect of evaluating information resources is deciding how to critique and compare incoming data from various sources. Traditionally special-interest groups have sent information, often unsolicited, to member offices. And sometimes a member who is searching for alternatives or unspiced evaluations or supporting data seeks another view of the same issue from the cognizant CRS subject division or a GAO study team.

Consider also the impact of critical information that is now available only through such services as the New York Times's Information Bank or the Congressional Information Service Index. Most recently a computerized file providing comprehensive access to the *Congressional Record* has had its debut. Whether under the aegis of a governmental service—such as the GAO *Congressional Sourcebook* or the Department of Agriculture's Federal Assistance Program Retrieval Service (FAPRS) still under development—or within the commercial realm (the Lockheed or System Development Corporation online, multiple-file offerings), the congressional customer is now becoming attuned to paying for certain types of information that previously were free. Similarly, many paper products are being replaced or augmented by computerized or microform services.

Along with a broader base of information resources is the factor of direct access. The congressional leadership has taken steps to help provide the membership with equipment and/or financial support to purchase computer services. More than three hundred offices in both chambers now have their own terminals, and although these do not provide universal access to all valuable data bases, it is a critical first step. Whereas some of the traditional gatekeeping of congressional data has been replaced by terminal access to computerized files, a new awareness of the importance of file security and protecting the confidentiality of data has arisen. To what extent the Congress will choose to operate in time-honored modes and in which areas it will rely upon the technology is not yet fully determined.

Nothing can replace the personal networks that have served Capitol Hill so well for so many years. Only the nature of some of the information brokers and their panoply of resources may evolve.

Action to Improve Information Support

Beginning with the two-chamber action to formulate the second Legislative Reorganization Act (in 1965), a number of members in both parties sought to enhance congressional information support. Extensive hearings were held and numerous documents, articles, and other communications were received by the Joint Committee on the Organization of the Congress. Among the areas stressed was that of improved information services, with suggestions forthcoming from representatives of management, labor, the academic community, and government (including the Congress itself). A summary listing of projected applications, prepared at the time, included:

Summary Listing of Projected Applications of ADP in Support of the Congress

The Congress as a unit

Status of pending legislation
Lobbyist activity information
Direct access to legislative research
Legal literature/information
Automated index/catalog of congressional documents
Payroll accounts of employees of Congress
Up-to-date legislative telephone directory

Each chamber as an entity

Current information on issues up for vote
Postvote analytical information
Electronic (remote) voting by congressmen

The committee or subcommittee

Current schedule of committee meetings and hearings
Histories of committee action
Exclusive file for each committee
Information on federal contract awards
Appropriations statistics and information

The individual congressman

Exclusive file for each congressman
Selected readings of interest to congressmen
Constituent information.[9]

When the revised bill (HR 17654) finally was passed in 1970 as Public Law 91-510, it made several provisions for Congress to receive better information. For example, Title II stated that fiscal and budgetary data should be collected, maintained, and analyzed in an executive branch automatic data processing (ADP) system. This system, it was hoped, would upgrade the ability of its users to make more useful comparisons between the costs of federal programs and their benefits.

Although often by implication, the act identified the importance of advanced information-handling tools and techniques in authorizing the Congressional Research Service to take on several new duties. As defined, these would encompass both a refinement of analytical and advisory services and would provide for better files, with the ability to retrieve from a variety of indexes, digests, and full-text forms:

1. Assist committees in analyzing, appraising, and evaluating advisability of enacting legislative proposals and alternatives thereto and estimating their probable results; maintain continuous liaison with committees.
2. Inform committees of programs and activities scheduled to expire in the current Congress.
3. Provide committees with lists of subjects and policy areas suitable for analysis in depth.
4. Upon request, prepare concise legislative histories of measures upon which committee hearings are to be held.[10]

Throughout the late 1960s, bipartisan support for introducing computers in a centralized facility took the form of individual bills introduced (but not acted upon), speeches, and news releases. In addition, several members participated in seminars and symposia stressing the role to be played by systems analysis and ADP in the legislative process. These members—including Representatives John Brademas, Richard Bolling, Robert McClory, William Moorhead, Jack Brooks, and Joe Waggonner—recognized and articulated the role that information technology must fulfill if governmental processes were to cope with a complex world.

The tactic employed by Representative John Brademas to initiate activity in this area within the House of Representatives was a resolution that was endorsed by the Democratic Caucus: "Resolved, that the Committee on House Administration be fully supported by Democratic members in efforts to improve the efficiency of operations of the House of Representatives, and we urge that these efforts include, but not be limited to, the use of computers and of a centralized mail processing system."[11] The responsibility to develop a plan of action was assigned to the House Special Subcommittee on Electrical and Mechanical Office Equipment. In the spring of 1969, a Working Group on Automatic Data Processing was created by the Special Subcommittee; it included senior personnel from the Office of the Clerk of the House, CRS, and GAO. In undertaking this effort, Chairman Joe D. Waggonner, Jr., promised that "we will do our best to establish standards and ground rules to provide the coordination needed to create a system we can all be proud of."[12]

During the 1969-1970 period, the Special Subcommittee issued its First Progress Report, which reviewed suggestions for the use of ADP and some possible alternatives for forging requisite services into a "unified, compatible system geared to serving the Congress."[13] Following a survey of House members and staff aides regarding their information needs, a Second Progress Report was published, succeeded by a Special Reporting treating a projected House addressing and mailing system. Another activity involved eight contractors who assisted the working group in studying the information and analysis needs of the House and developing a plan for managing the design, implementation, and operation of the services.

In the Senate, meanwhile, the impetus was developing in a more measured way. Following Senator Hubert H. Humphrey's earlier admonitions to consider the role of computerized information handling systems, Senator Hugh Scott pointed out that "the electronic computer and the systems techniques connected with its use are simply tools for use by the decision maker. They are designed to help provide that information which is necessary to make balanced, accurate decisions."[14] In 1970 the Senate Committee on Rules and Administration, chaired by Senator B. Everett Jordan, authorized a study of the role of data processing in legislative operations and established the Subcommittee on Computer Services.

Shortly after the Ninety-second Congress was convened in 1971, the pace quickened insofar as information systems development was concerned. Representative Wayne L. Hays consolidated all of the House automation activities under a new House Information Systems (HIS) office reporting to his Committee on House Administration. This entity has grown markedly in size and scope of service during the ensuing years. More than two hundred staff members now provide support to the House membership and its committee structure through such key services as a chamber electronic voting system, an office that supplies current information on bills by telephone, calendar preparation support for committees, and assistance to the House committees on the Budget and Appropriations in working with fiscal-budgetary data.

Senate responsibility for ADP-type functions is shared by three long-standing functionaries: chairman of the Committee on Rules and Administration, secretary of the Senate, and sergeant at arms of the Senate. Their combined efforts have resulted in the establishment of an online network serving all senators' offices, a powerful addressing and mailing capability, a computerized voting statistics file, and, like the other chamber, the automation of payroll and personnel records. Both the House and Senate computer centers have been instrumental in preparing computerized indexes to microfilmed files of campaign expenditure data in order to be responsive to the Federal Elections Campaign Act of 1971 (PL 92-225).

The major legislative branch support groups—GAO, CRS, and the Government Printing Office (GPO)—also furnish information to the Congress.

The Congressional Research Service, supported by the Automated Systems Office (ASO), another entity within the Library of Congress, maintains a series of computerized files; 725 terminals throughout the legislative branch have access to them. Operating under a sophisticated information retrieval package, SCORPIO (Subject-Content Oriented Retriever for Processing Information Online), the system offers both in-house files and, through separate access, data from external holdings. Among the in-house files are those containing legislative information (bill content and status), bibliographic citations (books and periodicals), and essential elements of information about key issues. External data files include the New York Times's Information Bank, Justice Retrieval and Inquiry System (JURIS), MEDLINE service from the National Library of Medicine, and the fledgling services offering information from the *Congressional Record* and on federal information services and systems.

The GAO, primarily through its Program Analysis Division, not only continues to generate reports concerning ADP use by the federal government but monitors the executive branch creation of a standard classification system for government programs and the role of computers in supporting that program. In addition, the GAO uses ADP in its internal management and in preparing audits of other agencies. Staff members skilled in systems analysis, statistical sampling, ADP, and actuarial science performed 504 audits and studies in one year in response to congressional requests.

Hard pressed to meet the mounting congressional and executive branch work load, the GPO continues to modernize its massive plant. Joining the LINOTRON devices capable of handling magnetic tape input data are the newer VIDEOCOMP units. Eleven computer programs are used in the Congressional Index system, with four tapes resulting: subject index, House of Representatives by committee, Senate by committee, and joint and special committees. From these a Bill Number Index is also produced. Through arrangements with the HIS group, some automated House calendar material is now directly inserted into the electronic photocomposition system.

The Congress, sometimes collectively or on a chamber basis, has created official groups (such as the House Select Committee on Committees) with missions that include an examination of information support for members and other congressional personnel. And through major legislation, it has created the Office of Technology Assessment (PL 92-484) and the Congressional Budget Office (PL 93-344), which are charged with rendering assistance in areas of critical oversight concern.

Such significant congressional efforts, reflecting an awareness of the importance of establishing an up-to-date, highly responsive information support capability, are chronicled in figure 1. Of particular note is the creation (in 1977) of the Policy Coordination Group—comprised of senior

FIGURE 1 Key Steps Toward Improved Congressional Information Support

1965–1966	Second Legislative Reorganization Act hearings
1966	First bill to create a congressional computer facility (HR 18428, Eighty-ninth Congress)
1967	CRS automates Bill Digest information
1968	CRS computerizes first House calendar operation
1969	House acts on Brademas resolution by empowering Special Subcommittee on Electrical and Mechanical Office Equipment to study ADP uses
1970	Passage of Legislative Reorganization Act of 1970 (PL 91-510)
	Senate establishes Subcommittee on Computer Services; authorizes study of ADP uses
1971	House Information Systems office created
	Potter administrative survey of offices of the secretary of the Senate issued
1972	House and Senate campaign expenditure data systems implemented
	New House chamber voting procedures approved
	GAO *Budgetary and Fiscal Information Needs of the Congress* published
	Technology Assessment Act of 1972 creates OTA (PL 92-484)
	Library of Congress ISO begins SCORPIO development
1973	Senate commences pilot test of CRS online files
	House electronic voting system becomes operative
	CRS and Senate tie in to New York Times Information Bank
	CRS establishes links with MEDLINE and JURIS systems
1974	Congressional Budget and Impoundment Control Act of 1974 creates CBO and chamber budget committees (PL 93-344)
	House Select Committee on Committees makes recommendations (HR 988)
1975	House Commission on Information and Facilities establishes pilot member information network
	Senate provides terminals for all member offices
	House Committee Order 23 authorizes $1,000 monthly expenditure (from clerk-hire funds) by each member for computer services
	Temporary Commission on the Operation of the Senate established
1976	Temporary Select Committee to Study the Senate Committee System created
	House Commission on Administrative Review formed
	Expansion of Senate, House, and Library of Congress computer capabilities
1977	House Policy Group on Information and Computers established
	Trial videotaping of House chamber proceedings by Select Committee on Congressional Operations
	Policy Coordination Group authorized by Committee on House Administration and Senate Committee on Rules and Administration

FIGURE 1 *(continued)*

1978	First Annual Report of the Policy Coordination Group for Technology Development
	Audiotaping of Senate debate on Panama Canal treaty
	GAO Congressional Sourcebook files incorporated within SCORPIO system
1979	Congressional Clearinghouse of the Future features month-long series of seminars, workshops, and demonstrations on Information and Communications
	Videotaping of all House chamber proceedings attains operational status

Hill staff members—to guide the development of technology-supported information systems. This monitoring mechanism was authorized by the chairmen of the Committee on House Administration and the Senate Committee on Rules and Administration.

With the strengthening of the Capitol Hill information underpinning, there has been a sharp upturn in member and staff curiosity about how some of the innovative tools and techniques can help them. For example, Representative Charlie Rose in his role as chairman of the House Policy Group on Information and Computers has taken steps to determine how best to use television. In addition to displaying summaries of floor action on videoscreens, he took steps to have CRS create pilot documentaries (of ten to fifteen minutes each) on videotape cassettes for use by members prior to committee or subcommittee sessions and floor votes. Meanwhile, the Select Committee on Congressional Operations conducted a ninety-day trial videotaping of House chamber proceedings.

Thus, in many ways, the modernization of the Congress regarding improved information support may be viewed as a continuum. Accompanying the use of computer, videoform, microform, and telecommunications technology over the past decade has been a trebling of congressional staffs. If the volume of Congress's work continues to increase, then an even greater premium will be placed on developing information-support mechanisms of the highest quality.

Information in the Future

If those who prognosticate about the social and economic dimensions of our nation in the coming century are at all accurate, the Congress of that era will have to cope with a spate of technologically inspired problems. But it will have improved resources to generate and convey information to the rest of the world. The legislators will be responsible for helping to alleviate the social uncertainty that is sure to exist—born of innate global complexities that tax human capabilities—by disseminating information and knowledge so that people everywhere may comprehend and survive.

The omnipresence of technology forces those who govern to plan better. Among the devices and techniques already identified for future use by the Congress are these:

1. Computer-supported models capable of manipulation by nontechnical staff personnel.
2. An elaborate congressional watch center featuring displays that can call up key data from microform and computerized files for crisis decisions and the consideration of alternatives.
3. Access to both federal and state legislative research files from member district or public terminals.
4. Television monitors of chamber and committee proceedings allowing members to work in their offices and still be cognizant of ongoing legislative business.
5. Video and audio cassette devices for use in providing members with quick briefings on key topics prior to participation in floor debate or committee or subcommittee deliberations.
6. Quick availability of selected information, using satellite transfer capabilities, from files and human information resources around the world.

A premium will be placed upon extensive technical training of large numbers of staff members and an effort to stretch the horizons of the decision makers (members and senior staff aides) regarding what information technology can do for them.

An increasing number of private homes will be equipped with the kinds of information-handling equipment—computer terminals, microfilm reader-printers, inexpensive duplicators, more versatile television-radio units, and perhaps even devices allowing use of credit cards or banking services—that will revolutionize both working patterns and the relationship between constituents and those in government. Indicative of the attention being paid to the area of two-way contact between the citizen and the official is the George Washington University project, funded by NASA, which tests the feasibility and utility of congressional video conferencing through use of a commerical satellite.

A related realm for revised social interaction and control is that of public decision making. In his foreword to *The Future of the U.S. Government,* Daniel Bell talks about "nonmarket public decision making": "The layouts of roads, the creations of jetports, the planning of cities, the organization of health care, the financing of education, the cleaning up of the environment—these are all public concerns and become the subject of public debate. Often, they have to be settled by public decision."[15]

These enhanced reasons and mechanisms for cross-talking have permeated our way of life. Legislative-executive exchanges of information, for example, have become increasingly critical in recent years. Often it seems that traditional adversary relationships are evolving into more cooperative postures as the OMB planning-programming-budgeting cadre seeks greater accommodation with both its departmental counterparts and the legislative oversight forces. And since information should allow better judgments to be rendered, it seems propitious to ask if there is sufficient institutional encouragement of the individual's development of knowledge that could allow the exercise of initiative or responsive action.

On the legislative scene, are we perceiving and assessing the side effects that information technology has on the legislative process? One Capitol Hill group with a responsibility to do just this is the Futures Research staff of the Congressional Research Service, which has been instrumental in preparing such reports as *Computer Simulation Methods to Aid National Growth Policy.*[16] An awareness of such aids, together with an appreciation of their benefits and shortcomings, is critical as the technological is melded with the political in the cauldron of policy formulation. Richard C. Dorf places in a useful perspective the viability of this burgeoning technology: "Thus a model is to be developed where a list of alternatives has been generated, each complete with the social, political and economic portions of the model and the program plan. The actual implementation of any such program requires decisions on priorities. *It is at this point that the political processes assume the decision-making responsibility* [italics added.]."[17]

The role of information and its technology in government and society has been given its due. While the outpouring of data is, and should be, a cause for genuine concern, a serious effort is being made to utilize the information-handling capabilities that embody advanced technology. Packaging and distribution are the objects of special attention as the focus on outreach is intensified.

The prime consideration in this so-called "Age of Information" is a renewed affirmation in the responsiblity of each man and woman. Underscored in Rexford G. Tugwell's "The Shaping of the Constitution for 2000" is the premise that the new objectives in such a document would "not only protect the individual from oppression but match this right with a duty to participate . . . contribute and encourage others to contribute."[18] If the United States is to register continued progress under the guidance of a farsighted, responsive Congress, its leadership must use ingenuity and determination to employ both traditional and innovative methods in the fulfillment of governmental responsibilities and goals.

Information technology increasingly is seen as a servant that can be relied upon by legislators. Proceeding on the assumption that the effectiveness of Congress can be improved to a discernible extent through the use of computers and related advanced technology, then the requisite investment is merited. And if the past is prologue, this trend toward technology utilization should help govern the ways in which Congress determines its priorities and conducts its business.

Notes

1. Hugh S. Sidey, presentation before the America in the Information Age Bicentennial Conference, Washington, D.C., April 13, 1976.

2. Richard C. Dorf, *Technology, Society, and Man* (San Francisco: Boye & Fraser Publishing Company, 1974), p. 19.

3. John Brademas, "Congress in the Year 2000," in *The Future of the U.S. Government,* ed. Harvey S. Perloff (New York: George Braziller, 1971), p. 322.

4. U.S. Congress, House, Select Committee on Committees, *The Congress and Information Technology,* prepared for the Select Committee by the Science Policy Research Division, Congressional Research Service, 93d Cong., 2d sess., p. 10.

5. Richard Bolling, "The Management of Congress," *Public Administration Review* 35 (September-October 1975): 492.

6. "Congress in the Information Age," special issue of the *Bulletin of the American Society for Information Science* 1 (April 1975): 8-24.

7. *Washington Post,* September 14, 1976, p. A15.

8. Jerome B. Wiesner, "The Computer and Society," *The New York Times,* April 24, 1966, p. 15.

9. U.S. Congress, Joint Committee on the Organization of the Congress, *Organization of Congress,* Hearings before the Joint Committee, p. 15, appendix. Robert L. Chartrand, *Automatic Data Processing for the Congress,* 89th Cong., 2d sess., 1966, p. 2314.

10. U.S. Congress, Public Law 91-510, An Act to Improve the Operation of the Legislative Branch of the Federal Government, and for other purposes, H.R. 17654, 91st Cong., xx sess., 1970, pp. 42-46.

11. Andrew J. Glass, CPR Report: Congress Moves into Computer Age but Divides on Control of New Systems," *National Journal* 2 (May 30, 1970): 1152.

12. Joe D. Waggoner, Jr., remarks contained in the transcript of the videotape presentation at the Fall Joint Computer Conference, Las Vegas, Nevada, November 18, 1969, pp. 29-30.

13. U.S. Congress, House, Committee on House Administration. *First Progress Report of the Special Subcommittee on Electrical and Mechanical Office Equipment,* prepared by the Working Group on Automatic Data Processing for the House of Representatives, 91st Cong., 1st sess., 1969, p. 1.

14. Hugh Scott, press release, January 19, 1967.

15. Daniel Bell, foreword to Perloff, *Future of the U.S. Government,* p. xv.

16. U.S. Congress, House, Committee on Merchant Marine and Fisheries, *Computer Simulation Methods to Aid National Growth Policy,* 94th Cong., 1st sess., 1975.

17. Dorf, *Technology, Society, and Man,* p. 8.

18. Rexford G. Tugwell, "The Shaping of the Constitution for 2000: An Exercise in Putative Prognostics," in *Future of the U.S. Government,* p. 287.

3

NEAL GREGORY

Changing Information Needs of Congress

The Congress needs information on facts and figures, a comparison of this year's budget request with last year's spending, an impact analysis on the member's constituency for each vote he or she must cast—this and much more. Members may feel overwhelmed with the sheer volume of paperwork that descends on their desks each day, but there is no such thing as too much information. The basic problem in Congress is one of a lack of organization, a failure to sort out the facts and figures, the budget comparisons, and the all-important reactions of the voters.

Congress's information needs have changed during the two centuries that it has been making legislative decisions. More information comes into congressional offices, and it comes faster because of improved communication and transportation facilities. With most major business and academic organizations now headquartered in Washington, lobbyists and legislative representatives are easily available for answering questions on specific issues.

The legislative process encompasses more than the special-interest views of the issues under debate. Even the objective viewpoint of the Congressional Research Service of the Library of Congress or the analyses of the organizations representing the majority and minority leadership will not suffice if the issue is one of overriding importance to a segment of a member's constituency.

Edmund Burke defined the role of the legislator in his speech to the electors of Bristol, declaring "it ought to be the happiness and glory of a representative to live in the strictest union, the closest correspondence, and the most unreserved communication with his constituents."[1] While Burke also urged a nonparochial view for parliaments, no one will deny that members of Congress—particularly those in the House—are representatives of their districts in the strictest sense of that word. Running for office every two years guarantees that members must be in tune with the thinking of their constituents. Advocates of campaign reform frequently list advantages of the incumbent: newsletters, district offices, long-distance telephone allowances, a large staff, and trips home.[2] But each of these benefits—if properly applied—should make the members more informed and consequently better legislators.

Representative Charlie Rose (D-N.C.), chairman of the Policy Group on Information and Computers of the Committee on House Administration, reminds his colleagues that the people they represent are the most important information source of all and that communication is a two-way street.[3] Any staff member can confirm that there is a direct ratio between the volume of constituent mail and the communication modes a member uses. Scientific polling and extensive use of questionnaires add to the store of knowledge about constituent sentiment.

The information flow is triggered by more than the member's action. Anti-Vietnam War demonstrations, Watergate, the impeachment drama, and other important events have made Americans more aware of Congress. People—many for the first time—wrote to their congressmen during those dramatic times, and they have kept on writing. The volume of mail has more than doubled in most offices over the last decade. Staffs have increased to cope with this information explosion, but the efficiency of the office has not necessarily kept pace.[4]

Administrative Practices

Computer technology is clearly the tool for harnessing the information explosion and the corollary need for a better way to operate the legislative branch. The House of Representatives and the Senate have adopted different approaches to providing computer services for their members. The Senate has divided responsibility among the secretary of the Senate, the sergeant at arms, and the Committee on Rules and Administration. The House has placed all of its major computer applications in the Committee on House Administration and has also made it possible for each member to make his or her own decision on applying the computer to individual office needs.

Mail to the House is still delivered in the way it was decades ago. A red sign, not unlike the flag one hoists on a rural mailbox, is still placed at the door of House offices to indicate that mail is ready for pick-up. The new Phillip Hart Senate Office Building will also have an automated system of small carts (measuring 18 by 12 by 10 inches) running on an enclosed track to deliver mail to offices from a central switching area.[5] But how mail is handled in each office after delivery will still be determined by each office manager.

Each member of the House receives the same salary ($57,000 annually in 1979), the same number of staff members (eighteen in 1979), and the same benefits and allowances. The size of their work space is determined by seniority, but they all are furnished offices in Washington and in the home district.[6] They all represent approximately the same number of people (475,000 in 1979), but these constituents may be urban or rural, activist or complacent, have access to good media coverage or be relatively isolated. Similarly their congressmen may be newly elected or may have been in Congress for a decade or more.

How members communicate with their constituents is individual, and how members are applying computer technology to their offices is a matter of choice. Some have automated lists permitting them to identify certain employee groups (such as teachers) for a special mailing. Others maintain a base of form letters or standard-reply paragraphs to speed up letter writing. Other applications include file systems using a minicomputer or time-sharing through which a member can see at a glance on a video display screen the case history of each constituent's communications.

So far more than half the members have applied a portion of their clerk hiring allowance for computer services through contracts with private vendors, a practice permitted since July 1975 by House Administration Committee Order 23. New rules of the House, adopted in January 1977, continued this practice but gave members the option of transferring funds among various accounts. Although the overall dollar amount of the perquisites and benefits of members was not increased, the flexibility permitted in managing congressional offices plus new publicly available reports of expenditures should dramatically increase efficiency.

As more and more office managers concerned with the correspondence deluge are moving into the computer field by acquiring word-processing assistance, other congressional staff members are making extensive use of online information retrieval. Available at no cost to those offices with terminals are data bases from the Library of Congress. With SCORPIO (Subject-Content Oriented Retriever for Processing Information Online), the Library supplies digests of bills, briefs on legislation, scientific and technical abstracts, bibliographic data, a daily index to the *Congressional Record,* and files from the General Accounting Office.[7] The House Commission on Information and Facilities, assisted by House Information Systems, had a pilot project operating in thirty House offices during 1976 to provide members with bill status information, schedules of floor debate for the day and for the week ahead, and a running summary of proceedings from the

House floor.[8] Now operated by the Committee on House Administration, this member information network has been expanded to all House offices and other information data bases are being developed.

Tracking the Status of Legislation

Defining its internal problems is not a new task for Congress. In 1966, a bill proposed using electronic computers for the collection, formation, and maintenance of key information relating to each public bill before the Congress. Three years later, the Committee on House Administration, through its Special Subcommittee on Electrical and Mechanical Office Equipment, established the Working Group on Automatic Data Processing to survey the information needs of the House. The group concluded that the most important need was an improvement of available information on the status of legislation.[9]

The newly formed House Information Systems was given the task of implementing an approach to tracking and cataloging information. In early 1973, the first operational version of the Bill Status System was at hand.[10]

The system provides a historical record of legislative actions that have occurred, giving the status of legislation and including basic identifying information on each measure introduced in either the House or Senate. Identification data include such information as the bill number, cosponsor, date introduced, committee to which referred, subject index terms, and official and popular titles. Status data include specific action taken on the bill or resolution, such as comment by executive agencies, reporting the bill to the floor, passage or rejection by House or Senate, action by conference committees, and veto or signing by the president. Some 159 actions are possible as a bill moves through Congress.[11]

Since its start, the Bill Status Office has gathered data from official sources by telephone for input into the system at the end of each day. Initially data were retrieved by a battery of operators who sat before video display terminals translating telephone requests into computer queries. As the Ninety-fifth Congress opened in January 1977, the House and Senate reworked the Bill Status System into a new Legislative Information and Status System (LEGIS), maintaining a network of terminals in each committee and legislative office to provide source data. The telephone service has been maintained, but individual congressional offices with terminals are now able to have access to the data directly.[12]

Automated Voting

The slow speed with which the Congress reacts to change is well illustrated by the practice of voting on the House floor. A verbal roll call of 435 names is a time-consuming process, taking more than a half-hour to accomplish. Since a record vote in the Committee of the Whole can be demanded by as few as twenty members, nuisance delays have been common.

The concept of automated voting was first introduced in a House resolution in 1914, but it was not until the Legislative Reorganization Act of 1970 that "the names of Members voting or present may be recorded through the use of appropriate electronic equipment." And in 1972 the Rules of the House were actually amended to provide the electronic voting system. The system was first used on January 23, 1973. During the remaining months of the Ninety-third Congress, approximately five hundred hours that would have been spent on verbal roll calls were saved.[13]

This computerized system, more sophisticated than those used in most state legislatures, permits members to vote by inserting a plastic card into one of several voting stations located around the House floor. The vote is recorded on a display panel and included in the final tally when the fifteen-minute time period for voting ends. When the vote is declared final, printed copies of the results are available immediately to legislative leaders, the media, and the Government Printing Office for inclusion in the *Congressional Record.* During the voting, the leadership of both parties can monitor results on display terminals and deploy their whip systems to round up absentees or implore colleagues to change votes. The computerized sytstem also maintains the official voting record history for each member.[14]

This almost daily personal interaction with a computer as they cast votes has eliminated much of the fear many members have toward permitting computers to play a larger role in the legislative process. The new hands-on approach, with direct access to data through a computer terminal, is breaking down this barrier even more.

Uses of Government Data Bases

At hearings in early 1976 on funding the computer operations of the House, members of the House Administration Committee expressed support for sharing other data bases of the federal government. The program that most sparked members' interest was the Federal Assistance Program Retrieval System (FAPRS), providing a method for ascertaining which federal grants specific communities are eligible to receive. Developed by the Department of Agriculture, the system permits local officials to answer a series of multiple-choice questions and match their needs with six hundred grant programs via a computer terminal. This system eliminates hours of search time through the bulky *Domestic Assistance Catalogue* and should provide small towns an equal opportunity to participate in programs that formerly were available only to areas able to afford a large research staff or consultants.[15]

Legislation to expand this concept to include urban programs and to establish a full-fledged Federal Program Information Center was introduced in the House and Senate during 1976 (S. 3281, sponsored by Senator Edward Kennedy and Senator William V. Roth, Jr., which passed the Senate, and HR 13186, sponsored by Representative Charlie Rose). The Office of Management and Budget was opposed to the concept. No doubt hundreds of consultants from the health-education-poverty complex also fear the availability of direct access to data that only they could provide before, and bureaucrats are alarmed at the prospect of a huge increase in applicants for these limited grants. In the past, the complexity of application procedures had kept the number of applicants down. Moreover sponsors of the legislation ultimately want this information center to tell local communities and Congress how much money is left in each program at the time of application, a concept that would completely upset the delicate pork-barrel balance.

It is not just the executive branch's systems that members of Congress want to join. At least a score of other bills were introduced in the Ninety-fourth Congress directing executive agencies and departments to computerize information so that Congress and the public can find their way through the data. Included were energy information, national resources materials information, government operations records, jury selection drawing, government lease information, securities uses of data processing, and criminal justice information.[16]

The Federal Budget Process

The most logical extension of automated information involves the federal budget process. More and more members of Congress want to look behind the OMB budget tapes and obtain data used by the various agencies to justify their funding requests.

The House and Senate Committees on the Budget and the Congressional Budget Office have brought three hundred new people to Capitol Hill and a huge new demand for automated data. Other committees have hired computer-oriented staff members, who are asking new questions of the executive branch. Congressional econometric modeling is underway in such diverse areas as agricultural marketing, oceanography, and monetary policy as members demand more and more analytical data.[17] In the not-too-distant future, congressional oversight committees will find it routine to ask agencies for data obtained from their econometric models so they can go beyond the prepared testimony to find out why certain assumptions were made to develop agency policy. The executive branch will oppose linking its computers with those of the Congress. In the past, battles over executive privilege have been compromised through selective editing and other devices that may not be practical in the computer age.

There will be internal opposition in the Congress as well. Most of the power that now resides in certain committees results from the special expertise that comes from intimate knowledge of a specific area of policy. To share information—to make information on the budget easier to understand, for instance—is to share power, and this is something most committee chairmen and senior members are reluctant to do.

The Future of the Computer in the House

Edward Schneier of City University of New York contends that having computer consoles in every office to provide decision-making information ignores the political aspects of information obtained through the committee hearing process:

> The advantage of using committees rather than computers to process information is that the committee, unlike the computer, is "programmed" by those whose role orientations, social origins, and political problems are remarkably similar to those of the men who need the information. An information source that deals only in objective facts is not likely to be very useful. If "there is no point in preparing vast volumes of general data to be added to the tomes congressmen already have not time to read," then there is no point in preparing yard upon yard of computer output to be added to the material that congressmen already do not understand.[18]

Schneier need not fear. The political instincts of members of Congress will never be supplanted by automated data from their terminals. A member may never read a lengthy hearing transcript, but he or she may get a chance to look over a computerized abstract of a statement or the summary of a proceeding. Today most hearing transcripts and other documents available to members as information sources do not even have adequate indexes, but the computer is changing this shortcoming.

Since mid-1975, the Committee on House Administration has been attempting to remove the mystique surrounding computer technology. Through a series of seminars and newsletters, its staff has provided information and demonstrations showing the relative ease by which members and staff can access data online. Representative Rose has even acquired a portable terminal, which he has taken into the cloakrooms off the House floor to search for data on pending legislation. He and other members have taken the terminal home to their districts, sharing with local government officials information from FAPRS and SCORPIO. Rose contends that the only limit to computer applications in the Congress is the imagination and ingenuity of the members and staff.[19]

A major review of House information systems conducted in fall 1976 at the direction of Representative Frank Thompson, Jr., (D-N.J.), chairman of the House Administration Committee, has resulted in the shift of all policy decisions from HIS to the committee. The review also recommended moves toward an open shop and better communication in order to define congressional user needs.[20] Thompson has established a policy group headed by Rose to move toward greater efficiency in House computer operations and to set priorities for new and improved applications.

Meanwhile members and staff continue to experiment and test new approaches to the old problems. A minicomputer system is being installed by HIS to process texts of committee hearings transcribed by the official reporters to committees. Working with the Government Printing Office, this new application contemplates a savings of $3 million in the first year of operation and more than $10 million in the second. In addition, delivery of printed hearings by the GPO—now requiring three months—will be accomplished in three weeks as the computerized approach to typesetting replaces the old system.[21]

Representative Dave Stockman (R-Mich.), who came to the House in 1977, installed a full minicomputer in his office and hired a programmer with legislative experience as his administrative assistant. They have in place the most ambitious approach yet to a computerized congressional office. Applications include constituent casework maintenance, correspondence tracking, legislative files, scheduling, monitoring of various projects from press release use to status of federal grants, public policy analyses, and statistical comparisons.[22]

Staffs of members who are contracting with time-sharing companies for word-processing support are forming user groups to demand better service from vendors, to economize on their rather limited resources, and to share ideas for increasing congressional office efficiency.

A lengthy paper circulated among junior members during the organizing caucus of the Ninety-fifth Congress in December 1976 urged more efficient use of information systems and suggested a business orientation for the use of computers in the congressional office. The staff members who prepared the paper were highly critical of the current lack of data, particularly budget information. One wrote, "If Eastern Airlines can tell you in a couple of seconds whether you have reservations on next Thursday's flight to Miami, the Congress ought to be able to find out where the money goes. The necessary systems are strikingly similar, only Eastern has one and we don't."[23] While Budget Committee analysts might disagree with the analogy, the comment is symptomatic of the new computer awareness in the House.

As more and more new members and staff arrive in Congress, bringing their knowledge of information retrieval from the world of business and academia, they will demand more detail from the executive branch and insist that the computer refine these data into information that will aid in the decision-making process. New job specialties such as legislative programmers will be in great demand. There will be more use of modeling and other forecasting devices demanding computerized information.

The Congressional Budget Office is forcing members of Congress to look at the entire government spending package, instead of just focusing on their special interest. New information processing may also cause the Congress to focus on long-range programs and impacts, rather than the short-term remedies, which has been the norm.

Former United Nations Ambassador Andrew Young, once a member of the House from Georgia, has a story he frequently tells when asked about the progress of the civil-rights movement. His comments could also apply to the status of computer technology in the Congress: "We ain't where we want to be, and we ain't where we ought to be. But, thank God, we ain't where we used to be."[24]

Notes

1. Leslie M. Broughton, ed. *Edmund Burke: Selections* (New York: Scribners, 1925).

2. *Washington Star,* February 8, 1976.

3. *Information on Information* (newsletter of the Ad Hoc Computer Subcommittee, Committee on House Administration), September 1975, p. 1. See also biographic sketch of Charlie Rose, mimeo., September 1, 1975.

4. For discussion of mail volume, see testimony of House Postmaster Robert V. Rota before Subcommittee on Legislative Branch Appropriations, Committee on Appropriations, *Legislative Branch Appropriations for 1977,* pp. 621-637.

5. *Staff* (newsletter of the House Commission on Information and Facilities), Ninety-fourth Cong., issue 2, n.d.

6. U.S. House of Representatives, Committee on House Administration, *Regulations and Accounting Procedures for Allowances and Expenses of Committees, Members and Employees* (January 1977).

7. U.S. House of Representatives, Committee on House Administration, *Library of Congress Information Resources and Services* (April 27, 1976), pp. 34-34.

8. U.S. House of Representatives, Commission on Information and Facilities, *Final Report,* H.Doc. 95-22, January 4, 1977, pp. 18-20.

9. U.S. House of Representatives, Committee on House Administration, Special Subcommittee on Electric and Mechanical Office Equipment, *Second Progress Report,* October 1970, p. 5.

10. U.S. House of Representatives, Committee on House Administration, *The Bill Status System* (1975), p. 2.

11. Ibid., p. 5.

12. U.S. House of Representatives, report to accompany H.R. 1087, April 26, 1976, p. 16.

13. U.S. House of Representatives, Committee on House Administration, *The Electronic Voting System,* January 31, 1975, p. 1.

14. Ibid., p. 2.

15. U.S. Department of Agriculture, press release, "New Computer System for Rural Community Development," March 12, 1976.

16. *Information on Information,* March 30, 1976, p. 3.

17. Ibid., September 1975, p. 1.

18. Edward Schneier, "The Intelligence of Congress: Information and Public Policy Patterns," *Annals of the American Academy of Political and Social Science* (March 1976).

19. U.S. House of Representatives, Committee on House Administration, *Computer Based Information Resources,* September 1, 1975.

20. "A Review of House Information Systems," report by Coopers & Lybrand and Arthur Young & Co., prepared for the Committee on House Administration, October 1, 1976.

21. Representative Charlie Rose to Frank Thompson, Jr., Chairman, Committee on House Administration, January 25, 1977.

22. Interview with Representative Dave Stockman (R-Mich.) and his administrative assistant, David Gerson, December 9, 1976.

23. Earl Young, "Targeting Mail and Information Needs for the House," typescript, December 1976.

24. Remarks by Representative Andrew Young before Peabody-Edmunds Parent-Teacher Association, Washington, D.C., August 31, 1976.

Part II

STATE LEGISLATIVE INFORMATION PROCESSING

As Robert Chartrand and Jane Bortnick indicate in the lead chapter to this part, state legislators are being inundated with a constant flow of information, which requires structuring, analysis, and assimilation. This deluge of information, coupled with outdated legislative practices, has made extensive legislative revitalization necessary. The legislators, by acknowledging that information is at the crux of their problem, have been able to organize human and computer resources and put them to good use. Chartrand and Bortnick also discuss the ten major activities supported by state legislators (each to a different extent) and the patterns of growth that have developed in the early 1970s. They further describe the organization and management of information support services, the utilized hardware and software, access methods, system security precautions, and cost considerations.

Each of the three state legislative information-processing systems described in this part—Florida, Virginia, and Washington—includes details concerning the working operation of its system. The authors discuss their states' methods and procedures for handling bill status, preparation of legislation, online inquiry, text processing, photocomposition, indexing, and fiscal and budgetary accounting. They each note to some extent the historical developments leading to system design and implementation, the conceptual framework and design criteria, and future plans.

4

ROBERT LEE CHARTRAND and
JANE BORTNICK

An Overview of State Legislative Information Processing

State legislatures are undergoing change in the face of complicated pressures. Their genesis stressed the guarantee of individual flexibility and freedom while still rendering a few critical collective services, and the legislatures customarily convened for relatively brief sessions, rarely dealing with more than a handful of lawmaking and oversight problems. But members today must be knowledgeable about scores of issues, some quite complex and ranging in scope from regional to local.

In a sense, state legislators find themselves sharing the problem enunciated in *A Nation of Strangers:* "A great many people are disturbed by the feeling that they are rootless or increasingly anonymous, that they are living in a continually changing environment where there is little sense of community."[1] This situation has occurred in part due to the unprecedented problems that arise from governing and responding to the multifaceted needs of a technology-oriented society. Those who govern and are governed often must yearn for the simplicity of Jefferson's era. Increasingly, the crux of the modern legislative dilemma is recognized correctly as one of information—reliable and relevant and suitably packaged—and the ability of members and staff, often within severe time constraints, to assimilate, evaluate, and use that information.

The views expressed in this chapter are those of the authors and are not necessarily those of the Congressional Research Service or the Library of Congress.

Within the past quarter century, state legislatures have vigorously pursued a course of legislative revitalization designed to result in an ability to meet current crises and to plan for the future. Not only have relationships with the federal bureaucracy come to rival the Minoan maze, but they must "determine the boundaries, the legal powers and financial resources, the very existence of local governments."[2] Faced with this dual responsibility, the leadership in a significant number of legislatures has grasped the potential of modern information technology as an adjunct to improved legislative performance. There is general recognition that more effective legislative management and functioning, though obviously contingent upon perceptive human decision making, will depend upon the upgrading of information resources.

All legislatures, state and federal, continue to share a need for the assembly of salient facts and data, independently developed, accurate, as complete as possible, of maximum currency, and readily available for use; access to and an understanding of executive branch planning, budgeting, and program performance data required for effective review of governmental operations; and assistance in analysis of policy problems, which requires the additional capability to assess and apply policy-relevant information.[3]

The availability of information and its accessibility through employing online systems have become increasingly important not only because many states have curtailed operating schedules but because the volume and variety of information provided by the federal government, state executive branch elements, and outside interest groups can overwhelm existing information-handling capabilities. At the same time other legislative problems remain: the number of bills to be coped with still is too large and continues, in many instances, to increase; many systems surfeit the legislator with too many committee assignments; the turnover among legislators remains high, often precipitating information needs seldom found in more stable groups; strong pressures to deal first with more parochial matters rather than those of broader concern persist; and many states have sharply limited library and research support elements, which are often inundated during periods of peak demand. All of these factors are forcing State legislators to abandon the time-honored motto, *rebus sic stantibus* ("as long as things remain the same"), in favor of a stance more in keeping with the kaleidoscopic demands of our times.

The inventory of information tools and man-machine techniques now available is impressive and growing. The electronic computer offers a versatility that laymen are just beginning to appreciate. Minicomputers, do-it-yourself kits and a myriad of cassette-stored games that can be played on home television sets, are popularizing the electronic computer. When combined with the use of telecommunications technology, the user of an information system can tap into computerized files located far away. Word (text) processing technology, seen by many as having the highest potential for meeting immediate legislative needs, already has been incorporated into a number of bill drafting and prepublication processes. Microform technology, long viewed primarily as a space-saving storage medium, now is enjoying an enhanced image—and utility—with the advent of computer output microfilm (COM). And while recognized for its potential, video technology has yet to achieve a real breakthrough on the legislative scene.

Perhaps the most noteworthy ramification of the legislatures' commitment to the use of information technology is that it represents a tangible, tested form of support that can relieve some of the pressures on the lawmakers. Imbedded within the pattern of commitment to the use of information technology is a determination that it will be used to good effect, which can be assured by diligent legislative oversight and businesslike management of support services. And when one considers the many data-dependent legislative services, it is accurate to characterize information as the life blood of the legislative community, which in turn mirrors the diverse needs of our society.

Many information-handling problems are shared by the members of Congress and the state legislatures. Indeed a significant number of those now on Capitol Hill previously served in the state legislatures. Their awareness of what is possible and their experience in using systems on the state level have prompted them to urge and underwrite improved congressional support systems. Conversely the innovations undertaken by the U.S. Senate and House of Representatives are being observed closely by state legislative systems designers.

Sharing the needs of the leadership, committees and subcommittees, and individual members for sophisticated information-handling services are such traditional legislative support elements as the legislative reference bureaus, legislative councils, and state libraries, each of which has a set of well-defined requirements for improved information-processing devices and analytical services.

Applications of Information Technology

Although information technology has been experimented with and, in isolated instances, made operational in other legislative areas of activity, state legislatures have made significant progress in applying information technology to ten major activities within the legislative process: bill content and status, bill drafting, statutory retrieval, photocomposition, fiscal-budgetary, modeling (computerized), electronic voting, audiovideo, political redistricting, and administrative work.

Bill Content and Status

The monitoring of the content and status of pending legislation was one of the earliest applications of computer technology to the legislative process. Systems in use today vary from the distribution of daily or weekly journals to instantaneously accessed (online) videoscreen terminal networks. Most systems contain essential descriptive elements of bills and resolutions introduced during the current session of the legislature—for instance, introduction date, sponsor(s), title, abstract (or legal digest), and legislative action taken. Systems may also feature a legislative history, as well as an associated index.

Bill Drafting

The drafting of bills generally refers to the conception and phrasing of new legislation, any amendatory wording developed during the course of the legislative process, and the ultimate revision of the existing statutes. Although the professional skills of attorneys are of primary importance, much of the routine work of preparing these documents has been made less time-consuming and more cost-effective by the application of automated text processing. Generally the original draft of a bill is entered into a computer via a special typewriter or videoscreen terminal and is stored in machine-readable form, retrievable for later manipulation. Any additions, deletions, or modifications can be done at any time without the necessity of retyping and proofreading the entire document. Some systems are only bill-typing systems, but others have the capability to retrieve existing statutes and session laws from the computerized data base to use in the creation of new legislation.

Statutory Retrieval

Statutory retrieval was one of the first legislative areas to be recognized as having a high potential for the application of computer technology. The encoding of state statutes into a computerized data base was seen as a means of reducing the time-consuming search for relevant references and sections of the law. Typically requesters can design their own search through the use of key words or phrases, which, when matched with words in the full data base, will print out the appropriate sections. Search processes are either online or in batch mode, where a printed report, processed in a main computer center, is returned to the user. The reports may be citations of the relevant sections, the full text of the sections, or a Key Word-In-Context listing (KWIC), which displays every occurrence of a given word within the context of the surrounding text.

Photocomposition

Modern electronic printing techniques contribute to the reduction of both costs and the time required to publish the growing volume of legislative material. The combination of a graphic computer, phototypesetter, and developing processor produces camera-ready copy from information originally on magnetic tape. Once entered into the computer, information can be recalled and edited as needed, properly formated in pages on a cathode ray tube (CRT) terminal, phototypeset, and printed using high-speed equipment. The output also can be generated in some type of microform. The photocomposition of legislative documents is being employed increasingly with the greater availability of machine-readable data created in bill drafting and statutory retrieval systems. Similarly, the use of computerized phototypesetting is expanding in the printing of journals, brochures, newsletters, and bulletins.

Fiscal-Budgetary Information

Several new information tools support the state legislature's appropriations and oversight functions. Increasingly state bill status systems can tag those pieces of legislation with fiscal impact notes accompanying them, indicating an appropriations bill or an expenditure authorization. In many states, computers provide support in actual budget preparations. Reports, for instance, can show past budgets, a governor's initial budget request, and subsequent Senate, House, and Conference Committee versions. Users can perform various fiscal analyses, test hypotheses, and create columnar or graphic displays. The more innovative of these systems are capable of providing up-to-date information on expenditures and revenues of the state and various budget proposals.

Modeling (Computerized)

Legislators are beginning to employ modeling techniques to analyze their various alternatives for action. A model may substitute fictitious information for real events. By manipulating qualitative and quantitative information based on present or past activities, modeling techniques can hypothesize a particular approach to a problem and then analyze the effect that might result from its implementation. Policy makers can thus view a simulated long-term impact of the legislation they enact. Specifically modeling tools have been employed by state legislatures in the budgetary process, for evaluating educational funding alternatives, for analyzing tax structures, and for forecasting revenue and expenditures.

Electronic Voting

Since the development of mechanical vote-recording devices a century ago, mechanical parts have been replaced by electronic solid-state components in many state legislative systems, and in a few cases computers are employed to support complete voting-information systems. The basic voting system is composed of a voting station at each member's desk, wall display panels, voting controls at the presiding officer's desk, a printer, and a control logic unit. The votes can be displayed on a wall panel as they are cast or held until voting is closed. Most of the existing voting systems provide a printout of the vote when the roll call is taken. Some of the newer systems have the ability to capture the vote on magnetic tape to feed directly into a photocomposition system for the printing of daily journals.

Audiovideo

The use of audio and video media for transferring information has become increasingly popular in state legislatures. In some states, audio coverage of floor proceedings is transmitted to the offices of the leadership and legislative support personnel. In others, legislators can follow the debate in their own office. Both California and Oregon use in-house television for broadcasting activities on the floor and in hearings, and many states permit outside television coverage. Other audiovideo techniques—narrative slide shows, videotape summaries, overhead projectors, audiotape briefing, and computer-assisted instruction—are used to provide briefings to the membership.

Political Redistricting

The storage capability and computational abilities of the computer have been highly useful in supporting the redistricting process by producing districts with equal or nearly equal populations.[4] Two popular techniques, the Weaver-Hess and area partitioning algorithms, attempt to achieve compactness of districts as well as an equality of population. The computer is useful in balancing a number of critical elements, including natural boundaries, population contiguity and compactness, voter composition, existing districts, and current political entities. Some redistricting systems have operated in a batch mode, producing printed reports, and others have included online capabilities with videoscreen viewing of data about a specific district.

Administrative

Personnel, payroll, accounting, and inventory are computer applications in the administrative area that may not be as highly visible as certain legislative uses but are extremely valuable to the operating efficiency of the legislature and individual members. Other computer applications designed to assist legislators in handling an increasingly heavy and varied work load include scheduling committee meetings and hearings, keeping track of legislative appointments, monitoring legislative research projects, reporting on lobbyist registration, and printing mailing labels.

These ten major applications, with many implementing variations, have been worked on in a significant number of states. There have been some false starts, setbacks, and failures, but in virtually all cases, the exercise of looking afresh at a legislative support function has resulted in a newly perceived appreciation of the environment in which it occurs, the procedures currently used—many of which have been randomly added to or altered over the years—and the actual substance and user value of the service performed.

Patterns of Growth

Not only has there been an impressive growth over the past several years in the number and variety of technology-supported information systems within the state legislatures, but an ensuing refinement of the planning and management functions connected with these innovative developments has taken place. Fewer leadership figures and members now regard the computer and its companion technology with suspicion and resentment. Where higher-quality, more responsive service has resulted from the introduction of computer, microform, or word-processing technology, the enthusiasm of members and staff is evident. Similarly, where measurable savings have been attained, the legislators are quite ready to test other candidate systems. Gradually changes are taking place that feature the role of technology in facilitating the packaging and dissemination of legislative information. The literature describing these efforts is somewhat limited, but a few key writings chronicle the progress being made by the state legislators. They include:

1. "Modern Information Technology in the State Legislatures," a 1972 study prepared for the Joint Committee on Congressional Operations by the Congressional Research Service (Library of Congress).
2. A series of surveys by James S. Elkins, Jr., for the Council of State Governments; the 1974 edition, *State Use of Electronic Data Processing,* was updated in 1975.
3. *Comparative Legislative Information Systems,* edited by John A. Worthley (1976), which reports on selected state and congressional activities.
4. "Legislative Fiscal Information Systems," a 1977 report by the National Conference of State Legislatures, which focuses on one area of high-priority concern.
5. "State Legislature Use of Information Technology," a 1977 study prepared for the Commission on Administrative Review, U.S. House of Representatives, by the Congressional Research Service (CRS).

Since 1972, the number of operational information-support systems in the various state legislatures has risen significantly. Automated bill drafting systems increased 300 percent (from eleven to thirty-three) and computer-supported legislative printing systems went from ten to twenty-six (a 260 percent rate of growth). Other major applications such as statutory retrieval and bill content and status systems enjoyed more modest but nonetheless meaningful increases. Table 1 offers the comparative statistics for 1972 and 1977, showing both the operating systems and those either under development or firmly planned.

A useful overview of information technology utilization, featuring the ten major application areas in the fifty states, is shown in table 2. These data were obtained during the preparation of the 1977 CRS report for the House Commission on Administrative Review and include reports on visits to eleven state legislatures, combined with telephone questionnaire data and a summarizing mail survey covering all states, resulting in comprehensive and detailed information on the status of applications development or operation in the state legislatures.

In the light of this record of activity and achievement, it may be useful to reflect on the actions that are prerequisite to a successful integration of technology into existing legislative operations. Although not every step may be taken and the sequence of events may vary, the following have to be considered:

1. A sense of dissatisfaction on the part of members regarding the way in which a given legislative function is being performed must exist.
2. A willingness to explore alternative approaches to executing a legislative service must exist on the part of key leadership.
3. This need must cause a legislative oversight group—variously called commissions, task forces, or committees—to be established.
4. A professional staff must be recruited, for there must be in-house competence prior to undertaking any information system modification.
5. A priority list of legislative activities requiring identifiable improvement must be created—usually as the result of a member and/or staff survey—reviewed, and approved by the legislative oversight group.
6. An analysis of how to bring about better legislative support, either through adjusting manual procedures or using computer, microform, or other information-handling technologies, is required.
7. The trade-offs involved in building a permanent legislative information systems staff versus the utilization of external consultants and service bureau capabilities must be assessed.
8. A top-priority application area should be selected as a pilot experiment, allowing management to evaluate technical feasibility and user reaction.
9. After a careful evaluation of the worthiness of the projected new service, the legislative oversight group may then decide if a full-fledged operational system is to be established and the degree to which contractor support will be necessitated.[5]

This series of initiatives, trials, and assessments comprises a realistic set of guidelines for improving legislative systems: identifying the application as it now is performed, with an emphasis on elements involved, present information-handling procedures, and alternative paths to improvement.

TABLE 1 Legislative Applications of Information Technology

Applications	Operating		Under Development or Planned	
	1972	1977	1972	1977
Bill drafting and statutory revision	11	33	18	5
Statutory retrieval	25	35	11	3
Status of pending legislation	25	36	10	2
Fiscal-budgetary information	20	28	6	3
Legislative printing	10	26	14	4
Electromechanical/electronic voting	35	44	1	1

Source: U.S. Congress, House, Commission on Administrative Review, *State Legislature Use of Information Technology,* Report prepared for the Commission on Administrative Review by the Science Policy Research Division, Congressional Research Service (Washington, D.C.: Government Printing Office, 1977), p. 26 (fig. 7).

Oversight Responsibility and Planning

Since the early 1960s, a number of oversight and planning mechanisms have been created by state legislatures concerned with the orderly development and effective management of technology-supported information systems. In Florida, for example, the Joint Legislative Management Committee was formed in 1964, made up of three Senate and three House members, which still reviews and directs all computerized activities. New York, with legislative burdens often approaching that of the U.S. Congress, initially created the seven-member Legislative Data Processing Committee, including selected leadership from the Senate and the Assembly. The responsibilities of the original committee later were divided between the secretary of the Senate and his counterpart, the chief of staff of the Assembly, and the bicameral Legislative Bill Drafting Commission was created to control that vital activity.[6]

Washington state has placed its legislative information system under the Permanent Statute Law Committee, and in Pennsylvania the first initiative in this area was taken by the Commission for Legislative Modernization. This commission was comprised of private-sector representatives, which performed a study resulting in the publication of recommendations "designed to make the individual legislator more effective and to improve the operations of [the] General Assembly."[7] Later the Legislative Data Processing Committee was established, with membership drawn equally from the majority and minority of both chambers.

As the states one by one took action to introduce mechanization into such areas as the drafting and amending of bills and statutes, performing statutory retrieval, indexing pending legislation (by bill number, sponsor, and

TABLE 2 Information Technology Applications in State Legislatures, 1977

	Electro-mechanical Voting	Statutory Retrieval	Bill Drafting	Bill Status	Photo-com-position	Fiscal-Budgetary	Administra-tive—Payroll, Manage-ment, Mailing Lists	Political Redistricting	Modeling	Audiovideo
Alabama	X(H)			X			X	X		X[a]
Alaska	X	[b]	[b]	X	X	X	X			X
Arizona	X(H)						X	X		
Arkansas	X(H)									X(H)[a]
California	X	X	X	[b]	X	X	X	X	X	X[a]
Colorado	X	X	X	X	X	X				X
Connecticut	X	X	X	X	X	X		X		X
Delaware								X		X
Florida	X	X	X	X	X	X	X/X/X	X	X	X[a]
Georgia	X(H)	X	X	X	X		X	X		X[a]
Hawaii		X	[b]	X	[b]					X
Idaho	X(H)	X	X						X	X[a]
Illinois	X(H)	X	X	X	X	X	X/X		X	X(H)
Indiana	X	X	X	X	[b]	X		X	X	X[a]
Iowa	X(H)	X	X	X	X	[b]	X/X/X	X		X
Kansas	X(H)	X	X	X	X	X	X	X		X[a]
Kentucky	X(H)	X	X	X	X	[b]		X		X
Louisiana	X		[b]	X			X	X		X
Maine	X(H)		X	X				X		X
Maryland	X	X	X	X	X	X				X
Massachusetts	X(H)	X		X	X	X	X		X	X[a]
Michigan	X(H)	X			X	X	X			X[a]
Minnesota	X	X	X	X	X		X			X
Mississippi	X(H)	X	X	X		X		X		X
Missouri	X(H)			X						
Montana	X	X	X	X	X	X	X			X[a]

Nebraska	X	X	X		X					X[a]
Nevada	X	[b]	[b]	[b]	[b]			X		X
New Hampshire	X(H)			X		X		X		X[a]
New Jersey	X	X				X	X	X		X
New Mexico		[b]	X	X		X			X	X[a]
New York	(H)[b]	X	X	X	X	X	X	X	X	X[a]
North Carolina	X		X	X	X	X	X			X[a]
North Dakota	X	X	X	X		X				X
Ohio	X(H)	X	X	X		X	X			X(H)[a]
Oklahoma	X	X	X	X	[b]			X	[b]	X
Oregon	X(H)	X	X	X	X	[b]		X		X[a]
Pennsylvania	X(H)	X	X	X	X	X	X/X/X	X	X	X(H)
Rhode Island	X						X			X
South Carolina	X(H)	X	[b]	X		X	[b]			X
South Dakota	X(H)	X	X	X	X	X	X			X
Tennessee	X			X			X			X[a]
Texas	X(H)	X	X	X	X	X	X	X	X	
Utah	X	X	X	X			X			X
Vermont							X			X
Virginia	X	X	X	X	X		X			X
Washington	X(H)	X	X	X	X	X	X/X/X	X	X	X[a]
West Virginia	X(H)	X	X	X			X	X		X(S)[a]
Wisconsin	X	X	X	X	X	X	X			X
Wyoming		X	X		X	X				
Number of operational systems	44	35	33	38	26	28	29	24	11	46

Source: U.S. Congress, House, Commission on Administrative Review, *State Legislature Use of Information Technology,* Report prepared for the Commission on Administrative Review by the Science Policy Research Division, Congressional Research Service (Washington, D.C.: Government Printing Office, 1977), pp. 28-31 (fig. 8).

Notes: The information represented here is the result of a three-part telephone, mail, and follow-up telephone survey and is current to November 1977.

S refers to Senate and *H* to House.

[a] In-house broadcasting.

[b] Projected.

other features), legislative printing, and fiscal-budgetary data handling, several key issues emerged for consideration by every state:[8]

1. Should the data-processing facility supporting the legislature be within the legislative branch, with all of the advantages of having a dedicated capability?
2. Can acceptable priorities be established and a satisfactory level of responsive service be realized if the legislature relies on executive branch facilities?
3. Can the security of legislative information, often of critical importance to the leadership or committees, be guaranteed by the custodians of the data-processing facility?
4. Is it desirable to contract with outside firms to perform certain tasks rather than to maintain a legislative capability?
5. Can an objective determination of legislators' information needs be made—including the crucial decision as to whether a quick-access (online) system is justified—or would a less-costly service with a longer turnaround time provide members and committees with the data they need?

In recent years, two other significant queries have evolved:

1. Can new forms of information transfer, involving such relatively unfamiliar media as video and audio, result in better member orientation to issues and legislative processes plus enhanced retention of key information?
2. Will the increased use of videoscreen and typewriter terminals allow a decreased dissemination of the same or similar information in traditional printed forms?[9]

There is also a pattern gradually developing across the states of preparing long-range plans to deal with the inherently complex business of establishing and maintaining automated information-support systems. Illustrative of this strategic approach is the state of Illinois, which has been using a multiyear projection since 1970, thus enabling the Illinois Joint Committee on Legislative Information System to function with maximum effectiveness and more realistically project the resources necessary to bring about new or expanded services for the legislature.[10]

As systems developers and their legislative overseers become more comfortable with long-range planning approaches, they can begin to act on applications originally considered too exotic or unattainable. Also, better predictions regarding improved services become possible as the potential of the hardware and software is more fully understood.

Management of Information-support Services

The evolution toward technology-centered legislative-support services has shown many variations regarding the structuring of facilities, personnel, and other related resources. Pennsylvania led the way in establishing a separate computer facility, allowing a degree of freedom and priority fulfillment rarely enjoyed elsewhere. In 1977, the Legislative Data Processing Center had an IBM 370/145 central processing unit plus disk, tape, reader, communications, and printing units, supported by a budget of $850,000. An array of thirty-two CRT and ten typewriter terminals is in service, and the system is operated by two analysts, four programmers, and seventeen data-entry operators.[11]

In Georgia, control of automatic data-processing (ADP) activities is vested in the State Computer Service Center, established in 1966 with "the mission and objective of service outreach to smaller state agencies and commissions which, because of their relative size, are not able to justify economically . . . a data processing facility for themselves."[12] The center's top priority has been the design and development of a legislative information system.

In Mississippi, the legislature took the initiative in 1970 to create the Central Data Processing Authority (CDPA) "to promote sharing of the computing facilities of the State and to regulate the acquisition of computer related equipment and software packages."[13] Consolidation of nine computer centers into a single center that functions as a computer utility was possible through the use of a five-year master plan, and a small group of professional analysts and programmers was established to work with governmental entities lacking their own ADP staffs. The first legislative application—a statutory retrieval system—began operation in 1973 as the result of CDPA staff coordination and contractor effort.

Regardless of how management is organized and the various service functions eventually performed, the changing posture of legislatures in contemporary times has resulted in their membership's periodically examining existing support capabilities. While state-of-the-art improvements may offer far better ways of conducting some support functions, the problems related to effecting desired changes more often than not are nontechnical in nature. Yet technical considerations must be understood and coped with; for example, certain equipment costs continue to decrease, while those connected with software development tend to grow.

The legislative clientele is becoming more sophisticated, and therefore more demanding. In many states, progress in developing advanced information systems has been accompanied by both success and failure, but over time those guiding the introduction of information technology have realized that computer and microform technology has both strong points and limitations and must be employed accordingly.

Computer Hardware and Software Resources

While the array of tools, processes, and man-machine techniques associated with information technology is broad, the focus over the past score of years has been on computers. The hardware and software inventories of the legislatures today reflect both an enhanced user familiarity with available options and the manufacturers' efforts to adapt emerging devices and programs to the needs of a growing market.

An overview of computer hardware installed to serve state legislatures as of the November 1977 survey is presented in table 3. It shows the dominance of the IBM Corporation as a supplier of mainframe computers. Of the forty-four states using computers to support their legislatures, only six are not served by that firm.

The minimal use of minicomputers by state legislatures is indicative of one technology lag in comparison to the high volume of minicomputer use in the business community. A minicomputer is the product of fourth-generation development of technology characterized by the miniaturization and integration of electronic components in the computer. The minicomputer has a smaller memory, fewer capabilities, smaller size, and—most importantly—much lower price than earlier computers. It is quite adaptable to lower-volume tasks and has been used widely in many business applications. State legislators, however, often view minicomputers as being more expensive than renting time on other state agency computers. Thus only California (with a Varian 73), New Hampshire (Data General and WANG System 20), Illinois (IBM System 7), and Oklahoma (IBM System 6) reportedly have purchased minicomputers or word processors.

Software, because it is the instructional base upon which all operations grow, often is readily adaptable by legislative computer programmers. Indeed as table 4 illustrates, several of the states have adapted or modified commercial software packages to their own use. Slightly fewer than half of the programs reported in use were purchased from commercial firms, 10 percent were created by other state agencies or universities, and 42 percent were either created or modified in-house. It should be noted, however, that in-house staff sometimes consisted of or were supplemented by personnel on loan from universities or state agencies.

Some of the prevalent software that performs specific tasks suitable to the legislature are ATMS (Advanced Text Management System), an IBM-created software package for text entry and editing, which permits the entry, storage, retrieval, and modification of textual material, such as bills and other legislative measures; STAIRS (Storage and Information Retrieval System), a package designed by IBM for searching full-text documents stored in a computer, using specific words and phrases, employed especially in legal research and statutory retrieval; ATS (Administrative Terminal System), a text-editing program (available from IBM) providing a capability for remote entry and processing of textual and numeric data files, storing existing formats, and producing final copy from rough draft input with page headings, numbering, and column justification; ALTER (Automated Legal Text Entry and Revision), a computerized text entry, retrieval, and revision system, created by DRC, offering manipulation, correction, deletion, and addition of material without the need for retyping; SIRS (Statutory Information Retrieval System), a search program developed by DRC for textual data files, which can seek and retrieve the occurrence of a specific word and root word in combination with or to the exclusion of other words over the whole data base or portions of it, with outputs of full text or limited listings for use in drafting legislation; QWIK-DRAFT, created by Aspen Systems Corporation as text manipulation and editing software; and ASPENSEARCH, Aspen System Corporation's full-text document retrieval system providing output in several formats.

User Access to Information Resources

Many legislators would insist that ready access to key information resources is the most vital component of legislative support. Each new innovation brings about changes to procedures that may have existed for decades. Just as the telephone and duplicating machine gradually became standard office equipment, the computer, microfilm, and video technology now are having an impact on daily practices in both business and government. In *The New Utopians,* Robert Boguslaw notes that "computers are not found in nature. . . . They must take their places within a framework of existing systems."[14] As the legislative work load increases, often exacerbated by unrealistic demands and deadlines, the need for special packaging of information has grown apace.

Many state legislatures, like the Congress, have found it useful to survey the legislative community to determine the scope and nature of information needs. This includes having members and staff specify the best ways of presenting desired data. Legislators or senior aides seldom have the time (much less the inclination) to analyze copious computer printouts or microfilm cassettes. The emphasis must be on delivering a usable product. The recipients seldom care about the effort required to collect, organize, and format the requisite information prior to its delivery.

Several types of information display or printing devices have been installed in legislative settings, including the popular videoscreen console, often referred to as a CRT (cathode ray tube). This device, used in thirty-seven states, can display both narrative and (with modification) graphic information, allowing laymen to use it after a minimal training period.

One special-purpose, input-only device is the optical character recognition (OCR) unit, which reads type fonts from printed or typewritten pages and in some cases from handwritten characters. Special output-only devices include microfilm or microfiche devices, plotters, and high-speed printers. Computer-Output-Microfilm (COM) produces images that would ordinarily be typed on microfilm (photographic roll film) or microfiche (sheet film with images

TABLE 3 Computers in State Legislatures

States	Computer(s)	Type Model	Legislative Control	Other State Agency	Commercial Service Bureau
Alabama	IBM	370/158		X	
Alaska	IBM	370/145		X	
Arizona					
Arkansas					
California	Varian	73	X		
	IBM	370/168		X	
	IBM	370/145	X		
Colorado	IBM	370/148		X	
Connecticut	IBM	360/40			X
Delaware					
Florida	IBM	370/145	X		
Georgia	IBM	360/158			
Hawaii	IBM	370/155		X	
Idaho	IBM	370/158		X	
Illinois	IBM	370/168		X	
	IBM	System 7	X		
Indiana	IBM	360/168		X	
Iowa	IBM	370/158		X	
Kansas	IBM	370/155		X	
Kentucky	IBM	370/168		X	
Louisiana	Honeywell	60/80		X	
Maine	do			X	
Maryland	IBM	370/158		X	
Massachusetts	RCA	Spectra 70			
Michigan	Burroughs	6700		X	
Minnesota	IBM	370/158		X	
Mississippi	IBM	370/155			
Montana	IBM	370/158		X	

Nebraska	IBM	360/65		X
Nevada	IBM	370/148		
New Hampshire	Honeywell	600		X
	WANG	System 20	X	
	Data General		X	
New Jersey	IBM	360/30		X
New Mexico	IBM	370/158		X
New York	IBM	370/158		X
North Carolina	IBM	370/158		X
North Dakota	IBM	370/140		X
Ohio	IBM	360/158		X
Oklahoma	IBM	370/158		X
	IBM	System 6	X	
Oregon	IBM	370/158		X
Pennsylvania	IBM	370/145	X	
Rhode Island				
South Carolina	IBM	370/168		X
	IBM	370/158		X
	IBM	360/65		X
South Dakota	IBM	370/158		X
Tennessee	Amdahl	470/V6		X
Texas	IBM	370/155		X
Utah	IBM	370/158		X
Vermont				
Virginia	IBM	360/158		X
Washington	IBM	370/145	X	
West Virginia	IBM	470/158		X
Wisconsin	IBM	370/145		X
	IBM	370/158		X
Wyoming	IBM	370/155		X

Source: Commission on Administrative Review. *State Legislature Use of Information Technology,* pp. 42-43. Data collected by Congressional Research Service in telephone and mail survey, November 1977.

TABLE 4 Summary of Software in State Legislatures

	In-house (Created or Modified)	Other State Agency	Commercial Package
ATS			3
ATMS			11
STAIRS			9
SIRS			13
ALTER			11
SEARCH			9
QWIK-DRAFT			4
WYLBUR	1[a]		
LEXIS			1
MITS			1
QUIC-LAW			1
Boeing EIS			1
Education funding	1		1
Fiscal-budgetary	13	12	
Bill drafting	4		
Modeling	2		
Bill status	32		
Bill index	2	1	
Statutory retrieval	3		
Total	**58**	**13**	**65**

Source: Commission on Administrative Review, *State Legislature Use of Information Technology,* p. 50. Data collected by Congressional Research Service in telephone and mail survey, November 1977.

[a]NIH.

in a grid pattern) in a greatly reduced size. Printers range from electric typewriters to high-speed printers operating at thousands of lines per minute. More innovative terminals permit users to alter the display by touching certain parts of the screen with their hand, a light pen, or some other device. These are especially useful when employing graphic displays of output information. Table 5 summarizes the peripheral equipment used in the fifty state legislatures.

Only two states do not control their own peripherals entirely, and one other has some equipment under the control of other state agencies. Each of the other thirty-eight states reporting use maintains control within the legislature. This locus is indicative of the lower price of peripheral equipment—relative to complete computer systems—as well as the time-sharing

TABLE 5 Summary of Peripheral Equipment in State Legislatures

	Legislative Control	Other State Agency
CRT	37	3
Teletypewriter	16	
Printer	11	1
Graphics plotter	2	
Microfiche reader	2	

Source: Commission on Administrative Review, *State Legislature Use of Information Technology,* p. 46. Data collected by Congressional Research Service in telephone and mail survey, November 1977.

Note: Only forty-one states reported use of peripherals.

and leasing arrangements that many legislatures have with other state agencies for the use of computer time.

In some state capitols, videoscreen units are used for retrieval and display purposes only; the insertion of new (or updated) information into the files is performed by special typewriter terminals. Among the states that provide terminal devices at several locations for members is Florida, with a network of 115 videoscreen, typewriter, and teleprinter devices.

Augmenting the online services in many states are such traditional means of handling information as line printers, card readers, and other devices designed to sort, correlate, assemble, or present desired data. Large high-speed printers in centralized computer facilities often are augmented by small printers adjacent to the videoscreen units. Thus legislators can take hard copy, which they usually prefer to use, to committee meetings or into the chamber.

System Security Considerations

The need to protect certain legislative information has been recognized from time to time, but formal, effective actions to ensure data confidentiality have been more infrequent. Both Congress and the state legislatures deal with certain categories of information that require protection: casework data relating to individual constituents, political data (contributors' lists, key civic groups, and mailing lists, for example), committee and subcommittee data (legislative planning and privileged hearings data, for example), and debate supporting data (privileged information supporting public debate).[15]

System security controls exist in some legislative support centers. They include visual control of computer room access, use of special key devices for entry to facilities after normal work hours, tape vaults, and burn bags. Procedural controls include separate handling and decentralized control of leadership and committee information, use of passwords, limited terminal access to a given file, and purposely generalized software descriptions.

Future alternatives for strengthening user protection include:

1. Strengthening security provisions of legislative branch regulations.
2. Establishing standards for need-to-know controls governing all persons having access to legislative files.
3. Developing descriptions of available file data and detailed restrictions as to its use.
4. Creating an enforceable legislative classification system.
5. Establishing an information service group to mediate users' information requests and enforce need-to-know and security regulations.
6. Preparing realistic management and service guidelines, which optimize file protection and inquiry fulfillment.[16]

Cost Considerations

During the planning or upgrading of a technology-supported information system the question of what it will cost arises repeatedly. But it is often difficult to answer accurately. Although some system cost factors are firm (such as equipment rental or the purchase of a software package), additional expenses often cause managerial and budgeting problems. For example, how much in-house project coordination effort is required? Is a significant amount of software modification involved? Once the user community tries the new service, will a demand ensue for additional products, which will cost more money?

Experienced systems designers are very careful when discussing the potential dollar savings that may result from employing information technology. Instead they emphasize improved user support through better system performance: improved rapid retrieval of relevant data, a lessening commitment (in time) by clerical staff, and strengthened information control.

In some instances, of course, the advent of ADP has led to significant savings. Former secretary of the Senate of New York, Albert J. Abrams, reported that new legislative procedures, featuring the use of ADP in storing, modifying, and retrieving key data on pending legislation, allowed 4,050 bills to be carried over from one session to another, resulting in a saving of nearly $1 million in printing costs alone.[17] In Illinois, modifications in the bill drafting operation have eliminated twelve man-years of typing and five man-years of proofreading annually for a saving of $204,000 and advanced photocomposition methods have saved $60,000 and substantially reduced documentation delivery time.[18]

Both the initial developmental and ongoing operation costs must be considered in determining whether technology-supported services are to be initiated, expanded, or curtailed. The following are examples of state contract costs, as noted in the 1972 CRS report to the Joint Committee on Congressional Operations:

Connecticut: $95,000 paid to IBM for the development of an automated capability to produce calendars, bulletins, journals, indexes, and other selected information.

Illinois: $50,000 for the establishment of a bill drafting system (including first-year operating costs).

Minnesota: $150,000 for the first year of operating a bill-drafting system; the statutory retrieval system cost $68,000.

Mississippi: $746,750 for the Lawyers Co-operative Publishing Co. to update and recodify the state's thirty-year-old statute system, to result in an ADP-supported capability that will allow selective retrieval of statutes, court decisions, and other legal material, ease bill drafting, and expedite legislative printing.

Nebraska: $60,200 for the in-house development of a combination bill-drafting and statutory retrieval system.[19]

Further insight into the investment required if information technology is to be used, based on data acquired during the most recent (1977) survey of the fifty state legislatures, was gained from these data:

Colorado: $186,000 funding for the CLEAR (Colorado Legislative Evaluation and Analysis Resource) system, which will feature financial data-base manipulation (including a graphic capability), fiscal note tracking, personnel data, work load statistics, and revenue forecasting.[20]

Maryland: $348,533 for producing the bills introduced in the 1977 session of the Maryland General Assembly; includes bill preparation and printing and represents an approximate first-year savings of $30,000 over previous manual methods.[21]

Massachusetts: $580,000 budget for the Legislative Service Bureau plus $90,000 to fund the data-processing support office.[22]

New Jersey: $25,000 to have Aspen Systems Corp. update the computerized statutory data base (1976).[23]

Virginia: $75,000 fee to use Aspen QWIK-DRAFT II software for text editing (on-line) plus $80,000 charge for ASPENSEARCH IV, which provides batch keyword retrieval; also $34,000 to Computype, Inc., for position software for phototypesetting.[24]

Reflections and Expectations

Although some state legislatures have not yet advanced beyond the most basic information technology, the majority are pursuing innovative approaches designed to provide better information to decision makers. When particular technologies were found to have merit, and perhaps even be cost-effective, other legislative applications, which might extend these benefits, came under scrutiny. However, the burden increasingly is on the requester and user of information, as noted in "The Computer and the Poet": "The biggest single need in computer technology is not for improved . . . containers, but for better questions and better use of the answers."[25]

At this juncture in the development of state legislative support systems, three important trends can be discerned:

1. The acknowledged impact of information tools and techniques on legislative decision making and their increasing value in facilitating two-way communication with constituent groups.
2. The value of a calculated move toward integrating the diverse information-handling devices and man-machine procedures into a mutually supportive legislative information system.
3. The acceptance by those involved of incorporating information technology into the network of personal and organizational relationships that comprise the legislative process.

Few will challenge the assertion that how well the legislators harness the information resources dealing with contemporary issues will, in the long run, determine the vital aspects of a legislative course of action. Information not only must be gathered and filed; it must then be meticulously formatted for maximum usefulness. A hopeful countertrend to that which has seen an emphasis on producing ever more data concentrates on the conversion of facts into intelligence, which legislative policy makers can use. The continuing reinforcement of urging legislators to understand all aspects of information more fully—its collection, structuring, manipulative potential, and options for accessibility—is a critical facet of legislative revitalization.

Among the methodologies gradually gaining acceptance are trend analyses and forecasting through alternative scenarios, both of which stress the graphic display—hence the consequences—of certain legislative proposals. The willingness to employ such techniques usually requires the hiring of staff personnel with technical backgrounds who are capable either of performing such tasks themselves or monitoring the work of external consultants. The use of experienced personnel prevents the legislature from being led into a technological dead-end and optimizes on-site evaluation of computer-assisted processes. At the same time the circle of those advocating and understanding the new technology widens.

Another aspect of information technology is that it is essential to interstate communication. The relationships among state legislatures in sharing information are far from fully developed, but there is growing awareness of their importance. The National Conference of State Legislatures has established a Legislative Information System (LIS) to inform states about research reports available for distribution. There is also a nascent effort to set up a computerized file of state statutory material (or pertinent indexes). Related to this type of exchange is an often articulated need for better information on federal domestic assistance programs, which may be fulfilled in the near future by arranging state access to the new Federal Assistance Program Retrieval System developed by the U.S. Department of Agriculture and now operated by the U.S. Office of Management and Budget. An expanded sharing of information resources by the state legislatures and the Congress, conducted sporadically and in limited areas over the years, also is under consideration in several quarters.

The essence of legislative effectiveness is seen by many as one of judicious decision making based on valid, appropriate information. Governmental performance in all realms must be measurable, which means building evaluative processes into existing legislative and executive organizations. The criticality of this action is underscored in *The Recovery of Confidence:*

> . . . government officials must be required to be specific about goals—that is, about outcomes that would have to be achieved to count a given activity successful; they must develop measures to determine whether those outcomes have occurred; and they must apply the measures systematically to performance—all to the end that they can say of any program, "It worked" or "It didn't work."[26]

The state legislatures, along with the Congress, may correctly hold great expectations regarding the future contributions of information technology. The resources required, together with the necessary empowering legislative authorization, can result in an unprecedented responsiveness by the legislatures to the needs of the citizenry and a surer delineation of policies ensuring future stability and prosperity.

Notes

1. Vance Packard, *A Nation of Strangers* (New York: David McKay, 1972), p. ix.
2. Citizens Conference on State Legislatures, *The Sometimes Governments: A Critical Study of the 50 American Legislatures,* 2d ed. (Kansas City: Citizens Conference on State Legislatures, 1973), p. 3.
3. U.S. Congress, Joint Committee on Congressional Operations, *Modern Information Technology in the State Legislatures,* Report prepared for the Joint Committee on Congressional Operations by the Automated Information Services Section, Congressional Research Service (Washington, D.C.: Government Printing Office, 1972), p. 1.
4. Robert L. Chartrand, "Redistricting in the 1970's: The Role of the Computer," *Law and Computer Technology* 5 (May-June 1972): 58-74.
5. U.S., Congress, House, Commission on Administrative Review, *State Legisla-*

ture Use of Information Technology, Report prepared for the Commission on Administrative Review by the Science Policy Research Division, Congressional Research Service (Washington, D.C.: Government Printing Office, 1977), p. 18.

6. Interview with Roger C. Thompson, Secretary of the Senate, New York State Legislature, Albany, N.Y., April 14, 1977.

7. Pennsylvania, General Assembly, Commission for Legislative Modernization, "Toward Tomorrow's Legislature: The Report of the Pennsylvania General Assembly's Commission for Legislative Modernization," letter of transmittal from the Commission to the members of the General Assembly, January 1969.

8. Joint Committee on Congressional Operations, *Modern Information Technology,* pp. 4-5.

9. Commission on Administrative Review, *State Legislature Use of Information Technology,* p. 53.

10. Recommendation concerning bill status, bill drafting, and the proposed five-year plan for the members of the Joint Committee on Legislative Information Systems, prepared by the Management Information Division, Department of Finance, state of Illinois, 1970, pp. 13-14. Also see Illinois, Joint Committee on Legislative Information, *Legislative Information System: 1976 Annual Report* (Springfield, Ill.: Joint Committee on Legislative Information, 1976), p. 10.

11. Interview with Richard E. Campbell, executive director, Legislative Data Processing Center, Pennsylvania State Legislature, Harrisburg, April 1, 1977.

12. James S. Elkins, Jr., *A Survey of the Use of Electronic Data Processing by State Legislatures* (Athens: Institute of Government, University of Georgia, 1971), p. 46.

13. John A. Worthley, ed., *Comparative Legislative Information Systems: The Use of Technology in the Public Policy Process* (Washington, D.C.: National Science Foundation, 1976), p. 98.

14. Robert Boguslaw, *The New Utopians* (Englewood Cliffs, N.J.: Prentice-Hall, 1965), p. 182.

15. Clark R. Renninger and Dennis K. Branstad, eds., *Government Looks at Privacy and Security in Computer Systems,* NBS Technical Note 809 (Washington, D.C.: Government Printing Office, 1974), p. 15.

16. Ibid.

17. Interview with Albert J. Abrams, Secretary of the Senate, New York State Legislature, Albany, N.Y., November 25, 1970.

18. Illinois, Joint Committee on Legislative Information, *Legislative Information System,* p. 4.

19. Joint Committee on Congressional Operations, *Modern Information Technology,* p. 13.

20. Interview with Lawrence Leftoff, director, Colorado Legislative Evaluation and Analysis Resource, Colorado State Legislature, Denver, Colo., August 4, 1977.

21. Orin J. Durey, Assistant to the president and the speaker, Maryland General Assembly, to Jack Klasnic, president, Graphic Arts Consultants, April 29, 1977. Subsequent CRS interview with Anthony L. Merlo, manager, Computerized Legislative Processes, Maryland State Legislature, Annapolis, Md., August 22, 1977.

22. Interview with Anthony J. Burke, director, Legislative Service Bureau, Massachusetts State Legislature, Boston, Ma., April 13, 1977.

23. Questionnaire data provided by Samuel A. Alito, research director, Law Revision and Legislative Services, New Jersey State Legislature, Trenton, N.J., August 12, 1977.

24. Charles M. Hubbard, Legislative MIS Director, Division of Legislative Services, Virginia State Legislature, to Jane Bortnick, analyst in information sciences, Congressional Research Service, March 1, 1977.

25. Norman Cousins, "The Computer and the Poet," in *Perspectives on the Computer Revolution* (Englewood Cliffs, N.J.: Prentice-Hall, 1970), p. 500.

26. John Gardner, *The Recovery of Confidence* (New York: Norton, 1970), pp. 40-41.

5

DOZIER JOHNSON

Legislative Data Processing: Florida

The Florida legislature has been using various forms of electronic data processing for many years. In 1964 Florida pioneered the development of a data-processing system that would provide legislative members with current and accurate information about the bills before them by reporting the daily actions on each bill. Over the following few years, this system became the very heart of legislative sessions. It grew from a batch reporting system to an online data-entry and inquiry system accessible statewide both by WATS facilities and data-terminal inquiry.

This Bill Status System was designed, developed, implemented by legislative personnel, and operated at an executive branch data center. Because of the success of bill status, the concept of computers and data processing became more accepted by the legislative members, and the computer was recognized as a necessary tool for meeting the information-processing needs of the legislature and its staff.

In spring 1973, the legislative leadership determined that a computer was needed in the legislative branch and that one should be installed at the earliest possible time. The computer was ordered, and an organization to manage and operate it was set up. The machines were installed in November 1973 and were operational for the 1974 session, which began April 2.

The Conceptual Plan

After having been involved in data processing with the Bill Status System on an executive branch data center for several years and having been involved with consultants and specialists on urgent projects, there was a general realization by the leadership and staff that data-processing machines can be used to help solve the information needs and data-processing requirements of legislators. Hence the legislative leaders requested their technical staff to study the data-processing activities already being conducted within the Florida legislature, determine the feasibility of applying automation technology to meet the legislature's other urgent information needs, and propose a plan for implementing a comprehensive information and data-processing system. The study was made, and an implementation plan covering a five-year period was proposed. The plan was accepted in spring 1973, money was appropriated in May 1973 to acquire staff and equipment, the organization was set up in August 1973, the computer equipment was installed in November 1973, and systems were operational online for the 1974 regular session that started April 2.

The study identified online data processing for bill status and appropriations and batch processing for statute search, ombudsman, and educational funding. In addition, the auditor general was carrying on significant data-processing activities in accounting and auditing. Real needs were identified to enhance and extend the online bill status and appropriations systems, to provide a more timely and economical means of updating the statute search file, and to provide the full text of the Florida statutes for other uses, such as bill preparation and statute publication. The needs were broadly classified into three categories: (1) legislative process, (2) support to legislative process, and (3) other support.

The legislative process category indicates those systems that have direct interplay with the lawmaking process. As shown in figure 2, the online systems for bill status, appropriations, bill preparation, roll-call vote recording, engrossing of passed bills, and lobbyist registration comprise this category. Future plans are to include automation of the calendar and journal preparation processes.

Support to the legislative process category includes systems that provide support to the lawmaking process and to the information processing systems. Examples of these systems are statute search and update, data-base management system, analytical-statistical utility system, text composition, and generalized text entry/edit system.

The third category includes administrative and management functions, support to various legislative organizations, computer program development and maintenance, and data processing of the State Courts' Administrator.

As schematically shown in figure 2, the center's system is online processing via a data communication system and a legislative information data base.

Summary of Conceptual Plan

The development of the Florida Legislative Information and Processing System was envisioned in three developmental phases covering a period of

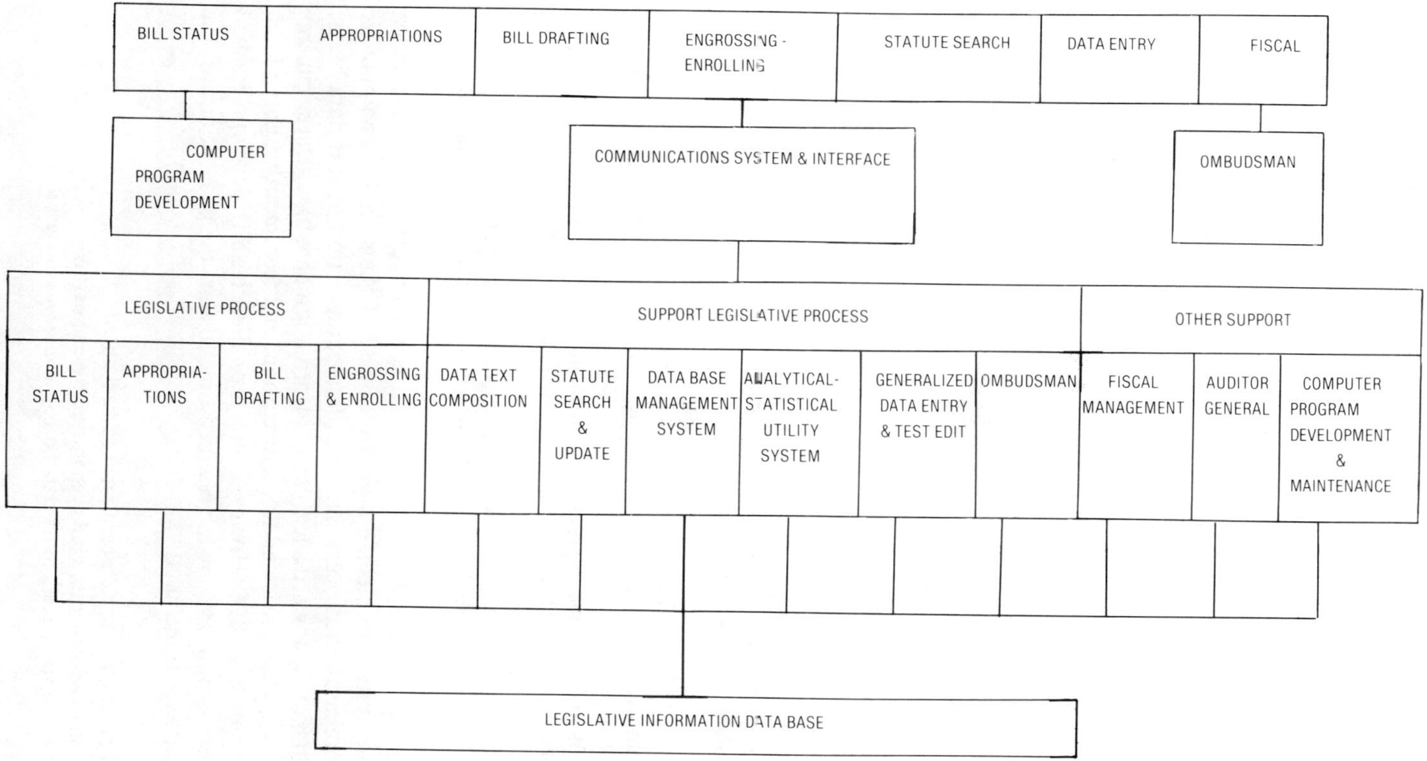

FIGURE 2 Florida Legislative Information and Processing System Conceptual Design

about five years. The conceptual plan is extensive and comprehensive and calls for the development of major information processing systems on a computer supported by skilled staff.

The first phase of development was to accomplish the computer equipment installation, technical training of the systems and data-processing staff, and the transition from an executive branch data center to the legislative center. This phase of development was projected to require about eighteen months to complete, but it was completed significantly ahead of schedule, prior to the 1974 legislative session. Some of the tasks accomplished were:

- Required computer equipment was determined and ordered.
- A site to house the equipment and build the physical facilities was provided.
- Staff to write computer programs and operate the computer were recruited and organized.
- Technical staff were trained.
- Computer equipment was installed.
- Generalized data communications system was installed.
- Data communication network was designed and installed.
- Online bill status system was resystematized.
- Online appropriation system was converted.
- Online ombudsman system was developed.
- Text entry/edit online system was installed.
- Data base of the full text of statutes and index was constructed.
- Statute update was provided for and the index experimentation was photocomposed from batch mode.
- Online fiscal management system was implemented.
- Data processing support was provided to the auditor general, an independent agency of the legislature.
- Analytical and statistical programs were provided as required.
- Computer program development and maintenance of programs was provided.

The second phase of development was conceived to extend the information processing system to include in-house update of the statutes, computerize the bill preparation process, provide photocomposition of text data bases, and begin moving toward a legislative information data base. Developments in this phase were projected to require about eighteen months, going from early 1975 to late 1976. However, much of the Phase II development had already been completed by the planned time to start the phase. Some of the work for Phase II included:

- Phase I developments were continued and enhanced.
- The initial developments in bill preparation were undertaken.
- Update of the statute and index data base in-house was undertaken.

- Preliminaries for photocomposition were begun.
- Preliminaries for batch data-base management system were begun.
- Implementing the data base of legislative information was begun.

Several accomplishments were made in addition to the planned developments and were successfully completed:

- Lobbyist registration online from both House and Senate was accomplished.
- Senate bill preparation (except for local bills) was accomplished in a production mode.
- Senate bills were engrossed and enrolled.
- House roll-call votes were captured online.
- A data-processing system to handle case disposition reporting for the state courts was developed and implemented.

The final phase of development of the Legislative Information and Processing System is the completion of the conceptual design. This phase was projected to require about twenty-four months, starting in late 1976 and continuing through 1978. Projected work for the final developmental phase includes:

- Continue the enhancement and implementation of developments of Phases I and II.
- Complete the computerized system for House and Senate bill preparation, engrossing, and enrolling.
- Automate calendar and journal preparation for photocomposition.
- Automate the capture of roll-call votes for journal preparation.
- Develop text-processing and photocomposition system for statutes, index, session laws, pamphlet laws, and so forth.
- Develop statute search system with in-house update.
- Implement data-base management system as required.
- Implement analytical-statistical utilities online as required.
- Implement online generalized text entry and edit system.
- Implement adequate data communications system that operates independent of data processing programs.

Some of the final phase developments have already been undertaken and successfully achieved, among them, photocomposition, statute update, capture of roll-call votes, and bill preparation. In addition, the full text search of the Florida statute data base is operational on the legislative computer. The revised, conceptual design, which more accurately reflects the last phase in the development of the Legislative Information System, is shown in figure 3.

Major and significant accomplishments have already been achieved and realized in the planned development of the Legislative Information System.

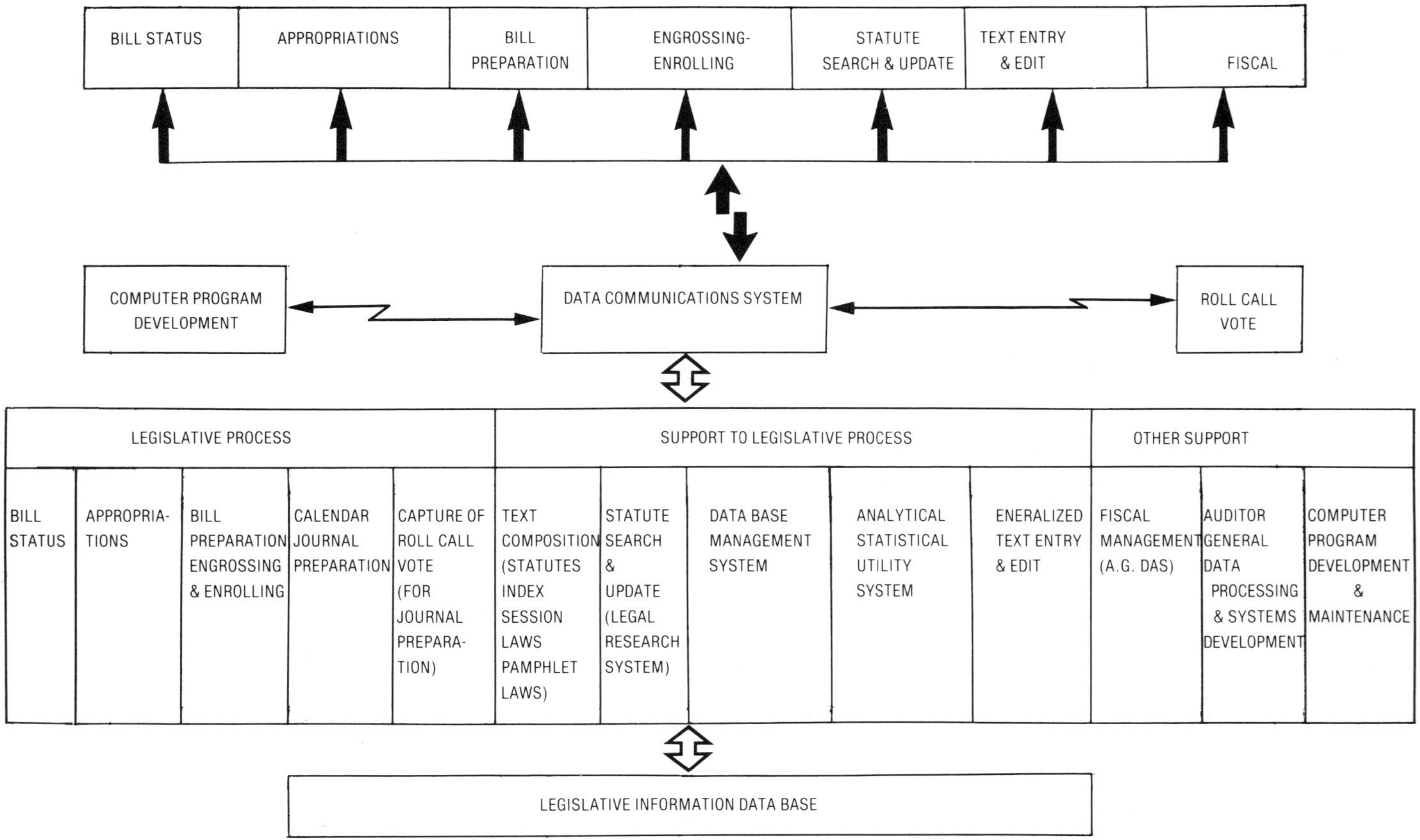

FIGURE 3 Florida Legislative Information and Processing System Conceptual Design (Revised)

The accomplishments have exceeded even the highest expectations and have progressed much faster than the most optimistic planning schedule.

The Joint Legislative Management Committee

The Joint Legislative Management Committee has the responsibility and authority for administering the joint functions of the House and Senate as determined by the committee, with the consent of the presiding officers of both houses. The committee is composed of three members of the House, appointed by the speaker of the House, and three members of the Senate appointed by the president of the Senate. Chairmanship of the committee rotates between the House and Senate each year. The committee sets the broad and general policies and provides uniformity and consistency to the management of legislative activities and functions. The committee oversees the functions of the following divisions: administrative services, legislative library, statutory revision and indexing, legislative information, and systems and data processing.

The administrative services division provides six functions and services to the legislature:

1. The fiscal section processes legislative vouchers for payment, prepares monthly financial statements, assists in budget preparation, and maintains accounting records for audit purposes.
2. The personnel section recruits new employees upon request of legislators and department heads. It also provides for periodic employee service ratings, background checks on new employees, updating of the uniform work regulations for legislative employees, and maintenance of confidential personnel files.
3. The payroll section processes legislative payrolls and contractual payments, provides for insurance and credit union deductions, processes retirement refunds and certifies employment for retirement purposes, maintains leave and attendance records, and submits monthly payroll reports.
4. The purchasing section coordinates and consolidates legislative purchasing to ensure best pricing through maximum discounts and volume purchasing. Legislative purchasing is done through a system of requisitions, purchase orders, and receiving reports. State laws on bidding and advertising are complied with.
5. The law book distribution section annually distributes sets of the Florida statutes and sets of general laws and special acts.
6. The legislative clinic administers emergency treatment to legislators and capitol center employees. Also, medication is dispensed and treatment is given that would prevent loss of time from work.

The legislative library division exists to secure, communicate, inventory, and store information needed by the members of the Florida legislature, the legislature's committees, and the committee staff. Its reading rooms in the basement of the Holland Building and other library centers in legislative offices in the capitol and Holland Building contain material primarily in the legal and public administration fields. Its librarians provide a reference service to the legislature, securing needed information by inquiry, loan from other libraries, or purchase. It catalogs, and maintains for the future use of the legislature, research performed by legislators in other states and acquired through interstate exchange, as well as research performed by study committees and commissions in Florida, which deliver their files to the library when they cease operations. Its up-to-date files of the reports of current committees provide a convenient source of public information on these activities.

The Statutory Revision Division performs several functions. It edits and publishes the *Florida Statutes* following each regular session of an odd-numbered year and the *Supplement to the Florida Statutes* following each regular even-numbered year, and it publishes the *Laws of Florida* (session laws) following each regular session. It also prepares indexes for the various publications of the Joint Legislative Management Committee, including *Florida Statutes* and *The Laws of Florida* (session laws); prepares and publishes *Digest of General Laws,* following each regular session; carries out the continuous revision and improvement of *Florida Statutes,* including the preparation of reviser's bills; and processes all requests for computer search of *Florida Statutes.*

The director serves as ex officio secretary and member of the Florida Commission for the Promotion of Uniform State Laws, and a staff attorney serves on the Suggested State Legislation Committee of the Council of State Governments. The division also maintains liaison with the Florida Law Revision Commission.

The legislative information division provides data to the various information systems of the legislature, thus providing the members, staff, and general public current information on all bills prefiled in the interim and introduced during regular and special sessions from one central source. This division serves as liaison with data center personnel implementing present and future legislative data-processing applications. It prepares and distributes the following reports during session:

- Bill status books (including journal page numbers of all actions); books are printed daily and distributed throughout the legislative offices.
- Subject index, updated daily in report form and included in bill status books.
- Sponsor report, updated daily in report form and included in bill status books.
- Citator: all bills and joint resolutions introduced in current session pertaining to any statute or article in the Constitution (updated daily in report form and included in bill status books).
- Prime sponsor report: weekly listing for each member giving last three actions on all bills of which he or she was shown as the prime introducer.

- Committee progress report: daily report on bills in committees.
- Committee summary report and statistics on all bills referred to committees.
- Passed bill report: daily listing and status thereafter of all bills after passage by first House.
- Final bound status book: full history of all bills; distributed widely after adjournment of session.

Its online network includes videos, direct-line typewriter terminals, and dial-up terminals located strategically in the capitol and across the state with inquiry capabilities for information on the title and full history of bills, status of a bill and its companion (if there is one), last three actions of a bill, last action on maximum of ten bills (string response), sponsors by bill number, last action of all bills by member, and bill citator to statutes and constitution.

The division also:

- Prepares and distributes list of all passed bills in numerical order and subject index order, immediately upon adjournment.
- Provides this information on prefiled bills during interim as during session (short titles, citator, companion or similar bill data, final disposition of identical or similar bill).
- Maintains complete file on all bills introduced and engrossed in both houses dating back two sessions.
- Periodically prepares and distributes interim subject indexes of prefiled bills.
- Serves as both a coordination point for the legislative and executive branches of government and as a central input point for the computerized appropriations process.
- Provides inquiry capability on video for each data record.
- Provides hard copy to aid in printing the following for the Senate, the House, and the Department of Administration: summary reports, comparison reports, governor's recommendations, narrative explanation of recommendations, legislative appropriations bills, and legislative letter of intent.
- Maintains complete file on all administrative documentation of appropriations system.
- Provides assistance to other legislative systems.
- Provides twenty-four-hour incoming WATS line service for citizens of Florida during regular sessions.

The systems and data-processing division has the responsibility of providing computer data-processing support to various legislative activities. The legislative computer is housed in and operated by the staff of the division. Computer systems analysts and programmers of the division perform the tasks of maintaining computer programs and systems of programs, developing new computer programs as required to meet legislative needs, analyzing future needs and requirements for information processing, and planning and coordinating the implementation of information systems on the legislative computer. Some of the uses of the legislative computer are:

- The Bill Status and Information System, which is managed by the legislative information division to provide members, staff, and others interested current information on all bills.
- The full-text data base of the Florida statutes for revision and update for publication and for use in bill preparation.
- The Legislative Appropriation System used to aid the formulation and preparation of the General Appropriations Act each session.
- The text-processing system used in the Senate bill-preparation process.
- A computerized system to aid and facilitate registration of lobbyists and to maintain current lists of registered lobbyists.
- A computerized system of capturing roll-call votes on bill passage in the House for a postsession summary report.

The computer is also used by various House and Senate committee staff for data processing.

The Systems and Data Processing Division

The systems and data processing division is organized into four functional units: planning and analysis, systems and techniques, systems design and programming, and operations.

The planning and analysis section has responsibility for short- and long-range planning of data processing activities and support, systems analysis and research necessary for optimum utilization of computerized technology, and providing consulting services to various legislative committees in formulating information processing requirements. In addition, the section assists with formulating operational standards within the division, performing evaluations of new hardware and software products made available by the electronic data-processing industry, and performing other related work to ensure sound planning for the effective operation and management of information-processing activities. The section is staffed with systems analysts (nonprogrammers) and a section chief, who is a computer programmer analyst.

The systems and techniques section has responsibility for maintaining the computer operating system and other systems software and program products, evaluation of the performance and acceptability of hardware and software obtained from suppliers, and determination of the hardware necessary and best suited to meet the data processing requirements. The section also maintains the system reference library and monitors system performance to ensure effective and efficient utilization. The section is staffed with systems programmers.

The systems design and programming section has responsibility for assisting in the definition of problems that incorporate computerized techniques design, and development of computerized systems; performance of the detailed tasks of computer analysis; design, development, and implementation of application programs; and the monitoring of the performance of application programs for correction and revision as required. In addition, the section is responsible for maintaining detailed documentation, in accordance with established standards, on all application programs. The section is staffed with computer systems analysts and computer programmers.

The operations section is responsible for the operation of all data-processing equipment, maintaining the scheduled hours of operation, providing data conversion as required, maintaining adequate inventory of supplies (such as cards, paper, and magnetic tape), enforcement of prescribed security regulations for the machine room, and maintaining procedures for the orderly flow of work into and out of the computer center. The operations staff also monitors the physical environment of the machine room and maintains detailed records of all equipment malfunctions. The operations section is staffed with a manager, communications coordinator, computer operators, control clerk, and keypunch operator.

Other legislative organizations are also directly involved in the information processing activities. Most notable is the legislative information division of the Joint Legislative Management Committee. The director of this division helped design and implement the original automated bill status system over ten years ago. This division provides all of the data terminal input to the online systems for bill status and roll-call vote capturing systems and the bulk of the input to the appropriations system. The data entry is in addition to the many other information service functions they perform, such as report dissemination, data screening and preparation, and operation of a WATS line inquiry service. Data entry is accomplished by a full-time staff of trained and skilled terminal operators. Some of these operators are assigned to a pool, which provides the work force for different areas at differing times of the year. For example, some of the text-processing system terminal operators are assigned to the secretary of the Senate to assist in bill preparation data for part of the year and are later shifted to the statute revisor to update the statute data file. In this manner, skilled and proficient terminal operators are retained year round.

Data-entry terminal operators are on the staff in other legislative organizations and in the budget office of the executive branch. The secretary of the Senate and the clerk of the House of Representatives each have terminal operators for input, edit, and update of online lobbyist registration. For both the Senate and the House, there are terminal operators for bill preparation and the engrossing of bills that were amended and passed. Data entry and update are also performed by terminal operators on the staff of the appropriations committee and the Senate Governmental Operations Committee.

The Systems and Data Processing Division provides a service that affords users the flexibility of managing their data while being responsible for its accuracy, its input, and its dissemination.

The Bill Status System

The Bill Status System was pioneered in 1964 and has evolved into a comprehensive information system for reporting the status of all pending legislation. The system provides both online and printed report information on the status and history of bills, a subject index for referencing and locating bills, and a citation by bill number to the state constitution article and Florida statutes section that may be affected by the bill.

The bill history subsystem is the heart of the Bill Status System; it tracks a bill from its introduction until its enactment into law or its rejection through the legislative process. This subsystem provides the complete history of all actions occurring to every bill introduced, identifies the sponsor of each bill, gives all bills sponsored by each legislative member, gives information concerning activities in House and Senate committees, and notes the present status as to whether a bill has passed none, one, or both houses. This information is available from online data terminals and in summary reports distributed by the Legislative Information Division each day of the session and at appropriate times during the interim.

The subject index subsystem provides the data entry, logging, and preediting of all subject index transactions. Subject index entries are derived from the subject matter of the short title of each bill by trained and experienced indexing personnel. Entries are made directly into the index data file from online video data terminals.

The citator subsystem provides the cross-reference between bills and the article of the state constitution or the section of the Florida statutes referenced or addressed by the bill. Citation entries are made via online video data terminals and are available for inquiry from both video data terminals and hard-copy terminals. The inquiry is made by constitution article number or statute section number, and the response is all bills referencing or addressing the given entity.

The Bill Status System is an online data communications information system. All information input into the system is from online video data terminals in the real-time environment of occurrence and first availability of the information. Information is entered into the system by video data terminals located on the floor of each chamber as soon as action occurs. During periods of debate and session recess, operators input journal page number references on bill status action and enter committee actions as they become official. Online inquiries are available from hard-copy terminals located throughout the capitol, House and Senate office buildings, and in outlying areas of the state. These terminals are used by the staff of the legislature and committees, staff in the executive branch, local delegations, government agencies, and the general public. The terminals for general use in the capitol and Senate and House office buildings are provided by the legislature. Executive branch agencies, local delegations and agencies, and the general public may subscribe to the data service; they may provide their own terminal or have it provided for them by paying the subscription fee. The fee also entitles subscribers to one copy of the final printed reports following the session.

During each annual regular session, the Legislative Information Division operates an in-WATS facility to serve inquiries by the general public who do not have access to the online facilities. The in-WATS facility is available twenty-four hours every day of the sixty-day session. This service is widely publicized in the newspapers and receives considerable use.

In addition to the online facilities for bill status information, printed report information is produced by the system, and the Legislative Information Division takes care of the reproduction and distribution of these reports. Each session day, reports are produced that list the action of that day, a report of committee actions, an action report on bills by sponsor, and statistics on bills introduced, reported out of committee, and passed in both chambers.

Appropriations

The first attempt at applying computer technology to the legislative appropriations process was solely for the purpose of using the computer as a high-speed typewriter to produce hard copy of the changing contents of appropriations bills. This experiment proved that computer technology could be applied to the appropriations process and that the speed of the computer could vastly multiply the analytical comparisons and computations of appropriation data. At the same time it could reduce to zero the man-hours of work by budget analysts in preparing these same comparisons and computations in the traditional manual way. Automation of the total appropriation process therefore was undertaken with the objective of providing computerized data analysis, hierarchically organized sufficient for detailed comparison and analysis, and the General Appropriations Act itself could be created automatically. The system meets these goals and objectives and has been enhanced to include both fund-major appropriation category reports and program-structured reports from one data base.

The appropriations process begins with the joint preparation of budget instructions by the legislative and executive budget analyst staffs. These instructions are the guidelines, form, and content of requests of the agencies for appropriation amounts by funding source and major category of expense. Using prior year data and estimated expenditures for the current year, each agency formulates its request for continuing current activities. New programs or services are also requested on the forms provided. The agencies submit their requests to the Budget Office of the Department of Administration (DOA) and the legislature simultaneously. The data are input as submitted via video data terminal into the computer system and processed for verification and audit purposes. Errors found are corrected from the online video data terminals, and the verification and audit cycle is repeated until the data base is complete and correct.

For comparison and analytical purposes, twenty-one data items are maintained in the data base:

1. Second prior year expenditure.
2. First prior year expenditure.
3. First year appropriation.
4. Current year appropriation.
5. Agency amended appropriation.
6. Agency report appropriation.
7. DOA modified appropriation.
8. Administration commission modified appropriation.
9. Adjusted appropriation.
10. Authorized operating level.
11. Current year estimated expenditures.
12. Agency request.
13. Agency amended request.
14. Governor's recommendations.
15. Governor's amended recommendations.
16. House subcommittee.
17. House bill.
18. Senate subcommittee.
19. Senate bill.
20. Conference report.
21. Other legislative appropriation.

The budget analysts of both the legislature and the executive branch use the computer system and data to compare, analyze, and formulate the General Appropriations Act and the governor's recommended appropriation, respectively. However, the legislature cannot use or have access to the data of the Budget Office until authorization for its use is granted by that office. Conversely, the Budget Office cannot use or have access to the data of the legislature until authorization is granted. Moreover, in the legislature, the Senate committee cannot use or have access to data belonging to the House committee, and conversely, until authorization is granted.

Video data terminals are located in the Budget Office, House Committee,

Senate Committee, and legislative information division. In addition, hard-copy terminals are allowed limited summary data after authorization for use has been granted.General access to appropriations data online is not allowed due to the nature of the information requiring explanation by the committees.

The appropriations system, although working well, is far from being complete. Future plans include constructing a full-circle system, which includes a comprehensive management accounting system, budget projecting and planning system, the appropriation system, and a budgetary system to annually initialize the management accounting system. This system will be supported with computer graphics and comprehensive trend analysis.

Bill Preparation

Perhaps the largest burden to legislative staff is the clerical typing and retyping of the multitude of bills filed for each session. In Florida approximately thirty-five hundred bills are introduced every annual session, the majority of which are new ones appearing for the first time. Prior to filing for the introduction, the bill has been researched and may have been typed and retyped many times. After it has been filed and introduced, it may be amended by any of several committees and amended on the floor of either or both chambers. All of these amendments require clerical work for retyping and modifying the bill. Since the bills are the product of the legislative process, the speed and accuracy with which the clerical work can be accomplished directly affects the session. For this reason, legislators are still seeking faster and better tools, computerized text processing notwithstanding, to speed their work product through the legislative process.

Florida uses the general purpose text processing system for various text processing requirements, including bill preparation. Advanced Text Management System (ATMS) is the tradename of the IBM program being used. It has proved to be effective and efficient in bill preparation, committee amending and substituting, and the engrossing of amendments made at the time of passage. The Senate started what was to be a pilot bill preparation project for the 1975 session. The pilot became a production system, and 1,760 bills were prepared via ATMS and five video data terminals over a period of about four months.

ATMS provides many powerful text processing capabilities ranging from security over data and terminal operators to generalized markup language (GML). GML allows a code to be defined and used throughout the text, and at selected points in the processing or printing output, the code is replaced by its unique definition. The definition can be another code (photocomposition), standardized phraseology, or an entire document defined elsewhere in the system. The full text of sections of the Florida statutes is available in the ATMS data base for use in the bill preparation process. The keyboarding work load for preparing bills is significantly reduced by using statute text already available in the ATMS data base.

The printed output capabilities of ATMS give the system added flexibility for hard copy of the processed text. These capabilities permit and facilitate format changes for width and depth and single or double spacing. The text data can also be output in a form acceptable for photocomposition purposes. Printed output from ATMS was used as copy master by a commercial printer to make photographic plates for printing pamphlet bills. The method worked well and speeded up the availability of these bills.

Capture of Roll-Call Votes

Perhaps the greatest need is in the area of text processing and high-speed, good-quality print. Examples of the magnitude of this need are found in the daily preparation of calendars and journals. A few states have partially met these needs in some automated way that serves their need. We plan to approach the problem in a step-by-step fashion by solving portions of the overall problem one step at a time. One of the major problems is getting the roll-call vote composed and typeset in the daily journal.

Since our plans are to use computerized text processing for journal preparation and photocomposition for production of camera-ready copy for printing, roll-call votes must be captured in computer-readable form and formatted for the text-processing system. Our capturing system is the first segment of this lengthy and complicated process.

Indicator panels showing member name, vote, and the bill being voted on are located in the House and Senate chambers. The panels display to the chamber and the audience how each member has voted and record the vote by punching small holes in a preformated vote sheet readable by member and vote. A copy of this vote sheet goes to one of the video data terminal operators assigned to enter votes. The operator, using a light pen attached to the terminal, enters the vote on the video screen, which has been formatted with the member names. The fewest votes are recorded by selecting whether the yea or nay votes are being indicated, and those not indicated with the light pen are recorded as opposite votes. Nonvotes are always indicated with the light's marking the nonvote character opposite the nonvoting member's name. After the votes are entered, a printout is produced from the data file for use in proofing and verifying the data. The next step, which has not yet been developed, is to format the recorded votes into the text processing system.

A significant by-product of this system was realized following the 1975 session in that the voting records of all House members were published and distributed. The publication gives the vote to report out of committee by member of the committee and the vote on bill passage in bill number sequence and by member alphabetically by bill number. The publication appears to be popular among legislators, students, and the general public.

Capture of the roll-call votes in this manner still may not be fast enough to meet the requirements of daily journal preparation. The light pen terminal is very fast for entering the data, but the printout still must be proofed and verified. When there is a high number of roll-call votes taken on a session day, they must all be reflected in the journal for that day; hence the data entry, proofing, and verification must be completed before the text processing and photocomposition can begin. We are currently investigating alternative means of data entry for the roll-call vote.

Text Processing of Statutes and Index

The first exposure in Florida to text processing of the statutes came in 1968 when it was determined that the capability of computerized search of the full text of the statutes would be desirable for the upcoming reorganization of the executive branch. The search system of Data Retrieval Corporation of America was employed for searching, and the 1967 Florida statutes were converted to the computer-readable data file required for this system. SIRS, as the system is known, served the intended purpose very well and provided desirable features for searching statutes. The system was abandoned in 1970 because of updating problems caused largely by the annual sessions of the legislature.

When the legislature acquired its own computer in 1973, we immediately began preparations for creating a new multipurpose data base of the Florida statutes. The goal was to construct a full-text data base of the statutes that could be searched for research and updating purposes, that could be maintained and updated by in-house staff, and that could be used for photocomposition of camera-ready pages for commercial printing. Such a data base has been built and is being used for these purposes.

Our full-text search system is IBM's program product, Storage and Information Retrieval System (STAIRS), an online search system that provides conversational dialogue to query the data base. The users of this system praise it as being superior to the batch systems by virtue of the interactive capabilities of the online system. STAIRS allows many data bases to be searched at one time. Although only the statute data base is available for searching, we are making plans for a legal research system that would contain, in addition to the statutes, Attorney General opinions, case law, and other pertinent data. Any one of these data bases or all of them can be selected for searching in a conversational mode from the terminals.

The statute data base was created from the 1973 Florida statutes. The data base was almost immediately updated in-house from video data terminals with the laws passed during the 1974 session. While this update was going on, the 1974 supplement was being prepared for photocomposition using the data base. Both the update and the photocomposition were successful. The statute data base and the index data base are being updated by in-house staff and will be photocomposed. This will be the first time for the statutes and the second time for the index.

In addition to the searching and updating of the statutes, they are used in bill-preparation processing, and chapters of the statutes are printed by computer for specific uses, such as pamphlet laws. New laws therefore are available in print before the published volumes appear.

Lobbyist Registration

The online lobbyist registration system was designed and developed with the objective of providing improved facilities for registering, classifying, and reporting the lobbyists. The system has met the design goals and provided additional abilities by addressing mailing labels and reducing printing costs.

Video data terminals are located in the clerk of the House office and the secretary of the Senate office for use in entering registrations and maintaining the name and address file of the lobbyist and the principal or principals represented. The system provides easy access to the data files for update and reporting both data file activity (update), new registrations, reports by area of interest, and reports by principal. Employees of executive and judicial branch agencies are required to register as lobbyists when they appear before any legislative committee or hearing. Reports on state employees who appear before committees are available from the system.

The Auditor General

After playing a significant role in the initial planning of the legislative data center, the data processing staff of the auditor general set about to transfer computer programs from the executive branch data center to the legislative computer. Amid the programming conversions, the staff participated in much of the same technical training as did the staff of the legislative data center. The conversion was accomplished efficiently and speedily, thus giving the required continuity to the auditor general's data processing needs. Concurrent with the conversion and transition effort, the management systems division was reorganized and almost completely restaffed because many of the staff members had opted to go with the legislative data center.

Upon completion of the conversion of the computer programs, the auditor general's staff began designing and implementing an online accounting system. The accounting system includes facilities for project management, cost accounting, fixed asset (property records), personnel management including leave records, and online voucher preparation. The office of the auditor general and the legislature were the first to use the system from online terminals. Various enhancements and extensions are planned to improve the usefulness of the system.

In addition to the online management accounting system, other online applications were developed. For example, to assist in crucial assessment studies, online data verification and correction of data in the assessment files were provided. Examples of batch work performed include computer processing and analyses of accounting records for audit purposes, assessment ratio computation, and various projects of a consulting nature with a few executive branch agencies. Another project undertaken was to use the online text processing used in statute update and bill preparation for preparing audit reports. So far, only preliminary experimentation has been done.

The installation of the legislative computer has enabled the auditor general to meet his data processing requirements in a timely manner and efficiently and has provided the vehicle by which the development of the management accounting plan may proceed.

State Courts

Prior to the beginning of fiscal year 1974-1975, the state courts requested that they be permitted to use the legislative data center for their processing activities and the continued development of their Case Disposition Reporting System. After studying the impact of this processing on planned legislative data processing, the decision was made to permit the courts to use the center. In order to begin processing data already available, some fifty computer programs had to be converted to operate on the legislative computer. This task was accomplished by court personnel, with some consulting assistance from the legislative data center staff. Concurrent with this conversion was the definition, design, development, and implementation of an online data entry-edit-update system for inserting case disposition information. All of this work was accomplished within less than six months, and the online system was operational in mid-January 1975.

Eight remote data-entry terminals are in use in the court system. Since January 1975, 547,410 online transactions have been processed into a data file containing 1.5 million data records.

The Future

Information processing for the Florida legislature, though still relatively young in its development, has realized significant progress and success. The work already being done will be enhanced and carried on into the future. We anticipate developments in the following general areas:

1. Automation and computerization of the preparation of daily calendars.
2. Automation and computerization of the preparation of daily journals.
3. Capture of roll-call vote online directly from the roll-call display panel.
4. Development of a comprehensive legal research system.
5. Application of data-base management system technology to various data bases, such as appropriation and economic data.
6. Development of the use of computer graphics to aid legislators in decision making.
7. Development of mathematical modeling for use with economic and financial forecasting.
8. Experimentation with creating indexes automatically from text data and computer techniques.
9. Application of operations research techniques to study the impact of proposed legislation.

It has been said that Florida is leading other states in the development of legislative information processing. If it is so, we hope to stay in that position and share our experience and the knowledge we gain with other states. The Honorable Dempsey J. Barron, president of the Florida Senate, has summed up the state philosophy in this way: "We in Florida are not attempting to impress the governments of other states by our use of sophisticated communication and data retrieval equipment. We believe the people of Florida we represent are entitled to the most effective use of modern methods and this we propose to develop."

6

JOHN A. BANKS, JR.

A Comprehensive Computer-Assisted Legislative Program: Virginia

The federal government has grown enormously over the past forty years. The first thirty years of this growth, beginning with drastic measures to combat the Great Depression, affected and greatly regulated every aspect of our national economy but had relatively little effect upon state governments. The Kennedy and Johnson programs of the 1960s—the New Frontier and the Great Society—were endeavors that ushered in literally hundreds of new programs for the delivery of human services. They involved state governments and forced rapid growth upon them. The majority of action in state departments of welfare today is spent in administering federal programs with federal funds. The same can be said equally, or to a lesser degree, of departments of health, mental health, vocational rehabilitation, highways, education, labor, employment, and many other state agencies, where federal grants, federal programs, federal funds, and federal requirements are often referred to. Additionally the states have taken the initiative in developing their own programs to deal with the myriad of complex problems in our modern society as our citizenry has come to expect more of, and rely more on, governments rather than on other institutions for solutions to societal problems.

The rapid and unusual growth in the administrative branches of state governments has led to a rapid and unusual growth by state legislatures, notwithstanding the propensity of legislatures to resist change. In response to this need, state legislatures have looked to modern methods and technology, including computer technology, in assisting such changes and growth. The experience of the Virginia legislature in the development and implementation of computer-assisted programs in its processes illustrates the value of such technology.

Bill Status System

In 1969 the Virginia legislature developed and installed for use during its 1970 session a computer-assisted Bill Status System for the purpose of maintaining a chronological history of each item of legislation introduced. This system employs video screen terminals that are located throughout the state capitol and legislative staff offices. An inquirer keys a particular bill or resolution number into one of the terminals, and the bill title, patrons, and history of the measure are flashed on the video screen. By noting the last entry, the inquirer can determine the current status of the measure as it moves through the legislative process. Significant enhancements have been made to this system since its development.

Instant Online Updating

When the Bill Status System was first installed, the data within it were brought up to date twice daily—once at noon and again at the end of the working day. On each occasion, the system had to be shut down so all legislative action that had taken place since the last update could be entered into the system. Now the operators of special input terminals are housed with direct communications to the chambers of both houses. Any action taken on any bill in either chamber is instantly keyed into the input terminals and immediately becomes part of the system.

As soon as amendments are adopted by either house, the text of each amendment is keyed into the system and becomes part of the retrieval history. If the amendments are substantial, a reprinting of the entire bill is required.

Aggregate Reporting

Refinements to the system include reporting on various categories of action on legislation. For example, the inquirer can have the terminal report all bills that have passed either house or both houses, all bills that have been vetoed, all bills that are in conference, or all bills with title amendments. The system will also report on daily committee schedules, giving the time and place of meetings of all standing committees of both houses.

Expanded Batch Reports

Large volumes of information can be documented rapidly on high-speed printers. After each legislative day, all information in the system on all bills and resolutions (including the title, patrons, all actions, and text of accepted amendments) is printed in a report in numerical order and distributed to legislative staff offices.

Minijournals

A summarized journal of the proceedings of each chamber is available from this system either online from a video terminal or in batch-printed form. The journal reports both the current legislative day's activities and also those of any previous legislative day during the current session.

Expanded Number of Users

Although the Bill Status System was initially designed as an aid for the processing of legislation by the legislature and its staff, its effectiveness has been recognized by many other state and local governmental agencies. These agencies purchase or lease their own typewriterlike terminals and tie into the system by dial-up telephone lines. Other users include county and city governments, planning districts, colleges, and universities. Users in the most remote parts of the state can receive notice of any action on a particular bill at almost the instant that the action takes place. Terminals are also located at legislative information booths in the capitol and legislative buildings, where any citizen can inquire about the status of a bill; information is retrieved by the terminal operators. Terminal operators also respond to citizen inquiries made by letter or telephone.

Bill and Resolution Status

The number of steps in the legislative process that a bill or resolution can pass through and that the system tracks has grown from about 70 to 215. The 190 steps in the system today coincide with the House and Senate journals and are used for preparing the indexes to the journals.

Preparation of Legislation

In the late 1960s when substantial legislative growth became inevitable, the Virginia Legislative Process Commission was established to provide for such growth and to ensure that it proceeded in an orderly and efficient manner. After considerable study of many potential applications of computer technology to legislative procedures, this commission recommended in 1972 that the Joint Rules Committee include comprehensive computer-assisted techniques in the legislative process. In the following session, implementing legislation was enacted.

The commission specifically recommended that Aspen's QWIK-DRAFT, a computerized text-editing system specifically designed for the preparation of legislation, be installed as a starting point. After an attorney drafts a bill, it is keyed via a display terminal into the computer system, where it is stored and may be quickly recalled for editing, amendment, revision, or for any other future reference. The keying process is displayed on a video screen, and after completion, a printout is made for proofreading and editing.

The computer also permanently stores, for quick recall, the entire Code of Virginia. Whenever a bill amends one or more sections of the code, those sections can be recalled by the terminal operator and edited to conform to the amendment without the need for keying the entire code sections. Since the vast majority of bills are amendatory, this feature has proven to be a very effective time and labor saver. Many other features are built into the system for the incorporation of standard provisions or changes with little effort. For example, line centering, indentation, and spacing can be done with fewer key strokes than would be necessary on a typewriter; boilerplate material appears by a simple command without the need for complete keying; and the striking through of existing statutory language that is to be deleted by the bill or underscoring of text to indicate new language can be accomplished, regardless of the length of the deleted or added language, with just a few keystrokes.

Approximately six months were needed for the planning and implementation of the system. First, a contract for a license to use the system was executed with Aspen Systems Corporation. This contract provided for the furnishing of all necessary software, testing of equipment, training of terminal operators and computer technicians, and maintenance of the system for one year once it became operational. And another contract was executed for leasing the computer terminals. Ten Computer Optics terminals were initially installed. At the present time fourteen terminals are leased from Sanders Data Systems (now Harris). This contract, of course, includes service maintenance on these terminals.

Several adjoining office rooms in the legislative staff offices had to be modified for use as a computer terminal room. The walls between these rooms were removed. A raised floor to afford access to wiring below it was installed. Separate air-conditioning, heating, and humidity units were installed for this large computer terminal room to ensure that the temperature and humidity limits for the equipment were maintained at all times. Special telephone cables to connect the equipment in this room with the computer, which is located in a computer data center at a remote location in the city, also had to be installed.

A high-speed Mohawk Data Sciences (MDS) printer, with control equipment, capable of printing three hundred lines per minute, was purchased and installed. The standard model was modified to include a special upper- and lower-case print train and a section symbol for legislative draft preparation. A service maintenance contract for this equipment also was negotiated. Whenever this printer was out of operation, one at the computer data center was substituted. Transporting this printed material between remote locations hindered efficiency, so an additional MDS printer, capable of printing 760 lines per minute, has been purchased and installed. The older printer remains as an on-site back-up. Either can also be used as a batch-job processing terminal.

After the computer terminal room was completed and the equipment installed, the training of terminal operators proceeded much more smoothly than anticipated. Some of the clerical personnel who were responsible for typing legislative drafts were quite apprehensive at first about the apparent complexities of this new system. However, after just a few days of training, the operators gained a great deal of confidence and realized that they were gaining a new time-saving, useful skill. Training of new operators by experienced operators no longer presents any problem.

To guard against primary computer failure for an extended period of time when the Virginia General Assembly is in session, a contract for back-up support was entered into with a private computer company. Communication lines between the legislative computer terminal room and the computer company's remote location also had to be installed. This back-up arrangement is no longer utilized because a state computer data center, which has two IBM 370 computers, supports the system. In the event of the failure of one mainframe computer, back-up support is available on-site with the other computer.

The text-editing system was installed and tested several weeks prior to the session, which began in January 1974, and it has served as an excellent foundation for a comprehensive computer-assisted legislative process as recommended by the Virginia Legislative Process Commission.

The Text-Editing System

Upon introduction of a bill or resolution in either house of the Virginia legislature, sixteen hundred copies are ordered printed. Considering the large amount of legislation introduced within a relatively short period of time, the need to have the printing accomplished within just a day or two of introduction has always posed a large printing problem. To add to this problem, after setting the type by a hot-lead process and initial printing, the large volume of type used had to be stored throughout a particular legislative session for correction and for printing of the legislation as finally passed. These requirements could be met only by a very large printing firm capable of turning out large volumes of work on a twenty-four-hour-per-day basis and capable of storing great amounts of lead type. As the volume of legislation increased during recent times, no firm in Virginia could meet these requirements, and it was necessary to contract with a large printing firm in Baltimore, Maryland, for these services. The copy had to be sent to, and the printing returned from, the Baltimore firm by bus.

As soon as the text-editing system was installed, a new means of printing became available and was quickly recognized. One of the largest photocomposition service companies in the country is located in Richmond just a few blocks from the state capitol. Computer tapes generated by the text-editing system could be used for quickly and efficiently preparing printer's copy (camera-ready copy) via a photocomposer of bills and resolutions and could be subsequently printed in a fraction of the time required by the traditional hot-lead process. This modern, automated system reduced printing turnaround time and gave better control by dealing with a local firm.

After legislation is introduced, little human effort is required to prepare the printer's copy except to convert the legislation, which is already on computer files, from a form for introduction to a form for printing. This work is done on the computer terminals by adding the appropriate bill or resolution number, the date offered, committee referral, and patrons. At the end of each legislative day, all legislation introduced during that day is referred to the computer terminal room for conversion, and converted computer tapes are sent to the photocomposition company for typesetting and printing. Unless there is an unusually heavy load, all of the printing is returned the following day.

During the four years that this outside composition service was used, legislative composition costs steadily increased. In spring 1976, the clerks of the House and Senate and the director of legislative services directed its computer staff to determine the feasibility of accomplishing composition and/or printing in-house. The analysis resulted in a recommendation being made to the Joint Rules Committee of the House and Senate to proceed with a project to bring composition in-house and to provide camera-ready copy to outside printing firms on a competitive basis. This recommendation was approved and the following steps in the resultant project have been accomplished:

1. Specifications for acquiring a photocomposer in the form of a request for information (RFI) were prepared and sent to approximately twenty vendors for response.
2. An experienced manager for the composition operation was employed.
3. Responses to the RFI were received and analyzed, and an award was made to Autologics for delivery of an APS-5 Photocomposer.
4. The APS-5 was installed in January 1977.
5. An analysis for acquiring composition software was begun in September 1976. Several software options, including in-house development, were considered.
6. Upon completion of the software analysis, a contract was entered into with Computype, Inc., which installed in early February 1977 a composition software system (JCP) customized for outputting to the APS-5.
7. The Legislative Composition System now consists of QWIK-DRAFT for text editing, JCP for postprocessing text for composition purposes, and the APS-5 phototypesetter. To date journals, journal index, the index to the acts of Assembly,

and digests are being photocomposed. By 1978 most legislative composition was accomplished in-house.

Composition costs are being substantially reduced as this system is being used for other state printing work such as college catalogs, class schedules, and reports of Virginia Supreme Court cases.

In addition to the preparation of legislation for introduction and the conversion of computer tapes for photocomposition and printing of such legislation, many other uses of the text-editing system have been developed.

Study Report

One of the most obvious uses of this system is in the preparation and printing of interim legislative study reports. The first draft of each such report is keyed into the system. Computer printouts of the drafts are distributed to members of a drafting subcommittee of the particular study group. As each draft is amended by the drafting subcommittee, the previous draft can be recalled on the computer video screen terminal and edited to conform to the latest amended version. When a final draft is accepted by the study group, the text can be composed and printed.

Engrossed Bills

Generally an engrossed bill is defined as one in the form in which it passes its house of origin. In Virginia a bill is most often amended on its second reading and is engrossed as amended after its second reading prior to its third reading and voting on its passage. It can also be amended on its third reading. If it is, the bill will be reengrossed immediately after passage by the house of origin. The engrossed bill is transmitted to the opposite house, where it is referred to a committee for further action. In years past, only one copy of the engrossed bill was available as it was processed through the opposite house. It was read aloud both in committee and when it was reported to the floor of the opposite house since individual copies were not available to each legislator for close inspection. A legislator who wanted to examine the details of an engrossed bill had to go to the appropriate committee clerk or the clerk of the opposite house and review the bill in the presence of the clerk.

The increased printing capability offered by the text-editing system now allows engrossed bills to be prepared and printed in sufficient numbers for each legislator to have a copy. When a bill is ready for engrossment in its house of origin, all accepted amendments are keyed into the bill through the computer terminals. Engrossed bills are printed overnight, and copies are distributed the following morning. House-engrossed bills are printed on green paper and Senate-engrossed bills on yellow paper to distinguish them from initially introduced bills, which are printed on white paper.

Special symbols are used in the engrossed bill to indicate amendments made by the house of origin.

Enrolled Bills

An enrolled bill is one in the form in which it has passed both houses of the legislature. After a bill has passed both, it is transmitted to the computer terminal room and converted for printing as an enrolled bill. Unless there were substantial changes in the second house, this conversion process is fairly simple. After photocomposition and printing, the bill is presented to the presiding officers of both houses for their signatures and then to the governor for approval or veto. When signed by the governor, a bill becomes an act.

Acts of Assembly

As each enrolled bill is signed by the governor, it is assigned a consecutive chapter number and becomes a chapter in the Acts of Assembly, an official document comprising all laws enacted at a particular session of the Assembly. As these chapter numbers are assigned, they are referred to the computer terminal room where the numbers are included in the bill tapes, and the tapes are used for photocomposition and printing of the Acts of Assembly.

Bill Summaries

As soon as a bill is introduced in either house of the legislature, an attorney from the Division of Legislative Services prepares a brief summary outlining the substantive provisions of the bill. The summaries are keyed into the computer terminals, and the tapes generated are used for photocomposition and printing.

Digest of Acts

After each session has concluded and the governor has acted on all bills passed, the Division of Legislative Services prepares a digest of all acts, keying all such digest notes to the appropriate section of the Code of Virginia. The primary purpose of this document is to alert all users of the code to changes being made in state law and what sections of the code are specifically affected. As soon as the draft of this document is prepared, it is keyed into the computer terminals for editing, photocomposition, and printing.

House and Senate Journals

As in most other states, the Virginia legislature does not record verbatim debates in its chambers, but both houses do maintain journals of all chamber activities. The journal of a single house may be as long as twenty-seven hundred printed pages for a sixty-day session. The text-editing system is a great aid in preparing and editing these documents and, at the same time, producing computer tapes for photocomposition. The increased capability enables portions of these journals to be keyed and composed on a regular installment basis rather than waiting until the end of the legislative session for accomplishing the entire document.

Online Search System

In the late 1960s, Aspen Systems Corporation was contracted to keyboard a full-text data base of Virginia's Code and Constitution, to make the data base searchable, and to provide legislators and their staffs with printed results of various keyword search queries into the code data base.

The initial queries were mailed to Aspen and processed, and the results were mailed back to the requester, generally within about two days.

As needs increased, a contract option was exercised and resulted in the Aspen search software's (called ASPENSEARCH) being installed on a state of Virginia computer system in Richmond. It thus brought in-house the ability to process search queries.

In order to maintain a current data base, Aspen was contracted after each session of the General Assembly to keyboard legislative changes, update the full text, and generate the various other files to facilitate query processing. This arrangement for updating was followed through the 1974 session.

Beginning with the 1975 legislative session the Virginia code data base has been updated utilizing composition tapes generated by the Michie Company, which prints the replacement volumes and supplements to the Virginia code. Various volumes of the code that do not exist on composition tape are updated by selecting amended and added sections from the text-editing data base. These few volumes must be edited by legislative staff.

The demand for practically instantaneous turnaround for queries into the code data base plus expanded computer technology allowing one to converse with the computer in an online dialogue fashion precipitated the pursuit of a computerized system to meet this demand. A small number of the more sophisticated computer companies had developed online key word search systems. Inquirers can enter key words or combinations of key words via a video screen computer terminal. The words or combination of words will immediately flash on the video screen, indicating certain statistics, such as the number of times and the number of documents in which the word or words appear in the data base. The online capability greatly enhances the speed at which key word searches can be made. If the key words selected appear in an impractically large number of documents, refinements can be made online to derive a more manageable situation. After the search is completed, the documents of interest can be viewed on the video screen and/or printed to meet hard-copy requirements.

Various systems were analyzed, including IBM's STAIRS, Data Retrieval's SIRS, and a home-developed system. The decision was reached to develop a system, and in 1975, Charles Hubbard, management information systems director for the Virginia legislature, developed Virginia's own online key word computer search system, OSCAR (Online System for Computer-Assisted Research).

Major factors entering into the decision to develop OSCAR instead of acquiring a commercial product were the high cost of acquiring, installing, and maintaining the other systems; investment in a technology had already been made and OSCAR was an extension of this technology; and OSCAR provides flexibility for incorporating other textual data bases by various means, including selection from the text-editing data base.

This accomplishment is typical of the contributions of the professional computer staff of the Virginia General Assembly, which have caused it to be ranked high among all other state legislatures with respect to computer-assisted operations.

Computer-Assisted Indexing

One of the more difficult tasks facing producers of textual matter is the preparation of meaningful and usable indexes. In many cases, an index may be almost as voluminous as the material it is intended to index.

Virginia's initial involvement in computer-assisted indexing used the computer mainly as a high-speed printer; most other tasks were accomplished manually. But specific problems developed; individual indexes were keyboarded numerous times; arranging the index to a document was a manual process; corrections, insertions, or deletions were cumbersome and had to be accomplished on a line-by-line basis, even if only one character needed attention; and updating was done in a batch mode.

Today indexes are keyed, maintained, and corrected via the text-editing system in an online environment. The computer is programmed to use as input to the textual data base, along with other parameters, and then to arrange and provide the required index. Although the changes made thus far have greatly improved the system, a great deal more must be done to utilize the computer to its fullest extent in preparing indexes.

This procedure is used in preparing accumulative subject indexes for bills and resolutions, index to the Acts of Assembly, and the indexes to the journals of the House and the Senate. Edited and proofed indexes can be directed to the legislative photocomposition operation.

Future plans are to utilize the computer in deriving indexes from full textual matter. The need and feasibility for growing into this automatic indexing are very apparent.

Possibilities for the Future

Anyone who has attempted to plan future automated systems or strategies meets with frustration. Once a direction or strategy seems unquestionably clear, someone comes along with a new product or innovation that antiquates plans overnight. In Virginia certain time-proven system areas are under development or consideration.

Mailing System

Various distribution categories will be maintained in an online environment by the computer system, which will generate various optional outputs, including gummed address labels and continuous form envelopes. Selected categories can be processed when a mailing distribution is needed.

Photocomposition

Developing new areas in composition will be a demanding and continuing undertaking. The approach to date has been to use the text-editing system to key and maintain text and then to postprocess this text with a composition software system that generates a magnetic tape to drive the photocomposer operating in a slave mode. This system has been successful and will be pursued in the future. However, some composition requirements need a more direct solution, such as that provided by an integrated system consisting of display terminals designed and software supported specifically for page composition, programmable minicomputers, specialized software, various peripherals, and the installed photocomposer. The feasibility of this system is being analyzed.

Reapportionment and Redistricting

The computer will be used to support this legislative requirement, which must be accomplished in 1981 after the 1980 census. Certain innovative suggestions have been made pertaining to the reapportionment system, such as utilizing a display terminal with a light pen to accomplish manipulations of data and various geographic boundary alignments. To date, a system has not been designed. However, certain components will be supplied by the U.S. Census Bureau.

Computer Output Microfilm

Virginia's legislature is no different from most others in the sense that it is inundated with information. Microfilming is used for permanent recording and storage of printed matter. Most of the microfilming processes used to date have been labor intensive. The technology in microfilming, coupled with the fact that most textual matter is maintained on a computer system, makes computer output microfilm an attractive approach. Plans are to pursue this avenue by either taking advantage of an existing state contract with a local company, which would supply microfiche, or by using an existing in-state capability that provides roll film.

The microfiche versus roll film decision has not been made even though most users prefer microfiche. The situation is further complicated by the announced microfilm output capability of the Autologic APS-5 Photocomposer, which will generate roll film.

Various other computer-supported areas have been discussed or rationalized but not defined to any large degree. One of them is financial management. Virginia uses computer technology to some degree in this area, primarily in the executive branch of government. There needs to be computerization blending legislative perspectives into the system. A few systems have been demonstrated by outside vendors. The more appealing of these utilize online terminals with graphics capability to show the data in the financial data base in various graphical representations rather than just in numbers. Another area is computer-assisted visual aids. Clerks in each house who explain amendments to bills and resolutions could be aided by projecting information displayed on a video screen to a larger screen or screens so that all members in the particular chambers could view the information. This information might be a bill with a proposed amendment, and the amendment could be superimposed on the text of the bill via the video screen so that the viewer could readily see the impact and in-context meaning of the amendment.

7

RICHARD O. WHITE,
EDWARD C. MILLER and
ROBERT FITCHETT

A Legislative Information System: Washington

The effort to establish a legislative information system for the state of Washington began in 1966 with the creation of a steering committee to explore the possibility of a comprehensive system involving a myriad of legislative and legal data-processing applications. The committee consisted of the secretary of the Senate, the chief clerk of the House, the code reviser, the legislative auditor, the director of the legislative council, the state law librarian, and the attorney general's administrative assistant. With the approval of the Senate and House leadership, each of the agencies represented on the committee contributed $25,000 toward the development of a plan. The committee believed from the beginning that no single application, such as law search, was sufficient to justify the high cost of data conversion. Any plan to be developed needed to be general and diverse. At the same time, in order to gain practical experience and visibility in the legislature, we executed a minor contract with the IBM Corporation for the services of a programmer to automate certain small portions of the legislative record. This work was accomplished in time for the 1967 legislative session.

In 1967 several events coalesced to provide a favorable climate and the necessary technical and economic support to enable us to begin developing a comprehensive, multipurpose, integrated system. First, a state data-processing advisory committee was statutorily created for the purpose of coordinating the uses of automated data processing throughout state and local government. This committee was composed of thirteen persons representing the three branches of government. Although the furtherance of the legislative information system was not a specific objective of this act, the three members representing the legislative branch persuaded the committee to allocate a portion of its developmental funds to this purpose. Second, the Department of Institutions inaugurated a keypunch training program for women inmates at the Walla Walla state penitentiary and made its services available to capture the Revised Code of Washington in machine-readable form. Third, comprehensive programming in support of automatic data processing (ADP) information retrieval was made generally available from vendor sources. And fourth, a comprehensive system for applying data-processing techniques to legislative status reporting and other legislative record keeping was developed by the commonwealth of Pennsylvania and was offered free of charge for use in the state of Washington in a commendable and outstanding example of interstate cooperation. The transfer was accomplished by a visit to Harrisburg by our secretary of the Senate and others. A considerable amount of adaptation was required but we were thereby spared the work of developing the system entirely.[1]

In view of these developments, the committee sought and obtained technical and planning assistance from the Data Processing Advisory Committee, which resulted in a plan to implement both a computer search system on the Revised Code of Washington by utilizing the IBM Document Processing (batch) System and a legislative status and reporting system based on the commonwealth of Pennsylvania's system. A data-processing manager was hired to be directly responsible to the administrative officers of the Senate and House of Representatives and to the code reviser because these two initial projects related to the line functions of these officers. The manager was later assigned to the legislative payroll.

The keypunching of the Revised Code of Washington began in February 1968 and was completed in approximately six months. The search system on the Revised Code of Washington was available in January 1969. A basic legislative status system was installed for the 1969 legislative session, and significant capabilities requested by legislators and staff were added to it during that session as rapidly as possible.

The 1969 legislature decreed that the operation and maintenance of the Legislative Information System should be made the responsibility of the Statute Law Committee. Major factors influencing this placement are believed to be the heterogeneous and bipartisan composition of this committee, its continuity (several positions have staggered six-year terms), and its history of conscientious and nonpartisan service to both houses of the legislature.[2]

The Statute Law Committee is part of the legislative branch of state government. It also performs many more administrative functions than the typical legislative committee.[3] Virtually all of the functions it performs are now computerized to some extent.

The activities of the Legislative Information System are supervised by the code reviser, who is the secretary and executive officer of the Statute Law Committee, with the assistance of a data-processing manager, who is the supervisor of the data-processing staff. The code reviser is also assisted by a staff data-processing coordinator who works directly with him and other users in planning the goals and projects for the technical data-processing personnel. The data-processing manager and the assistant manager both perform programming and analysis functions in addition to their administrative duties. Five additional programmers and two control technician-clerks, together with two computer operators, complete the legislative information system staff. The staff data-processing coordinator consults with users and potential users and then works directly with the data-processing staff to outline applications and coordinate their translation into automated functions. The coordinator is the initial point of contact for legislative and other present and potential users of the system. In addition, the coordinator acts as an information specialist in processing the search requests into the legal data files.

Staffing has not been a problem. In 1969, when responsibility for the Legislative Information System was vested in the Statute Law Committee, the manager who had been engaged by the Data Processing Advisory Committee resigned and was replaced by the then assistant data-processing manager, and upon his decease, he was succeeded by his assistant. All of the managers possessed strong technical backgrounds in interactive systems work and competency in administrative skills. Their role has been mainly concentrated upon the technical developmental and operational side of the shop with relatively slight work with the user groups. Each of them, however, became thoroughly acquainted with the legislative process and all of its facets and subtleties. The staff data-processing coordinator's skills and experience may derive from the other pole as they did in our case. Washington's coordinator started out as a bill drafter on the code reviser's staff during the early development of the Legislative Information System. A law school graduate with a strong knowledge of mathematics, he rapidly acquired sufficient technical understanding to be able to assist in defining the legislature's needs and translating them into systems design. A large measure of our success derives from this blending of interdisciplinary skills and offering them to the legislature under the aegis of an already established and respected legislative service agency. We have also been particularly fortunate in acquiring personnel capable of performing efficiently under the stress that characterizes legislative operation: tight deadlines, conflicting demands, and long hours. Since most of the recruiting for ADP personnel was performed by experienced legislative staff members within an established legislative service agency, applicants were thoroughly screened as to their ability to operate effectively in this sort of environment.

Design Criteria

By 1970 our staffing was completed, and design of the Legislative Information System began. Our design philosophy was to establish a highly integrated real-time system dedicated to performing the functions of automated research and the automated creation, collection, and dissemination of such information as the legislature requires, as well as the automated publication of the products of the legislature. We knew that we wished to provide a legislative information service (covering such things as legislative actions on bills, bills sponsored by legislators and subject index of bills) an automated law search service, and a relatively simple and very flexible text-processing capability. We wanted all three systems to perform simultaneously in a harmonious multipurpose environment. We wanted master data-base files, each capable of serving multiple functions, thus eliminating multiple file processing during updates. We also wanted our design to be general enough and flexible enough to accommodate future applications, both known and unknown. These desires reflected the wishes of legislative leadership and staff aides.

With these criteria in mind, we chose a general-purpose monitor—the Interactive Application Supervisor (IAS)—to coordinate the various subsystems and applications. It has proven very satisfactory. IAS allows multi-threaded shared use of interactive application programs through remote terminals. The word *interactive* implies that the applications involve people interacting with programs, with data, and with each other. This monitor is a batch job, running as a single task in the highest priority partition and provides subtasking for application programs under its control. The multi-programming facility of IAS is accomplished by roll-in of programs and roll-in/roll-out of working storage. The application programs are reentrant, written in BAL, and restricted to 2K; they interface with IAS through macros. IAS also provides communication between terminal and non-terminal processes.[4]

The Legislative Information System contracted with the Department of General Administration's data processing service center during the 1969-1971 biennium for basic computer hardware support. In June 1971, the decision was made to acquire a computer that would be located in the legislative building and dedicated exclusively to the use of the Legislative Information System. This system, operational by December 1971, at present consists of an IBM 370 model 145 computer with 756K-core capacity, six 3,330 disk drives, two 3,330 dual density drives, three tape drives, a high-speed printer with dual density upper- and lower-case type train, and a complement of typewriter and cathode ray tube (CRT) telecommunications terminals, along with their respective controllers. Because of unique peak demands associated with legislative sessions, the number of terminals tied in with the computer varies. The number of typewriter terminals permanently hooked up to the computer by dedicated telephone lines varies from sixteen to twenty-eight, and, in addition, four dial-up ports of entry are available for servicing in excess of six additional dial-up terminals. The CRT terminals are hooked up by permanent cables to the computer and vary in number from ten to twenty-four.

Legislative Information System

The Legislative Information System provides to the legislature and to the public timely reports as to bill status and legislative operations. Information is entered and played back through typewriter and CRT telecommunications terminals, which are strategically located throughout the capital complex. Long reports or reports destined for offset printing are routed through the high-speed printer.

The legislative status information file structure provides efficient and instant report production from files that are instantly updated as actions take place on the House or Senate floors. The bulk text portions of the legislative information, such as digest paragraphs, veto messages, status titles, and topical index entries, are all entered via telecomunications terminals and are maintained in files under the text-processing system. No batch programs are required in order to update the files prior to running the reports or to assemble these reports, except that a batch program is used to do the page formatting (putting together the headed and paged two-column pages) of the Digest Supplement and of the *Legislative Digest and History of Bills.* Most reports are initiated and displayed on CRTs and are available at any time during the day concurrently as operators are adding information to the files of the system. The reports are also available in hard copy.

Daily Reports

During legislative sessions, the following automated reports are published daily: Status of House and Senate Bills, Sponsor/Monitor Report, committee reports, Digest Supplement, Leadership Report, Fiscal Note Tracking Report, House Agenda, Senate Calendar, and roll-call vote transcripts.

The Status of House and Senate Bills Report lists each bill, initiative, joint memorial, joint resolution, and concurrent resolution introduced by number and short descriptive title, followed by an indication of the most recent legislative action, which is asterisked if that action occurred on the previous day. Additional information provided by this report points out which other measures, if any, are substantially similar to the listed one; whether the measure has been amended; whether the measure is available from the distribution center as a substitute bill or as a reprinted engrossed bill; at whose special request, if any, the measure was introduced (for example, the governor or the Legislative Budget Committee); and whether the measure has a state or local fiscal note. Normally two thousand copies are distributed daily and widely circulated. Citizens may obtain copies at the bill distribution center.

The Sponsor/Monitor Report is an individually tailored report furnished daily to each legislator and to each by-request sponsor, such as the governor's office or executive departments. It shows the status of all measures upon which the person is a named sponsor. The receivers of this report may also request a daily list of additional measures of particular interest to them. This part is referred to as the member's *trap-line* or member's profile of interest. The executive agencies make extensive use of this service in tracking legislation related to the agency or its divisions. About seven copies are distributed weekly to members and staff to aid them in responding to constituent correspondence and to provide them with overall management information for the legislative process.

The Committee Report, which is delivered daily to the chairman of each standing committee, lists measures (initiatives, bills, memorials, resolutions, and gubernatorial appointments) under two categories. "Bills in" lists measures before the committee and shows the date that each measure arrived there. "Bills out" lists all measures reported out of the committee, together with the status of their latest legislative action. Additional copies consisting of the total combined committee reports of either the House or Senate are provided to key legislative leadership members in both the majority and minority of that house to assist them in managing the flow of bills in and out of the various standing committees. In addition, the House and Senate information centers, the House and Senate research offices, the legislative HOTLINE, and the four caucuses receive copies of the committee reports to aid them in their responsibilities. About forty-two copies are distributed daily.

The Leadership Report is designed to give leadership a summary of the accomplishments of the current session. This report lists the following categories for both the House and Senate:

1. Measures that are before the opposite house, including ones that have passed the original house but have not been introduced as of yet in the opposite house.
2. Measures that have passed the opposite house, including measures in dispute or in conference between the two houses.

3. Measures that have passed the legislature, including the signing by either of the presiding officers, the delivery to the governor's desk, the signing by the governor or his/her veto or partial veto, and the filing of joint memorials and joint and concurrent resolutions with the secretary of state.
4. Measures signed into law.

The exact daily status or last legislative action and the date of the last action are included. About fifty-two copies are distributed daily.

The Fiscal Note Tracking Report provides a comprehensive method for tracking bills having a fiscal impact. (The general and capital appropriations bills are not part of this system.) The impact might be the production of revenue or the making of an expenditure. Revenues and expenditures are broken down into six categories each to reflect the effect on various state government funds. The report essentially provides data in five different categories. The first category is measures before the house of origin, and the others are the same as those in the Leadership Report. This report is provided to both Ways and Means staffs plus others interested in the fiscal impact of bills. About nineteen copies are distributed daily.

The House Agenda and Senate Calendar are also prepared using the computer, drawing different information components from a variety of data banks and subsystems to create multiple copies of the order of business for the day. All of this material is in disk storage and is readily combined by a terminal operator who orders the sequence of the materials and causes the final product to be printed out on the high-speed printer for the creation of multiple masters. These documents also contain the digest paragraphs summarizing the bills under consideration and the digests for proposed committee amendments (if any have been offered) to such bills. The Senate utilizes the computer system to prepare an analysis on the bill, which is utilized during the committee hearing process and later published as part of the Senate calendar. Although this information is primarily for the benefit of the members, legislative observers also use it.

The Roll Call Transcript is usually produced on a daily basis and lists the day, the measure or bill number, the action voted upon, and the vote. The vote in the House is by yeas, nays, or not voting; the vote in the Senate is by yeas, nays, absent, or excused. Roll-call cross-references or index references are by the roll-call transcript number and the item number within in the transcript. The item number is located on the left-hand side of the page on the roll-call transcript. Numbers are assigned to any item of information in the roll call and are not assigned exclusively to the roll-call votes; for example, an item number is assigned to attendance information for morning, afternoon, and evening sessions, to attendance information reported during the call of the Senate or call of the House, and to information indicating that someone has been excused from the call or that someone has reported to the bar of the House or Senate. The House publicly distributes this report on a daily basis and provides an index at the end of the session for all roll-call transcripts for the session. The Senate provides a set of indexed roll-call transcripts to its members at the end of the session and will provide copy upon request during the session. At the end of each session both houses provide a computer typeset booklet of all rolls. This booklet is indexed by bill order.

The Digest Supplements are daily supplements to the *Legislative Digest and History of Bills,* covering the bills introduced the previous day and the bills substituted by the committee reports of the previous day. The Digest Supplement lists the sponsors, a short title, the digest paragraphs, which summarize the contents of the measure, and all actions on the measure that indicate to which committee the bill was referred. Revised digest paragraphs are published in the Digest Supplement on the day after any measure has passed a second reading in the house of origin. The index on the front cover cumulatively lists all of the new or revised digest paragraphs that have been published since the last edition of the *Legislative Digest and History of Bills.* Seventeen hundred copies are printed daily by the state printer from computer typeset copy.

Reports at Irregular Frequency

At varying intervals—from weekly to every several months as determined by the legislative leadership—all of the legislative information in the system is assembled and published as the *Legislative Digest and History of Bills.* Through the coordination of our staff, the state printer, and the legislative distribution center, we are able to supply copies of the *Digest* to the legislative members and others from one to four days after the last information is entered into the system. The time gap depends on the size of the publication, which may vary from a hundred pages at the beginning of the legislative session to two thousand at the end. The sponsors, titles, digest paragraphs, and legislative actions are listed for each bill, memorial, resolution, and gubernatorial appointment. A considerable number of other reports are also included, which categorize the captured legislative information into special reports according to the usage desired. Eighteen hundred copies are printed by the state printer from computer typeset copy.

The *Legislative Digest and History of Bills* contains several tables listing the statutes affected by the current bills. These tables are widely used by legislative draftsmen, as well as by all other attorneys concerned with the legislative process. They are computer products designed to assist the legal technicians in tracking the statutes generally and in discovering instances of potential multiple amendments to a given code section that, if enacted, would leave that portion of the law in a state of uncertainty. The information provided in these tables is collected by computer analysis of the title of the bill as it is placed in the bill storage files by the House and Senate workrooms. Changes brought about by amendment are reflected by a subsequent analysis of the title as the bill is engrossed or enrolled utilizing the bill drafting system.

The Statute Number to Bill Number Table lists the sections in the Revised Code of Washington that are the subject matter of current legislative measures and indicates the actions upon these sections. In addition to being included in the *Legislative Digest and History of Bills,* a daily printout of this table is provided to the code reviser's office. Symbols on the table indicate whether the amended section or new section has passed the legislature or has been signed into law or vetoed by the governor.

The Bill Number to Statute Number to Bill Number Table is designed to point out potential multiple amendments or repeals of an existing code section during the current session by reason of the section's inclusion in one or more bills. The primary value of this table is that it is designed to be entered by bill number rather than by statute number. A committee clerk may quickly check all bills on the committee calendar to determine which other bills before the legislature are in conflict with those at hand.

Another important feature of the *Legislative Digest and History of Bills* is the Topical Index to legislative measures. The index entries are prepared by legislative personnel and are entered into a permanent storage file via a telecommunications terminal. The availability of the text-processing facility for this purpose has immensely improved the ability to maintain the Topical Index. Prior to 1971, index revision or correction required deleting the old entry and keystroking the new entry. Under the new system, only the correction or revision need be made. A special feature in the maintenance of this index places the entry in a state of instant recall via a search query from a terminal. The Topical Index is published in every edition of the *Legislative Digest and History of Bills,* and daily copies are provided to selected legislative staff who need an updated index for research. Later editions also contain an index of measures enacted, reciting their chapter number. A weekly supplemental Topical Index is also published when the *Legislative Digest and History of Bills* is not published on a weekly basis.

Once bills have passed the legislature, an index of acts for the current session is published as part of the *Legislative Digest and History of Bills.* For those acts that have been signed into law by the governor, chapter numbers are set forth after each index entry. Those bills that have been vetoes or partially vetoed are noted by a V or PV. This index is published along with the supplemental Topical Index.

An Individual Member Roll Call Vote Report is published after every session. The accumulated roll-call vote information for each session is sorted into individual member voting records listing the measure number, the chapter (or act) number if any, the prime legislative sponsor other than a legislative committee, the status title describing the measure, a short phrase explaining the roll-call vote, the date, the member's vote, the vote of the body, and the roll-call transcript cross-reference number. After each session, every member receives a copy of his or her voting record, and the administrative officers of the House and Senate and the four caucuses receive a complete run on each of the members of their respective bodies.

Online Terminal Queries

A special feature of the legislative support system is the availability of online search query to the computer through terminal units. The search query will scan all information in the system up to the time of the query.

Legislative research terminal operators are located at the following locations: state library desk in rotunda outside doors to House chambers (this is also a public terminal); House and Senate rostrums; third floor of the House office building; Senate research; legislative HOTLINE; House speaker and leadership staff office in the legislative building; the governor's legislative tracking group; and the code reviser's office.[5]

Information is available on bills, joint memorials, joint resolutions, concurrent resolutions, gubernatorial appointments, and veto messages. Some of the information available upon request to the terminal operators includes:

1. All of the actions or the last action on a particular measure. The actions are up to date as soon as the action transpires on the floor.
2. The sponsors of a particular measure.
3. The digest paragraphs, which summarize the content of a particular measure. The measures are digested on the day they are introduced, but a hard copy of digest paragraphs will not appear in the Digest Supplement until the next day. Once the digest paragraphs are keystroked, they are available from the terminal. Efforts are also made to digest proposed amendments, which in effect substitute a new bill for the original bill and adopted amendatory changes once the bill passes off second reading in the house of origin. These revised digest paragraphs are available soon after the official floor action.

   Digest paragraphs as revised by the committee staff are also available after the committee reports the bill out of committee with amendments.

   An analysis of all Senate and House bills being considered by Senate committees is available once the Senate committee is considering the bill. These are updated as changes are made to the bill during Senate committee processing.
4. Research on particular measures introduced, such as all bills relating to gasoline or a particular bill designed to reduce gasoline taxes. Upon request, each of the

terminal operators will conduct research relating to a particular topic or topics.

5. Various printouts relating to the business of particular standing committees. These printouts tell when the bill entered the committee, where the bill is, if it was reported out of the committee, and the sum of the bills both in and out of the committee. Some of the printouts available include bills in and out of a committee, bills in the committee, bills out of the committee, bills from the opposite house in the committee, and bills from the house of origin in the committee.
6. Bills sponsored by a given legislator or a by-request sponsor. This lists the bills, a short title, and the latest action on the bills.
7. The text of the veto message as returned to the house of origin by the governor.
8. Fiscal impact of the measure on state funds.
9. Various types of reports allowing the grouping of legislation by its fiscal impact upon the state revenue or state expenditures.
10. Various types of reports allowing grouping of legislation by status within the House or Senate.
11. A copy of the latest version of the bill.

These reports may be viewed at video display (cathode ray tube) terminals or printed out at telecommunications typewriter terminals. Hard copy of the reports coming out on the high-speed printer may be initiated at both types of terminal devices.

Text Processing

The text-processing subsystem of LIS receives text input through computer terminals, stores it in the computer, and composes text hard-copy output. The copy may be set in typewritten copy or in cold typeset copy. The stored material can be called into working storage at any time for purposes of revision. The mission of the text-processing system is to eliminate reiterative keystrokes and proofreading, thus reducing total effort and turnaround time and increasing accuracy.

As late as 1955, the enactment of a bill into a statute and its subsequent inclusion in the official code required from four to ten keystroking and proofreading iterations, and usually reiteration of the entire bill.[6] Currently the original entry and proofreading can carry the bill through all of its stages to its ultimate inclusion in the official code. If revisions are required at any step of the procedure, only the portion revised needs to be entered and proofed. Thus one set of keystrokes has a potentially infinite life cycle, beginning with a legislative bill and carrying over into the official code, which, in turn, is available as the ready-made data base for future amendatory drafting. Accuracy is increased because we can now afford to give the existing code double or triple proofings and once perfected, it will remain so. Proofing effort can then be concentrated on revised material, and any carry-over material may be ignored. The computer even conducts a spelling check and notes exceptions to its known vocabulary.

In Washington, drafting requests for all bills, substitute bills, conference reports, and most of the proposed committee and floor amendments are funneled through the code reviser's office for drafting and entry into the data bank by means of typewriter telecommunications terminals. Until introduced by their sponsor, they are treated by the reviser's office as confidential material. Upon introduction, the measures are transferred to House or Senate storage files, where they are available for revision by workroom personnel using similar terminals to effect the engrossing and enrolling processes. Incident to this transfer, a code section to bill number reference is extracted for all code sections being added, amended, repealed, or reenacted in the bill. These references are utilized to build several tables. Upon enactment, the enrolled measures are retransferred to the code reviser's storage for photocomposition publication in the session laws and the official Revised Code of Washington.

The text-processing system may be used for any process involving text creation and revision. It is currently used for many other applications, and potential applications are under study.

Automated Law Searches

The state of Washington has had the capability of searching the total text of its state statutes (Revised Code of Washington) since January 1969. Using successively the batch IBM Document Processing System and the online TEXT-PAC systems, the state has been conducting searches that have proven valuable not only to the legislature and its committees but to the other branches of state government as well. The statutory search system has saved a great deal of work and has made possible many projects in support of the revision and reorganization of the laws of Washington that previously were not feasible. Under the direction of attorney researchers, the computer has proven to be a powerful tool in supplementing traditional legal research. One of the more popular classes of search has been to direct the computer to print out all sections of the Revised Code of Washington in which the name of a given agency, department, or elected official appears. With regard to the *Washington State Supreme Court Reports,* the capability to search against the full text of the cases in the data bank not only permits rapid searches predicated on principles of law, but it also opens broad new opportunities for searches framed to reveal fact pattern similarities to an extent not possible with existing manual research aids.

Search files include the Revised Code of Washington, Washington Administrative Code, the state and federal constitutions, the organic and enabling acts, the formal and informal opinions of the state attorney general (dating from 1949), Rules of Court, and twelve volumes of the *Washington State Supreme Court Reports.* Computer programming and data capture are presently being done which will result in all the second series of the Washington Supreme Court cases (October 1939 to present) being available for search in 1980. The search system will have the total text for about half of these ninety-two plus volumes. The total text remainder of the volumes will be available except for the opinions by the justices.

In addition the *Supreme Court Reports* and *Court of Appeals Reports* are being published via our text processing and phototypesetting system. The publication data-base structure was designed so that the advance sheets and, later, bound volumes, would be easily added to a search data base.

An incremental update program has been developed to permit additions to search data bases without necessitating regeneration of the entire base. Updating may be done periodically for such data bases as the legislative bills and the Washington Administrative Code, both of which change quite frequently.

During the capture of the attorney general's opinions and the court reports, the various parts of these opinions were assigned text identifiers or tags to aid in building a flexible search system, as well as to afford the capability of sorting particular data on which to run special programs (such as creating a listing of a table of all decisions authored by each of the justices sitting at a particular term). Thus in addition to searching the main body of the attorney general's opinion, the search could be made on the citation, the subject heading, the syllabus or headnote, the date of the opinion, the query (including the name of the requester), the name of the author of the opinion, and the footnotes. The court decisions are capable of search by one or more of twenty text identifiers or tags. Thirteen tags are assigned to the statutes and regulations to enable searchers to focus on the actual text of the statute or regulation as opposed to the notes or other text materials associated with the section, or vice versa.

All state and local government agencies are encouraged to use the search facility. In order to acquaint them with this service, the Legislative Information System, during the first two years of operation, offered one or more free introductory searches on any subject the requesting agency chose. Generally searches processed by the code reviser's office for governmental agencies other than in the legislative branch are charged for at a rate of from ten to fifty dollars, depending on the amount of time spent by the information specialist to set up the question for computer processing (for example, performing manual statutory research on a nebulous question or developing a list of synonyms to aid in searching), the amount of computer search time, and the amount of computer printout in pages.

Legal information specialists have been trained to process searches for the office of the Washington state attorney general and for the state law library, which provides services for the Washington state supreme court. These specialists process searches on telecommunications terminals located in their offices. The Legislative Information System assesses no charges for the computer time used by these two terminal users.

Marketing of this system to state and local government is being aided through a computer mailing address label system. Private requests are also honored by the code reviser's office at rates of from $30 to $120.

Indexes and Tables

A major asset of the system is its ability to assist in the creation of indexes and tables in a myriad of applications. For instance, the Topical Index to the *Legislative Digest and History of Bills* is entered by means of the text-processing system. Following a legislative session, the entries relative to measures enacted are programmatically extracted from the larger file of measures introduced, and this extract forms the basis for the index to the session laws and the House and Senate journals.

The most significant index application relates to the index of the Revised Code of Washington, all of which is stored in the text-processing system and is capable of inversion from alphabetical to numerical order and vice versa. The numerical order, which prints out all entries in numerical code section sequence, enables a rapid updating of all entries related to an amended section. When agencies publish the laws related to their agency, we are able to create a specialized index by merely extracting from the master the index entries related to the laws so published in their publication.

The system also creates a variety of cross-reference tables; bill number to statute number and bill number to reviser's file number are two examples. One of the more valuable tables lists code section references that are embedded in the text of other code sections. This table thus enables users to ascertain quickly all other code sections citing a given code section or adopting it by reference. Knowledge of such references is essential to bill drafters so that they can consider whether the sections in which the reference appears require revision.

All of the Revised Code of Washington applications in the index and table area are or will be applied to the Washington Administrative Code preparation and publication system.

Legislative Oversight: Washington's Fiscal and Budgetary Information System

Through an innovative computer system, the Washington legislature has developed a comprehensive tool for analyzing budget proposals and for monitoring the flow of agency expenditures and revenues. The program, the Legislative Evaluation and Accountability Program (LEAP), is operated in conjunction with the House Appropriations and Senate Ways and Means committees. It was initiated in January 1975 as a direct access (online) computer system capable of filling the legislative need for rapid, accurate, and concise fiscal information.

LEAP is composed of a major computer unit and a number of terminal teletype stations that provide information in printouts or in graphic display form. The computer unit consists of a memory bank which holds fiscal data from the year 1970 to the present; a control unit, which locates and organizes information within the system; and a data manipulator, which is the statistician and graphics composer. As the most sophisticated part of the system, this unit has been able to expand the legislature's knowledge of the state's changing fiscal situation.

The terminal stations, which function as the request and receiving units of the computer, are located in the House office building and the institutions building. They are able to translate the stored data into report or graphic form. Two portable terminals can also be used during committee meetings to provide printouts on any questions that require an analytical report on information already programmed. A simple English command language is used to instruct the computer to perform the manipulation and reporting task. The computer response is made within a few minutes. Report forms can also be graphed on one of the cathode ray tube stations if visual illustrations will be helpful. Pie, line, or bar charts may be used to illustrate and compare different fiscal alternatives.

Because of the importance of providing for legislative analysis and control of the state's budget, a major program has been established with the computer system for this purpose. This program, BASE (Budget Analysis for Statewide Evaluation), is flexible enough to digest and analyze new information as different variables are put into each budget proposal. If an information request is on a new budget proposal or on a set of changing variables, such as a state employee's salary increase, the staff can write the new program and extract the information within a day or two. BASE also enables users to do other sophisticated analyses, such as historical comparisons using data from previous bienniums, as well as forecasting, trend analysis, time-series analysis, and setting up hypothetical models.

Certain general budget questions have been programmed into one-line formula requests to allow laymen to use the computer's services. These include cumulative-to-date expenditure graphs for agencies or objects and pie graphs, which divide program costs within an agency. A BASE book available to interested users illustrates the available graph and report forms.

In addition to providing for budget analysis and control, LEAP also serves to provide for legislative visibility over the budget execution process.

In monitoring state agency expenditures, revenues, and staffing, LEAP uses its monthly reports and graphs to signal when an agency is exceeding its budget. Line charts diagram actual monthly expenditures against estimated monthly expenditures. If the monitoring routine reveals a large potential overexpenditure or an unexpected reduction, the agency can be contacted and the cause of the budget shift analyzed. Keeping overall budget expenditures visible to the legislature is crucial. Because state agencies sometimes expend funds in excess of their monthly estimates and resultant deficiencies are often too large to be covered through resource reallocation by the executive branch, the legislature, to avoid making a large supplemental appropriation within a critically short time, can now monitor overexpenditures before they reach an uncontrollable level. LEAP also sets tolerance levels for expenditures within an agency at the program level so that only programs that are notably overspent or underspent need be reviewed. The LEAP monitoring system also has been structured to allow laymen access to the graphs and report forms available on agencies, programs, and objects of expenditure.

Through the formula reports and through its statistical ability, the range of its graphs, and the rapidity of its performance, LEAP is able to strengthen the legislature in its decision-making capacity.

Product Beneficiaries: Current and Future Applications

The Legislative Information System was planned from the outset as an open-ended, generalized, multifunction system. This breadth of planning has made possible a large variety of current and future applications that are supported or can be supported by the system. Much has been said in data-processing circles relative to the economies of scale. Equally as important but seldom mentioned are the economies of variety and versatility. The true cost of any system varies inversely with the number of substantial applications within its realm of capability.

Following a brief period of reliance upon the executive branch for some very basic planning and hardware support, LIS became an arm of the legislature dedicated to assisting with the information it requires to operate efficiently and effectively as a separate and coequal branch of state government. The system also freed the legislature from dependence upon private research groups, which formerly supplied digest and status reporting services. The Washington legislature, like most others in the last decade, has encountered an information explosion of gargantuan proportions, and the volume and complexity of the legislative burden have increased tremendously. Although the state's constitutionally mandated sessions are but sixty days every two years, the Forty-fourth Legislature was in session for 250 days. Automation arrived just in time.

The decision to acquire dedicated hardware was partly influenced by the cyclical nature of the legislature's activities, which would disrupt the operation of another governmental computer geared to more even loads.[7] The legislative acquisition not only avoided any such operational contention but also afforded our staff an opportunity to proceed rapidly with essential research and development, and provided the flexibility to enable them to quickly innovate applications as the occasions arose.

Several applications created for the legislative branch are now proving extremely attractive to the other branches as well, and we must now steer a course that will extend these benefits to them without subverting the primacy of the legislature's needs for service. Foremost among these are the various applications in the text-processing subsystem, which have enabled us to republish the entire Revised Code of Washington (eight-five hundred pages biennially) every two years on a more timely basis and at less cost than mere upkeep of our former looseleaf edition. Some other major uses of the text-processing system follow.

1. *Court decisions.* Beginning in January 1977, the advance sheets and bound volumes of the *Washington State Supreme Court Reports* were published using the system, and in April the advance sheets and bound volumes of the *Court of Appeals Reports* were published by the system. Both of these projects involve the cooperative efforts of the court reporter's office, the state printing staff, and the Statute Law Committee's computer staff.

2. *Governor's budget document.* During fall 1976, the budget and the state printing staffs utilized a system designed by the Statute Law Committee's computer staff to insert the general and capital budgets of all state agencies into the computer. In December 1976 the book was published. Although the last two-thirds of the book was not made available for phototypesetting until four days before the statutory mandated publication date because of late budget decisions, the new technology and the fact that offset presses were used enabled the book to be ready one day ahead of time.

3. *State agency publications on statutes and regulations.* We have assisted many executive branch agencies with their publication of departmental pamphlets containing portions of the Revised Code of Washington (statutes) and the Washington Administrative Code (regulations). The demand for this service is growing, and our personnel have been working with the state printer's staff to keep up with the demand for select publications.

4. *Administrative Law—Washington Administrative Code.* The code reviser's office implemented a new publication system on the Washington Administrative Code during 1978. The whole codified compilation of permanently adapted administrative orders was reprinted in a bound nine-volume set. This set will be reprinted every three to four years. Changes to the code between reprints will be published yearly in a cumulative supplement of one or more volumes. An index is provided with both the reprinted code and the supplement. This index is directed toward the subject matter found in each chapter.

5. *Administrative Law—Washington State Register.* This publication was started in January 1978. The content of the register is as follows: proposed, emergency, and adopted regulations, rules of court, public meeting notices by state agencies, and executive proclamations. The register is published by the third Wednesday of each month, and it covers materials filed by the first Wednesday of the month. The materials relating to regulations are set forth in full text. Amended sections of the code are set forth with deletions being shown by striking through and with additions being shown by underscoring. The monthly publication has a cumulative table showing code sections affected and a cumulative subject matter index.

6. *Administrative Law—order typing service.* Since November 1975, the code reviser's office has been aiding the promulgating agencies in typing their proposed, emergency, and adopted regulations. The agency actually files a computer-typed or possibly typeset copy as their final administrative order. The same techniques deployed in bill drafting are utilized in this system to prevent reiterative keystrokings by the agency, the code reviser's office, and the state printer.

The use of the text-processing system is evidenced by the growth of the materials being phototypeset: 1975—4,471 pages; 1976—14,389 pages; 1977—23,357 pages; 1978—31,100 pages; and 1979 (through March)—33,336. In response to our activity, the state printer installed an APS-5 phototypesetting machine by Autologic, Inc., in July 1976.

Although LIS is dedicated to the legislative service, its benefits rebound to all three branches of government. The philosophy of saving keystrokes is successful in many ways: The initial capture of codes, decisions, and budgets take full advantage of the computer's text revision capabilities in the creation of the original document, is subsequently available for publication purposes, and concurrently produces a ready-made data base for computerized search techniques.

Although the extension of services to areas outside of the legislature is logical and technologically sound, it tends to create administrative and accounting complexities, and care must be taken that service to the legislature remains LIS's primary responsibility. The development of this system was not without problems. In the initial stages of its development, our small staff of managers, coordinators, and software specialists were compelled to work inordinate amounts of overtime and to make many personal sacrifices. Their product has withstood the test. The truest measure of its success is that it is now taken very much for granted.

Notes

1. The Pennsylvania system was a QTAM single-thread application, which provided for online inquiry and online data collection but used batch processing to

update the various data files. This was rewritten in Washington as a multithread IAS application, which provided online inquiry, update editing, and update processing.

2. The Statute Law Committee consists of twelve attorneys. Five are appointed by the Washington State Bar Association, two each by the Senate and House judiciary committees (bipartisan), and one each by the governor, the chief justice of the supreme court, and the speaker of the House.

3. The primary responsibilities of the committee and the code reviser are to codify, index, and publish periodically the Revised Code of Washington and to revise, correct, and harmonize the statutes by means of appropriate administrative or suggested legislative action. The agency is also the official bill-drafting arm of the legislature and its various committees and prepares for the legislature all bills, memorials, resolutions, amendments, and conference reports.

Immediately following each session of the legislature, the committee indexes and publishes the temporary edition of the session laws and subsequently publishes the permanent edition. The committee also responds to citizens' requests for copies of recently enacted laws and reviews all initiative proposals prior to their being filed with the secretary of state. The committee administers the Administrative Procedures Act and the State Higher Education Administrative Procedure Act. It acts as official repository for the rules and regulations of the various state agencies and the institutions of higher learning, publishes the Washington Administrative Code, and administers the Legislative Information System.

4. See *Interactive Applications Supervisor Users Manual,* IBM program number 360D-05.2.010.

5. The legislative HOTLINE is a statewide toll-free telephone number available for information about bills or for passing on information to legislators. It is serviced by seven persons and handles seven hundred or eight hundred calls per day. Hours are normally 8:00 A.M. to 6:00 P.M. Monday through Friday and 10:00 A.M. to 2:00 P.M. on Saturday. In addition HOTLINE is operating at all times the legislature is in actual daily session. A taped message responds to calls logged in during nonoperational hours.

6. These iterations could be four or more of the following: original bill, substitute bill, engrossed bill, reengrossed bill, conference report, enrolled bill, session laws, and Revised Code of Washington. To this could be added committee amendments in the original and the opposite houses plus floor amendments in the opposite house plus the number of rough drafts of the bill before it is ever introduced.

7. Purchase price in 1971 was about $1,189,000 spread over five years. Some peripheral equipment of a primarily mechanical nature, such as a high-speed printer, remains on lease. The decision to purchase was favored by the legislature, which in 1969 had delegated broad authority to the State Law Committee: "The code reviser shall be in charge of and shall operate and maintain the Legislative Information System which shall provide automatic data processing services for the legislature and its various committees and, by agreement, for the judiciary and the legal or law-oriented agencies of the executive branch. All such operations shall be subject to the general supervision of the statute law committee. The statute law committee may employ or engage and fix the compensation for such personnel as may be

required to plan, supervise, operate, procure, or supply such services. Pursuant to prior consultation with the data processing advisory committee, the statute law committee may enter into contracts with public or private vendors or purchasers for the sale, exchange, or acquisition of data processing materials, services, and facilities."

Our financial projections based on our cost experience of the previous year indicated that acquisition would be more cost-effective than remaining a customer of the Department of General Administration. The department disputed this claim unsuccessfully.

Part III

INFORMATION PROCESSING AND THE LAW

In the lead chapter to this part, Joseph L. Ebersole discusses the four basic functional types of legal research: practice, doctrinal, fact, and nondoctrinal. Computer-assisted legal research aids lawyers in the first two functions, although the effect has not been revolutionary. Ebersole further describes the historical developments and current practices of textual information-retrieval systems and, specifically, of two commercial systems—LEXIS and WESTLAW. He explains how these developments and practices, along with the behavior patterns and established needs of lawyers, relate to the current subdued approach to automated legal research. Since the cost of computer-assisted legal research is decreasing, the quality of the research results is increasing, and the computer capabilities are improving, Ebersole believes that the use and success of computer-assisted legal research will grow in the future.

Karlyn Stanley and Theodor Herman describe how LEXIS and WESTLAW, respectively, operate, and Stanley O. Croydon, Jr., does the same for JURIS, the computerized legal-research system of the U.S. Department of Justice. Each of these authors gives the history, methodology, and uses of the system; details the types of users, available data bases, and access methods; and speculates on future plans.

8

JOSEPH L. EBERSOLE

The Emergence of Computer-Assisted Research as an Established Legal Tool

Only a few years ago, dramatic claims were being made about the computer as the solution to the problems created for legal research by the explosive growth in the volume of case and statutory law. Some heralded the arrival of computerized systems as an innovation that could make major changes in the practice of law. But today, advocates of computerized legal research systems have a more subdued approach. Now one seldom hears that the computer will completely change the nature of the legal profession or even that it will replace books. Certainly the vast majority of American lawyers do not use computerized legal research systems in their practice. The changes that have occurred, and those that will probably result from today's commercially available systems—LEXIS and WESTLAW—do not represent a major transformation in the profession. The effect has not been revolutionary. As in other disciplines and professions, however, there is evidence that the new tools frequently increase quality and sometimes lower costs. Indeed, a growing number of attorneys, students, teachers, and judges seem to be finding them a valuable addition to the family of legal research tools.

A number of terms are used to describe computer systems used for legal research. I prefer the multiword adjective *computer-assisted legal research* (CALR) to describe them. Two CALR systems commercially available in the United States are LEXIS and WESTLAW; references to where and how CALR systems could be, or are, used will apply to these two systems.

One should be able to assume that CALR systems have been carefully designed to meet well-defined, widely recognized needs of the legal profession. The degree to which this assumption comports with reality is of interest, both in providing a context and reference for the uses being made of these systems and for understanding the origins of some of the new services' key characteristics.

First we should disabuse ourselves of the notion that CALR systems should be able to handle every type of research or every research method. To some extent, that notion is like expecting the descriptive-word index approach to be able to accommodate every research need. Nevertheless, the assumption is often made that use of a computer system for legal research is questionable unless the system can work with concepts or unless it can think as lawyers think or arrive at legal conclusions.[1] Although such capabilities would be ideal, it is unlikely that we will see practical systems providing services of this type in the near future.

At a minimum, CALR can be viewed as a new bibliographic tool. Although the nature of legal bibliography is determined in many ways by the nature of the law itself, the nature of legal research is determined, at least in part, by the bibliographic tools on which it is based. Thus present legal research models are our context for seeing where CALR fits in. If present CALR systems ultimately change legal research, they will do so as a result of the ways they are used.

Models of the Legal Research Process

Four functional types of legal research can be identified: practice (the research typically involved in lawyers' practices), doctrinal, fact, and nondoctrinal (also known as interdisciplinary or behavioral research).[2] In this conceptual structure, legal bibliography is not a type of research but a study of the finding aids for legal information—indexes, digests, citators, and the like. Practice research requires finding written manifestation of the law, with some relation to the facts of the case and a place in the hypothesis upon which one is working. Doctrinal research, best typified by Corbin's work on contracts, Powell's treatise on property, and numerous other works of this ilk, is generally concerned with any kind of critical scholarship or study.

Of these four functional types, practice and doctrinal research are the areas in which CALR systems have the most potential for benefit, although the importance of finding aids is certainly substantially less in doctrinal research. One should not expect application of computerized case-law systems to fact research, because it does not involve case law. Case-law finding aids are of minor use in nondoctrinal research, which seeks to "(a) assess the impact of nonlegal events (e.g., economic developments, growth of knowledge, technological changes) upon legal decision processes; or

(b) to identify and appraise the magnitude of the variable factors influencing the outcomes of legal decision making in terms of value gains and deprivations for litigants, nonlitigants, and nonlegal institutions."[3]

A number of models for the legal research process as it is used in practice research and doctrinal research have been suggested. The report on Operation Compulex, a study of practicing lawyers' legal research needs, describes four phases in the legal research process.[4] First, the lawyer must assemble the facts and decide what legal issues they raise. Second, he or she must refer to secondary sources—the citators, abridgements, and encyclopedias—to search for the relevant legislation or judicial decisions. Third, the lawyer must examine their validity in the light of more recent decisions to determine their current legal status. Finally, the relevant law must be related to the problem at hand before legal counsel can be offered. Computer-assisted legal research systems can be used for parts of the second and third phases of this model.

A somewhat more detailed outline of the process may differentiate the use of bibliographic tools in a more revealing way. Assuming the existence of a problem or a need or desire to know the law in a given area, four steps can be delineated. Step one consists of general background reading in encyclopedias or annotated law reports. Step two narrows the inquiry to the consultation of treatises, hornbooks, law review articles, looseleaf services, and the like. The function of these first two steps is to educate the researcher, help spot issues, give ideas for arguments, and find cases on point. The third step is to bring the topic up to date via the digest system. The final step is to make certain the relevant cases are still good law and find other cases citing those that the researcher found. A CALR system would probably have limited use in the first two steps but should be helpful in steps three and four.[5]

A very illuminating view of the practicing lawyer's legal research process is provided by two models of creative legal research postulated by Buchanan and Headrick.[6] From the models, they deduce four stages in a lawyer's thought processes. The models do not fit neatly into any of the four steps described above, although an implicit premise of them is the existence of some knowledge on the lawyer's part that would preclude the need for general background research. In the first model, the factual situation has been set, certain events have occurred, and a client wants to know what his rights, remedies, and risks are. In the second, a client is looking for guidance for a future action, and the client can control the facts or events somewhat to suit his legal needs as assessed by the lawyer.

After delineating the models, Buchanan and Headrick identify four stages in the practicing lawyer's thought processes: (1) establishing goals and finding links from facts to rules to legal consequences in pursuing these goals; (2) recognizing and characterizing facts as suggestive of rules and using cases and rules to suggest the relevance and importance of facts; (3) resolving rule conflicts by identifying which of several rules applies to a factual situation and selecting the rules that best fit the facts and the objective; and (4) finding analogies where cases with similar facts cannot be found. In the first two stages, the attorney will look for the same or a similar factual situation. In the third, the attorney selects, from among several possibly applicable rules, the rule that best meets the objective. In the fourth stage, the attorney looks for cases with an analogous factual situation. A CALR system could be useful for the first two stages, would probably not be useful for the third, and would be useful for the fourth only if it had concept-searching capabilities.

Price and Bitner provide a summary of research approaches before delineating the steps of the research process.[7] These seven approaches are tied closely to manual case-finding aids. First is the table-of-cases approach, for which twelve different methods are given. This approach is used when an attorney has the name or other incomplete information about a case but does not have enough information to find the case directly. West Publishing Company's key-number approach, the heart of the West digesting system, is second. The third is the annotated-reports approach using *American Law Report* (ALR). The fact or descriptive-word index approach, useful for finding cases in digests, is fourth. Fifth is the analytical or topical method, which involves moving from broad concepts to relevant, specific subtopics. Sixth is the words-and-phrases approach, which can be used to find judicial definitions, legally significant words, and phrases in West's *Words & Phrases* and in digests and encyclopedias. Seventh is the treatise approach, which uses texts to lead the searcher to other sources of authority. Price and Bitner then outline a ten-step research process that includes stages that do not fit specifically into any of their seven basic approaches, an indication that any attempt to describe models of legal research processes may so oversimplify the process as to be incomplete, inaccurate, or misleading.

CALR as a Research Tool

CALR appears promising in the context of these seven basic approaches. Full-text systems are well suited for the table-of-cases approach, the fact or descriptive-word index approach, and the words-and-phrases approach. The WESTLAW system is also well suited for the key-number approach and the analytical or topical method. Thus, only the annotated-reports and treatise approaches are not available in one of the existing computerized services. (Even this statement may be conservative, since Lawyers Co-operative Publishing Co. was one of the first major law book publishers to computerize its operations, and ALR could be accessed via computer terminals. The fact that such a service is not commercially provided may indicate that this approach is better implemented using manual techniques involving books.)

Looking at descriptive models to see where CALR systems should fit treats the latter as the equivalent of a traditional finding tool, albeit automated. This may make CALR more understandable, but it may also distort the real nature of CALR capabilities. It does not seem a satisfactory way to gain understanding of CALR uses, perhaps because of defects in the models. We know so little about how lawyers conduct legal research that our models may be incomplete and oversimplified.[8] Models that appear in research manuals reflect ideal, not actual, procedures.[9] It was suggested as recently as 1972 that until more was known about legal research methods and lawyers' habits, little could be done to meet their research needs.[10] Yet two systems representing major commitments by two corporations are now on the market. Thus it is important to attempt to determine why today's systems have the particular capabilities they have.

It is relevant to inquire whether certain well-understood and widely accepted needs of the profession—in other words, weaknesses or voids in the capabilities of existing research tools—were met by the design of distinctively new finding tools that required computers for their operation, or whether CALR tools represent mere mechanizations of some old tools to make them more efficient. A strong case could be made for the contention that today's systems are mere mechanizations of existing tools. However, a strong case can also be made that what appear to be primarily quantitative differences do include qualitative differences—that CALR systems do amount to new and different finding tools and that they therefore affect the nature of legal research itself.

The Development of Full-Text Systems

The basis for today's CALR systems is the ability of modern computers to sort words efficiently—a much more complex process than the manipulation of numbers that earlier computation devices could perform efficiently. This technological capacity to arrange collections of phrases that define legal concepts or collections of single words in headnotes or opinions into neatly arrayed alphabetic sequences also determines the nature of computerized finding aids. It has become feasible to apply this capability because of advances in time-sharing, communications technology, and terminal devices technology, all of which resulted in dramatically decreasing costs. The application of this capability to legal research, however, might not have occurred if there had not been problems in collecting, collating, indexing, retrieving, and disseminating scientific information. These problems were a result of the science-information explosion that was accelerated by the "space race" of the 1960s, which in turn resulted in the funds to explore solutions for the science-information explosion.

Until that time, the indexing systems and finding tools of the law were much better than those of other disciplines.[11] The finding-aids revolution demanded by scientific needs and made possible through computer technology occurred more than a half-century after the revolutionary nineteenth-century developments in legal research tools.

It would be naive to assume that the new finding aids were developed following careful studies of the way in which people conduct library research. Although there were many studies of this ilk, the predominant development method was to use existing computer capabilities and find two types of matches: a matching of the computer and an existing manual tool, resulting in a mechanization of an existing system, and a matching of a newly developed use of a computer and an information need. The best example of the first type is the mechanization of the production of library catalogue cards. The best example of the second type is the development of the permuted indexing technique—itself a variation of the "exploded sorting"[12] technique—and its use for the production of rotated or permuted indexes[13] and Key-Word-In-Context (KWIC) indexes. Currently available CALR systems all use more refined and efficient variations of the original exploded sorting technique as an indexing method. This technique, in effect, provided indexing of every significant word. The next advancement was to tag each word with a unique set of identification numbers that specified the document number, the page within that document, the line number on that page, and the position of the word in that line. With this method all words—with their identifying numerical tags—are sorted as index keys. The text itself is separately stored in the form in which it appeared in the document.

The development of these techniques was not the sole reason for increasing the use of words in text as index keys. Indeed, research and development in the information-science field had been leading to single-word indexing—part of several research efforts—as one solution to the problems created by the quantum leap in the volume of information.

The Association of Special Libraries and Information Bureaus (ASLIB) Cranfield Research Project, which began in late 1957, was an investigation into the relative retrieval efficiency of four forms of indexing: the universal decimal classification as used in a classified catalog; an alphabetical subject heading system; a faceted classification; and the Uniterm system, used in its original form as a free association of elemental terms.[14] Although the early research found that each form of indexing had superior efficiency for at least one type of retrieval problem, overall the results supported Uniterm. Uniterm had the highest percentage of success in searches for relevant documents, and it was therefore the system with the least chance of searching failure.

The second stage of the project (Cranfield II) had improved methodology and was somewhat more focused, analyzing the effect of index language devices on recall and precision (performance) of an information retrieval system.[15] It represented by far the most extensive and complex effort undertaken in the field. As in Cranfield I, all search procedures were conducted manually. Here again, the best performance was obtained using single-term index languages. Those based on concepts gave the worst performance.[16] A slight improvement in performance of the single-term indexing was obtained by using a synonym dictionary to group true synonyms and a suffixing process to generate word stems. Current systems have the latter capability; the researcher must supply the former.

The single terms found to be the most effective for indexing, according to the evaluation in Cranfield II, were content words chosen from document texts. This method of indexing was found to be more effective than concept indexing or controlled-term indexing. These results, quite unexpectedly, were counterintuitive. However, they were supported a few years later by experiments with the SMART system that verified the Cranfield results.[17]

The nature of the concept indexing used in those experiments is not necessarily equivalent to any of the hierarchical structures used for legal indexing. Nevertheless the results did indicate that it was worthwhile to explore the uses of single-word indexing. The Cranfield method involved selection of words by a human indexer from the document. The indexer selected the group of words that best reflected—in the indexer's judgment—the subject content of the document. The SMART system (Salton's Magical Automatic Retriever of Texts) involved automatic indexing by the computer, using algorithms developed by the system designers. Both of these approaches were relatively expensive, and neither provided coverage of every subject in a document. This latter limitation of both human and automatic selection of words led some to suggest indexing every significant word in a text (what we now know as full-text indexing).[18] These indexing research results and the emergence of enhanced computer capabilities facilitated the movement toward full-text indexing, but other developments and trends were also influential.

In the late 1940s, an indexing method, Uniterm, was developed by Mortimer Taube. Uniterms, as opposed to subject headings, concepts, or topical headings—which were part of the Library of Congress system, the Dewey Decimal System, and so forth—were individual terms or key words that made up a subject heading. It was felt that combining these simple terms would allow better retrieval. The concept of formulating requests by combining simple terms and then matching them with the stored terms is now used in almost every computerized retrieval system.

The necessary partner to the Uniterm method was a new technique, coordinate indexing, which uses set theory. In effect, it works on the assumption that when one has a query for an information retrieval system, one can structure it so that it can be represented in terms of the intersections of circles representing sets (Venn diagrams). For example, all documents that contain both subject "a" and subject "b" would be that set of documents represented by the intersection of set "a" and set "b." Coordinate indexing differed from prior indexing methods in that it involved indexing at the time of searching by the person conducting the search.

In another development of the late 1940s, Calvin Mooers proposed a method, superimposed coding, which had the objective of representing the subject content of documents. In this format, many key terms are placed in coded form—a code for each term in a punched card—where they could be read simultaneously instead of having to be read from several different areas, thus providing an efficient technique for finding term combinations.

In the late 1950s, Hans Peter Luhn developed the first indexing system that did not rely on human judgment in selecting terms. The computer counted the number of times individual words occurred in a document. The more frequently occurring words were then used to index the document.[19] This is actually a more refined approach than the complete full-text approach but had limitations that precluded its widespread use.

While these techniques were being developed and while computers and library research were merging, changes were taking place in the relationships among components of indexing systems in all fields of endeavor. Examples of this were noted by Verner W. Clapp in 1962.[20] Whereas in 1909 there was a ratio of one cross-reference to each two subject headings in the Library of Congress subject-heading list, by 1957 this ratio had been reversed; there were then two cross-references for each single subject heading, a multiplication of four. Using a technical journal as an example, Clapp noted that in earlier volumes of *Chemical Abstracts,* each abstract was indexed by an average of three entries, and in later volumes (those appearing around 1960), each abstract was indexed by twelve entries.

Both of these changes were manifestations of the problems created by the explosive growth in the volume of information in general, especially in the sciences. Clapp commented in 1962 that he had "been impressed by the converging tendency of the requirements made upon indexing, a tendency to converge upon smaller and smaller units of analysis. . . . It requires an increasingly closer degree of analysis to distinguish between an increasingly larger number of artifacts of the same kind." He added, "I do not know what the ultimate of the trend may be, but certainly it is in the direction of more and more comprehensive indexing. Is it too much to suspect that it is in the direction of indexing every significant word?"[21]

Thus, with the arrival of the third generation of computers in the middle and late 1960s, with the trend toward more exhaustive indexing and the use of single terms for indexing, and with research results showing the efficacy of single-term indexing, a sufficient number of forces were in motion that full-text indexing could be predicted.[22] In fact, the Cranfield II results support the efficacy of full-text indexing, in that the single terms were content words chosen from document texts (as opposed to terms assigned by subject analysts or indexers). Thus, the terms used in the experiment were a subset of all those in the text.

Full-text research systems, then, although including more terms in the computer data base than might be necessary, do contain all of the content words that could have been selected by a human or automatic indexer in the Cranfield and SMART projects. One could conclude that the Cranfield II and SMART research results support the effectiveness of full-text indexing for retrieval purposes (although these results have nothing to say about the cost-effectiveness of full-text indexing because of the substantial difference between the number of indexing terms and the number of terms in the full text). This conclusion was strengthened by the first evaluation of a full-text (batch) system for legal research, reported in 1968, which found the system to be "as effective as human searchers in finding documents relevant to the questions presented to the computer."[23]

Other Factors Affecting Use of CALR Systems

It would not be unreasonable for someone unfamiliar with CALR systems to assume that using a computer should save time. Although even this assumption turns out to be questionable, it leads us to ask whether a savings in legal research time would make much difference to lawyers.[24] Certainly the use of CALR will be influenced by this factor.

There are very little data on lawyer research time. A Canadian study, Operation Compulex, found that "a figure of 20 percent of total time would be generous" and that "any reduction in time required to conduct legal research would be negligible (a saving of at best 3 percent of total time)." The researchers concluded that "reducing the time required to conduct legal research is a payoff of very limited value."[25]

These figures refer to the average time spent by the average lawyer in Canada. The data showed that although 47 percent of lawyers sampled spent 15 percent or less of their time researching, 14 percent of the lawyers spent more than 50 percent of their time on this activity, and 2 percent spent more than 70 percent of their time researching.[26] This distribution suggests that savings in legal research time for lawyers who spend a high percentage of their total time on research might be sufficient to justify a more efficient research tool.

Studies in the United States show somewhat similar results. In a study conducted by the Missouri Bar Association in 1966, it was estimated that 16.7 percent of a lawyer's time was devoted to research.[27] That study also found that office practice arrangements, field of specialty, and number of years' experience were the most important determinants of time devoted to legal research. The smaller the firm, the greater the number of hours devoted to legal research; the less specialized, the greater the hours devoted to research; and the longer a lawyer is in practice, the fewer the hours devoted to legal research. An economic survey of the Massachusetts bar concluded that for practicing lawyers, "the average amount of time spent in legal research is ten hours per month."[28] Applying this figure to a forty-hour-per-week base gives a figure of approximately 6 percent.

The three studies thus report estimates ranging from 6 percent to 20 percent of the average lawyer's time spent on legal research. Operation Compulex found that about one-third of this time was spent on retrieving the law, with the other two-thirds spent on analysis to determine relevance. Thus we can estimate that, on the average, the average lawyer spends anywhere from 2 percent to 7 percent of his or her time finding the law; those figures also represent the average outer limits for use of CALR systems.

In the most comprehensive study of CALR systems to date, the Federal Judicial Center found that federal court law clerks estimate that they spend nearly 50 percent of their time on legal research, and that 20 to 25 percent of this time is retrieval time. Users in this study estimated that use of CALR could save from 10 to 33 percent of total research time. In addition to these estimates, reports of time saved—if any—were made each time a CALR system was used in this study. Data from these reports indicate that an average of 86.7 minutes were saved each time a full-text CALR system was used. The user with three or four research projects a week thus would save four to six hours a week.[29] These data are more supportive of the efficacy of CALR systems, but the results are consistent with both the Canadian and Missouri studies. Users were in the equivalent of a small firm (a judge in the federal system typically has two law clerks—this is analogous to a small firm with one senior partner and two associates), they were nonspecialists, and they had just finished law school or had at most one or two years' experience.

Although the Federal Judicial Center study shows that CALR use in the federal courts saves time, there are no similar data on practicing attorney usage that would encourage the average law firm to use a CALR system. Even so, many firms would surely try it if the price were right compared to alternative research sources for which law firms could spend library funds. Here again, one encounters a factor that could impede use. In 1973 and 1974, LEXIS was the only CALR system commercially available. The minimum charge was $36,000 per year. This cost should be compared with the mean annual expenditures for law firm libraries, which in 1972, according to the only data available to the public, was approximately $60,000; for large firms, it was $82,000.[30] This meant that in 1973 the average firm would have had to increase its library expenditures by more than 50 percent to acquire LEXIS.

The picture is changing dramatically here, however. The LEXIS minimum was reduced to $18,000 in January 1975, and in January 1976, the concept of minimum use was eliminated. Even so, equipment and communications cost around $6,000 per year, and moderate usage would probably result in a total cost of at least $20,000 to $25,000 per year. A simple extrapolation of 1972 law firm library expenditures, based on changes in the consumer price index, indicates that the average firm is probably spending about $90,000 per year on its library, and the average large firm about $125,000 per year, exclusive of CALR costs.[31]

We can expect law book costs, library space costs, and salaries to continue to increase and the costs of CALR systems to continue to decrease. These two diverging trends will have a greater effect on the use of CALR systems than any other factor. Each year, more firms should find the cost of a CALR system to be a feasible addition to their budgets.[32]

The other major factor that should affect the use of CALR systems is limited capability. For example, Buchanan and Headrick emphasize that ideally lawyers would want a system that would produce legal arguments—the end products of their research.[33] None of the present systems does this. One study concludes that large resources should not be devoted to the maintenance or development of the types of CALR systems that exist now.[34] Among the limiting factors noted in that study were that these systems cannot operate by way of analogy, they may impose certain alien logical structures on the verbal symbols of law (thereby affecting legal thought and ultimately substantive law), and they do not allow for random conceptual searching and therefore cannot be used satisfactorily to retrieve legal concepts. The limitation on conceptual capability would not seem to apply to the WESTLAW headnote feature, since the key number system does incorporate concepts.

Other critics have emphasized the inherent limitations of full-text systems.[35] They point out that words in the text do not necessarily reflect legal concepts and that words are protean, both over time and without regard to time. Further, although traditional indexes and research tools are educational devices by which a searcher can become oriented and then work down a hierarchy, no such opportunity exists with a word-search system. Other, similar weaknesses of full-text systems are mentioned frequently, usually in writings that emphasize the importance and strengths of a hierarchical arrangement of material.[36]

This review of factors affecting CALR use suggests that the amount of time the average lawyer spends on research does not seem to justify use of a CALR system, although lawyers or firms that spend large amounts of time on legal research might be able to justify using one. But when the cost factor is considered, the justification for the use of CALR seems to be weak even for high-volume researchers. Here, however, diverging cost trends are changing the situation quickly. Finally, one finds numerous concerns, reservations, and claims about the inherent limitations of CALR systems, especially full-text systems. In short, one would not expect to find large numbers of CALR systems in use; where they are used, one would expect to find them given very restricted applications. One would also expect systems with hierarchical index capability (WESTLAW) to be more heavily used.

Actual Use

There is very little information on the actual uses of CALR systems in the legal profession. Two reported empirical studies have been conducted, but other than these, one must rely on personal observation, articles written by advocates of a system, and discussions with lawyers in firms that have CALR systems. All of these data reflect the use of LEXIS for full-text searching and the use of WESTLAW for headnote or digest searching only. The introduction of WESTLAW's full-text capability, which began in January 1978, may be leading to additional uses not reflected in experience to date.

The most comprehensive empirical study to date, conducted by the Federal Judicial Center, shows a pattern of use that is counterintuitive. It does not fit the traditional descriptive models of legal research and the inferences one can draw about CALR use in that context. Nor does it reveal the uses one would expect after having read articles about the weaknesses of computerized legal retrieval. Admittedly the legal research conducted by law clerks (which was the basis of this study) is different from that of practicing lawyers, but the findings of the center's study are consistent with data from observations of lawyer use.

Although CALR proponents have stressed that such systems are supplements to traditional research, the center study found that the purpose of more than 50 percent of CALR uses was "searching on [the] computer as a substitute [for manual research]"; in 29 percent of the uses, the purpose was "searching mainly for recent cases."[37]

Another part of the study analyzed the characteristics of search commands. It revealed that, on the average, more than 75 percent of the search commands involved a general area of law, as opposed to specific opinions or citation tracking.[38] After a year of use, law clerks were asked the types of research for which CALR is most useful. Full-text CALR is best for initial research, according to 16 percent of the respondents; 31 percent said that it was best for narrow issues; and 11 percent said that it is best for so-called exotic uses, such as finding opinions by a particular judge.[39]

The center study also addressed the issue of variability of usage. It revealed variations in usage of as high as one hundred to one (that is, some law clerks used the CALR system one hundred times as much as others).[40] This degree of variation could also exist for other measures we have examined. When one considers the hundreds of thousands of lawyers and thousands of law firms in the United States, it becomes obvious that a substantial number of firms could have research needs and budgets substantial enough that the cost of CALR service would be only a modest increment to existing expenditures. My own observations of CALR use in law firms and discussions with lawyers have led to conclusions somewhat similar to those of the center's study. I would have expected a rather fixed pattern that would involve use of a CALR system at regular points in the research process. For example, there were indications that in some organizations, the CALR system was used only after manual research was satisfactorily completed, to see if there were any recent cases on point.[41] (The center's study indicates that only 6 percent of the law clerks experienced in CALR use said searching for recent decisions is the best use of a system; 27 percent of the inexperienced users said this is the best use.[42]) I would not have expected a CALR system to be used to become familiar with an area of law. Nor would I have expected it to be used as a first step in the research process. Yet many attorneys start their legal research at a CALR terminal: If the Federal Judicial Center data—showing that this type of use increases with experience—hold true, we should expect to see more attorneys using CALR in this fashion.

Some attorneys divide CALR usage into traditional and nontraditional research. Nontraditional research encompasses those capabilities that are unique to CALR systems, such as finding out what cases an opposing law firm has been involved in; obtaining all opinions by a judge before whom the firm will soon be appearing; or obtaining all of a judge's opinions on a given subject to determine his or her position on an issue. Nontraditional research also includes uses that are not unique to CALR but are handled differently in a CALR system, sometimes with different results. Some lawyers estimate that half of their CALR use is traditional and half nontraditional. Others indicate that their firms view CALR as a general legal research tool, useful in a variety of ways.

The findings of a second empirical study, conducted for Search Group, Inc., indicate reasonable consistency with other observations and study findings.[43] The study concludes that a CALR system can improve the quality and efficiency of legal research in criminal justice agencies only under certain conditions. CALR is most efficient when there is a CALR specialist available, when users are experienced and have adequate training, when many individuals are using the terminals, and when the staff has had experience with computers prior to adopting CALR. The project's laboratory test results produced a negative assessment of CALR—that is, manual research is better—but the data show quite clearly that all users were still learning. They were steadily becoming more proficient at the end of the evaluation. The use period for this particular project was only six months; the evidence indicates this amount of time is insufficient to draw conclusions. Any future assessment of CALR use should be made only after at least one year of use.[44]

The Search Group study highlights another significant factor that has been found to be associated with the amount of use of a CALR system. This is the recently recognized importance of a CALR specialist who is available to help attorneys conduct research or to conduct research for them. LEXIS representatives, at least in the past, stressed the point that the best user was the subject-matter expert. An intermediary was considered unnecessary. Although not explicit on this point, sales literature on the new WESTLAW system seems to be directed to the attorney as direct user. Both empirical and observational data support the role of the specialist-operator. The Federal Judicial Center found that the presence of a specialist-operator resulted in increased usage among all users and that only 30 percent of users preferred to use the system themselves, whereas 50 percent preferred having an operator available even when they used CALR themselves. A substantial percentage preferred having the operator do the research.[45] In its preliminary conclusions, Search Group, Inc. found the specialist-operator to be essential for efficient CALR use. Conversations with law firms having a specialist-operator indicate that the presence of this individual sometimes as much as doubles the number of frequent CALR users in a firm. Increasingly, the specialist-operator acts as consultant, adviser, or researcher in legal research performed on CALR terminals.

Another major factor that has affected use in general, and has certainly been instrumental in the penetration of the commercial market, is research quality. There is impressive evidence that use of CALR systems results in increased quality of legal research. Quality can be measured by several indicators or variables. Certainly, finding a significant case on point—which helps an attorney win a lawsuit or allows him or her to advise a client that a certain course of action is proper—improves the quality of legal representation. In fact, CALR has improved legal research quality in all instances where case authority that was not found through traditional manual research methods was found using CALR. For almost all CALR users, this has happened enough times that users give CALR high marks on this basis alone.

The Federal Judicial Center measured quality in several ways. If CALR use did not find any new information, manual results were confirmed; such a result is an example of quality assurance. In different courts, anywhere from 4 to 15 percent of uses resulted in this finding.[46] Of more importance were instances where cases were found that definitely would have been overlooked without CALR. This occurred with full-text searching in one-third of all searches. An important related category is finding recent cases that would not have been located without CALR. Close to 50 percent of all uses fell into one of these two categories, providing impressive data to illustrate CALR use's effect on quality.

If legal research publishers revolutionize their publishing methods so as to eliminate the recent advantage of CALR systems, this quality advantage would diminish somewhat. The Search Group study has also generated data indicating that where specialists are used for research, the LEXIS system results in a higher quality of research than do manual methods.

Several aspects of CALR systems that affect usage cannot be compared to manual systems. Examples are up-time availability (a measure of the percentage of the time the system is working), response time (expressed as the percentage of all search requests that are responded to within fifteen seconds), and terminal and network reliability (indicated by the percentage of the time that terminals and the communications network are working properly). These are all critical factors for CALR systems, but not for books.

Conclusions

In spite of costs and claimed inherent limitations, CALR systems are being used by practitioners in a variety of ways and are beginning to be recognized as general legal research tools. In the 1950s and 1960s, research on the comparative performance of indexing systems pointed in this direction, and the decreasing relative cost of computers is steadily increasing cost feasibility. Trying to ascertain and allocate probable use based on traditional models of the legal research process is an unsatisfactory method of predicting use. It appears that the legal profession has a new tool that does not fit old paradigms. A complete understanding of how CALR systems fit into the legal system must wait for a definitive study of use that applies appropriate paradigms and new theories.

Until that time, we can perhaps rely on existing authority to describe the emerging uses of CALR. In response to the question, "What is legal research?" Justice Felix Frankfurter answered, "It is not a method, it is not an object, it is a behavior. . . . Research is the systematic indulgence of one's curiosity."[47] Such patterns as are emerging show this more and more.

Within a decade, we may see the introduction of systems that begin to approach the degree of sophistication desired by the critics of present-day systems. It is doubtful that these capabilities will emerge as a result of research on how lawyers conduct legal research and how lawyers think. Instead, they will be the result of research now being undertaken in such disciplines as artificial intelligence, information science, symbolic logic, psychological research, computer science, pattern recognition, and mathematical linguistics, to name a few. As is the case for present first-generation CALR systems, developments in the hard and soft sciences will result in techniques that will be applied to the law.

Second-generation CALR systems will have a greater effect on legal research and the legal profession than do first-generation systems because their capabilities will include detecting or recognizing concepts; expressing them in written form; and organizing, storing, and retrieving them. This is an express goal of much present research and theory development on automatic language processing and subject analysis of documents. A recent article describing the five levels of indexing is indicative of the types of research and theory building in this area. The first level is concordance—which is what a full-text system really is—and the fifth level is inferential; it deals with concepts that can be logically deduced from, although not explicitly stated in, the text of a document or opinion.[48] Certainly the latter capability will be of immense interest to the legal profession.

A cursory review of literature in the most relevant fields reveals a vocabulary that is new to lawyers. It starts with the umbrella term *subject analysis* and moves to such expressions as *heuristics, centroids, vector methods, dendograms, concept space, fuzzy sets* (one facet of an area of study called *fuzzy mathematics*), and *adhesion coefficients.*[49] Users of these systems will not necessarily have to understand these terms, but the concepts they represent will be important if they are to make adequate use of second-generation systems, just as an understanding of Boolean searching or natural language querying is important for any user of current CALR systems who wants maximum effectiveness.

The thrust of present research is illustrated by a review of progress in automatic subject analysis, which notes that "the problems of subject analysis are inextricably intertwined with the understanding of how we think, how we conceive concepts, how we communicate them, how we record them, how we save them for future use, how we use them, and how we reuse them in unlimited permutations and combinations to synthesize or conceive of new ones."[50] Solutions of these problems will clearly be relevant to second-generation CALR systems.

A complete description of the probable features of second-generation systems is beyond my purposes here. Perhaps the most important features that should be noted are that they will use the full text of opinions, and they will require mechanisms for entering and expressing questions and for displaying responses. All of these features were developed for first-generation systems. Present systems are clearly the necessary first step toward later generations of systems. Today's CALR systems thus represent not an aberration but the first step toward systems that may truly revolutionize the practice of law in our time.

Notes

1. Buchanan and Headrick, *Some Speculation About Artificial Intelligence and Legal Reasoning,* 23 Stan. L. Rev. 40 (1970).

2. Nycum, *Legal Research—The Unrecognized Legal Discipline,* at 81 in Sense and Systems in Automated Law Research (1975) (ABA Science and Technology Section).

3. Jones, *Some Current Trends in Legal Research,* 15 J. Legal Ed. 121, 130 (1962) as cited by id.

4. Department of Justice, Government of Canada, Information Needs of the Practicing Lawyer: Operation Compulex 9 (1972).

5. Some attorneys apparently use CALR systems to meet some of the objectives of steps one and two. See text accompanying note 41.

6. *Supra* note 1, at 45.

7. M. Price and H. Bitner, Effective Legal Research (3d Ed. 1969).

8. Buchanan & Headrick, *supra* note 1, at 40.

9. Cohen, *Research Habits of Lawyers,* 9 Jurimetrics J. 183 (1969).

10. Kolasa, *Systems Design and Research Techniques,* in Automated Law Research, Proceedings, First National Conference on Automated Law Research, 1972, at 166 (1973).

11. Cohen, *Computerizing Legal Research,* 14 Jurimetrics J. 3, 4 (1973).

12. Exploded sorting, as used in permuted indexing, is a technique whereby a given record, such as a title or a sentence, is recreated or duplicated in exact form once for each significant word in the record. Each word is in the sort field of one of the new records, thus allowing each record to be located in the alphabetic sequence of each word.

13. Sometimes also called Key-Word-Out-Of-Context (KWOC) indexes. The history of the development of these types of computer-produced indexes is an example of the "simultaneous discovery" phenomenon. Hudson Snowden Marshall, then with the Rocketdyne Division of North American Aviation, Hans Peter Luhn, then with IBM, and Herbert Ohlman, then with the RAND Corporation, were the inventors who independently but almost simultaneously (in the late 1950s), conceived and pushed the implementation of these concepts. Marshall, who had been working on concordances, called his tool a *cyclical permutation index,* and Luhn called his a *Key-Word-In-Context Index.* A Rocketdyne report on cyclical permutation indexing in 1958 was reportedly influential in persuading IBM executives to support Luhn's development.

14. Richmond, *Review of the Cranfield Project,* American Documentation, Oct. 1963, at 307.

15. Rees, *Evaluation of Information Systems and Services,* in 2 Annual Review of Information Science and Technology 65-67 (1967).

16. Cleverdon and Keen, *Factors Determining the Performance of Indexing Systems,* ASLIB Cranfield Research Project (1966); Cleverdon, *The Cranfield Tests on Index Language Devices,* 19 ASLIB Proceedings 6, at 173-194 (1967).

17. The SMART System—Experiments in Automatic Document Processing (G. Salton, ed. 1971); Scientific Reports No. ISR-11 to ISR-21, Dept. of Computer Science, Cornell University (G. Salton, ed. 1966-1972).

18. "Significant words" means all words other than articles and prepositions, conjunctions, and other specific words—proper nouns, for example—designated as not carrying subject information.

19. WESTLAW uses this technique in determining the probable relevance of a headnote or case to the search query.

20. Clapp, *Research in Problems of Scientific Information—Retrospect and Prospect,* American Documentation, Jan. 1963, at 1-9 (Keynote address at Gordon Research Conference on Scientific Information Problems in Research, July 2, 1962).

21. Id. at 7.

22. "Full text," as used in describing a type of CALR system, is shorthand for "full-text indexing."

23. Eldridge, *An Appraisal of a Case Law Retrieval Project,* Proceedings of the Computers and the Law Conference 1968, at 36, 59, Faculty of Law, Queens University (Kingston, Ontario).

24. Empirical tests have produced mixed findings. In one controlled experiment, the Federal Judicial Center found that CALR and manual research took approximately the same amount of time, but the sample size was too small to be able to make any conclusions. Laboratory tests by Search Group, Inc., found that manual research took less time than research on either WESTLAW or LEXIS, but other data in this study showed users were still learning, suggesting the results might not be the same after more experience was gained.

25. Department of Justice, Ottawa, Canada, Information Needs of the Practicing Lawyer: Operation Compulex 25, 26 (1972).

26. Id. at 65.

27. Cohen, *supra* note 9, at 191.

28. P. Slayton, Electronic Legal Retrieval 5 (1974) (prepared for Department of Communications, Government of Canada).

29. A. Sager, An Evaluation of Computer Assisted Legal Research Systems for Federal Court Applications FJC-R-77-2, 34, 37, 40 (1977).

30. Head, *1972 Statistical Survey of Law Firm Libraries and Librarians,* 67 L. Lib. J. 389 (1974). The response rate for this survey was low—34 percent—and it is not known whether those responding were a representative sample. Thus the reported costs may be wide of the mark. Further, no data are given on cost distribution, so it is difficult to determine how meaningful, or helpful, the average costs are. Nevertheless, these were the best data available.

31. The 1972 survey reported the budget allocation as 14 percent for new acquisitions, 44 percent for continuations, and 39 percent for salaries.

32. The CALR cost data for LEXIS were used in the preceding discussion because LEXIS has been in existence longer than WESTLAW. The conclusions about a downward trend for CALR costs, however, apply to both WESTLAW and LEXIS.

33. *Supra* note 1, at 51.

34. *Supra* note 28, at 25.

35. A good example is Blaine, *Computers and Legal Research,* Calif., St. B. J., March-April 1975, at 100.

36. An example is Comment, *Computer-Assisted Legal Research,* 51 Ore. L. Rev. 665, 672 (1972). However, even this article agrees that "sufficient ingenuity in the

use of the technique sometimes can permit searching for concepts rather than isolated words."

37. *Supra* note 29, at 62. In most instances, law clerk research starts after briefs from counsel have been read. This may explain the amazingly high percentage of CALR systems used as substitutes for manual research. Even so, a law clerk has to give the judge absolute assurance that research avenues have been exhausted, and use of CALR as a substitute thus meets a rigorous standard.

38. Id. at 75.

39. Id. at 113. One unknown factor here is the extent to which this initial research is similar to the initial research that would be described by a practitioner. This figure takes on more significance, however, when one notes that it seems to increase with increasing experience. This is somewhat parallel to the findings in a survey of Philadelphia lawyers that revealed the materials those lawyers sought most frequently were (in order of importance) court reports, statutes, encyclopedias, and treatises. Cohen, *supra* note 9, at 191.

40. *Supra* note 29, at 76.

41. This seems to be an area where CALR systems are clearly superior, since an opinion can be incorporated into a CALR data base within several days after a court issues the slip opinion; the same opinion may not show up in reporters and law-finding aids for several months. This situation may change in the future as publishers take steps to improve their competitive positions.

42. *Supra* note 29, at 113.

43. Search Group Inc., The National Consortium for Justice Information and Statistics, *Automated Legal Research: A Study for Criminal Justice Agencies; Technical Report No. 19* (February 1978).

44. *Supra* note 29, at 114, found that the strongest factor users thought would encourage greater CALR use was a higher level of skill with the system.

45. Id. at 104.

46. Id. at 60.

47. Frankfurter, Llewelleyn, and Sunderland, *The Conditions for and Aims and Methods of Legal Research*, 6 Am. L. Sch. Rev. 663, 664 (1930).

48. Jones, *Towards a Theory of Indexing,* J. Documentation 1976 June; 32(2): 118-125, ISSN: 0022-0418.

49. See, for example, Boreham and Niblett, *Classification of Legal Texts by Computer,* 12 Information Processing and Management 125, No. 2 (1976). A good summary of the concepts these terms represent is in Liston and Howder, *Subject Analysis,* at 81 in 12 Annual Review of Information Science and Technology (1977) (American Society for Information Science).

50. Id. at 102.

9

KARLYN D. STANLEY

LEXIS: Legal Research and Litigation Support

LEXIS is the full-text, computer-assisted legal research service developed by Mead Data Central, Inc. (MDC). It has been available to lawyers and accountants on a subscription basis since May 1973. Since then, computer-assisted legal research has changed from a technological innovation to an accepted tool used routinely by the legal and accounting professions. MDC has continued to improve and enhance the LEXIS Legal Research Service in order to anticipate the needs of the professions it serves.

Background

MDC developed the LEXIS Legal Research Service as the third generation of a service growing out of an experiment initiated in 1967 by the Ohio State Bar Association Automated Research Corporation (OBAR). By 1971, MDC was committed to building a national computer-assisted research service through which an electronic law library would be available to lawyers in the United States. This service was given the trade name LEXIS, and an intensive program was launched to define and build a wholly new retrieval system capable of manipulating huge data banks and supporting thousands of users.[1]

Consistent with its aim of making LEXIS available on a national scale, MDC has entered into sponsorship agreements with a number of professional organizations. These sponsors assist MDC in defining library content, monitoring system performance, and in a variety of ways ensuring that the service meets the needs of their members. MDC's sponsors are OBAR; the New York State Bar Association; MOBAR (an affiliate of the Missouri bar); TexLex (an affiliate of the state bar of Texas); IBAR (a joint affiliate of the Illinois and Chicago bars); the National Center for Automated Information Retrieval (NCAIR), a nonprofit educational organization composed of judges, lawyers, and accountants, which sponsors LEXIS for all federal law; and the American Institute of Certified Public Accountants (AICPA), which sponsors a library of accounting materials.

LEXIS Legal Research System

The LEXIS System

LEXIS uses two dedicated IBM 370/155 computers in Dayton, Ohio. Another IBM 370/155 is available for back-up. The LEXIS mass storage configuration is one of the largest in the world.

The lawyer's terminal has been designed specially for LEXIS and is custom built to MDC's specifications. The terminal consists of a cathode ray tube (CRT) resembling a television screen, a hard-copy printer, a typewriter-style keyboard with additional keys to simplify the display of legal materials, and a microprocessor to store some data and control the operation of the terminal. All of these components are housed in a desk that has been designed to meet high standards of human engineering and aesthetics.

The software has been custom designed and written entirely by MDC to permit rapid searching and retrieval in large textual data bases. For example, more than 90 percent of all search requests are executed in less than fifteen seconds, and response times for well over 98 percent of all commands other than search requests, such as those directing the display of documents, are one second or less. Without such rapidity of response, the functions of LEXIS could not be employed to their full advantage.

Fast, easy-to-use, online systems with extensive data bases are of little worth unless they are reliable. The central site availability of the LEXIS system is about 99.9 percent. The mean time to repair is about four minutes. Should the system hardware fail, search results for users who are online at the time are automatically saved. Thus the only inconvenience to the user is an average delay of roughly four minutes for repair and restart of the system.

LEXIS Libraries

Materials in the LEXIS Legal Research Service are divided into a number of libraries (data bases), each covering a discrete body of law. LEXIS today has a library of general federal law containing the U.S. Code and decisions of the U.S. Supreme Court, courts of appeals, and district courts, as well as specialized libraries of federal tax law, federal securities law, federal patent and copyright law, federal trade regulation law, and federal and state cases construing the Delaware corporation law. Libraries of the law of the states of California, Florida, Illinois, Kansas, Kentucky, Massachusetts, Missouri, New York, Ohio, Pennsylvania, and Texas are also available.

These libraries constitute the largest collection in the world of full-text legal materials available for computer-assisted research—over ten billion characters and growing rapidly. The federal case law files, for the time periods spanned by the contents, are the most complete collection of federal cases available in any form, whether stored in a computer or printed.

Augmentation of the LEXIS libraries is a continual process. Several new state libraries were made available by the end of 1977. MDC is also expanding the case law files in existing libraries to include older decisions. LEXIS will ultimately provide lawyers with electronic access to comprehensive bodies of federal law and the law of the fifty states.

The LEXIS library of accounting materials, sponsored by the American Institute of Certified Public Accountants, contains nearly eight thousand corporate annual reports, accounting research bulletins, accounting principles board opinions, statements on auditing standards, and all pronouncements of the Financial Accounting Standards Board.[2]

Conversion to machine-readable form of large quantities of textual material at a high level of accuracy and at a reasonable cost has been one of MDC's most significant challenges. Back materials that were not available in machine-readable form were converted in large-scale keying operations in the United States and abroad. Current materials are captured by a variety of techniques, including the use of machine-readable tape produced as a by-product of photocomposition and the scanning of documents typed (for example, by a judge's secretary) with an optically scannable font.[3] MDC has implemented a system of computer-assisted error detection and correction, comprising hundreds of individual programs, to ensure that the converted data are at the required accuracy level.

LEXIS Users and Their Training

MDC, under the auspices of NCAIR and sponsoring state bar organizations, has entered into subscription agreements regarding LEXIS with law firms, accounting firms, corporate law departments, state government agencies, bar associations, law schools, federal agencies, U.S. district courts and courts of appeals, as well as the U.S. Supreme Court. There are hundreds of terminals in daily use, and nearly thirty thousand lawyers, judges, and tax accountants, as well as over twelve thousand law students, have been trained to use LEXIS. These ranks are growing rapidly.

To give lawyers confidence in their use of LEXIS, MDC has developed a three-phase training program: introduction to mechanical operations, exploration of search strategy, and practice use. Completion of the training program requires between four and five hours. A review session held at the lawyers' own offices after the training session services to reinforce the skills learned. MDC provides lawyers with a comprehensive reference book and other printed training materials.

How Lawyers Use LEXIS

LEXIS is a full-text research service, which means that the computer searches the full text of all of the documents stored in its data base when a search request is entered. No digests or indexes come between the researcher and the language of the law. One lawyer who uses LEXIS regularly commented, "Our experience indicates that the LEXIS system may uncover research data which is not otherwise searchable under traditional methods, due to the present system of indexing (or, in some cases, lack thereof) by the reporting services."[4]

The way the LEXIS system works is perhaps best described with an illustration. A lawyer's client, a pharmaceutical company, has developed a drug that it claims is effective in curing cancer. However, the drug has toxic properties and is potentially harmful to those who use it. The U.S. Patent Office refuses to grant a patent for the drug to the pharmaceutical company on the ground that the drug is unsafe and, therefore, not useful. (Section 101 of the patent law requires an invention to be useful in order to qualify for a patent.) The pharmaceutical company wishes to assert its right to a patent.

To research with LEXIS the specific legal precedence regarding usefulness and safety of pharmaceuticals, the lawyer sits at a LEXIS terminal in his office and dials the LEXIS computer in Dayton, Ohio. He then enters his private identification number, which allows him access to the system and provides for billing information. The lawyer then chooses the Patent, Trademark, and Copyright Library for searching from the list of libraries presented.

In less than a second, the files available in the library appear on the lawyer's terminal screen. The lawyer selects the Court of Customs and Patent Appeals file for searching and transmits this request to the computer. The terminal keyboard is a standard typewriter keyboard, with special function keys added to facilitate the transmission of requests to the computer from the researcher. The terminal console also includes a video screen for viewing retrieved documents. A high-speed printer on the console enables a paper copy of a document or a list of citations to be reproduced from the screen and carried away from the terminal for use at a later time.

The lawyer is now ready to enter his first search request in the Court of

Customs and Patent Appeals file. He types in the request, "patent and 101 and useful! or util!"[5] and pushes a button to transmit the request to the computer. In approximately three seconds, the computer responds on the video screen that 201 cases contain some combination of those words.

To limit the documents retrieved to ones specifically dealing with the problem at hand, the lawyer decides to enter more search terms to modify his search request. He types in this phrase: "and safe! or unsafe or health! or danger! or toxic!" The more complex search reduces the number of cases retrieved to forty-six. He can view them in several formats, such as FULL, which will show him the full text of each case, or KWIC, which will show him the Key-Words-In-Context—his search terms in a window of text surrounding them. After looking through several documents in KWIC, the lawyer decides to refine his request further by specifying that the already entered words "safe or unsafe or health or danger or toxic" appear within ten words of a reference to pharmaceutical or drug. He does this by entering the following request, "w/10 pharm! or drug," and transmitting it to the computer. The lawyer ascertains quickly that five of the eight documents retrieved are relevant and two of the cases are precisely on point. A 1975 case states that "unless the claimed composition can be used safely, it becomes useless."[6] It is apparent in the opinion of the case that "safety" implies a balancing of benefits and risks. The opinion of the court relies on a 1962 case (the other case in point retrieved by LEXIS), which states that

> with regard to . . . the nature of "safety" in the field of drugs and medicaments, we take judicial notice that many valued therapeutic substances or materials with desirable physiological properties, when administered to lower animals or humans, entail certain risks or may have undesirable side effects. True it is that such substances would be more useful if they were not dangerous or did not have undesirable side effects, but the fact remains that they are useful, useful to doctors, veterinarians and research workers, useful to both human and lower animals, and so are useful within the meaning of 35 U.S.C. 101. The use of drugs in medicine is frequently a matter of balancing risks to save a life.[7]

The lawyer makes a copy of the two cases in KWIC format by using the printer on the terminal and then concludes his research. The total time for the entire research session was less than fifteen minutes.[8]

LEXIS Litigation Support Service

One indicator of the impact that LEXIS has had on the legal profession has been the growing demand for special computer assistance in litigation, especially by lawyers who are accustomed to using LEXIS. Hardly any large-scale litigation or agency proceeding begins today without some form of computer assistance. More and more frequently, such assistance is used even when the flood of paper in litigation—documents, depositions and trial transcripts, briefs, motion papers—does not seem overwhelming. Many considerations other than the volume of paper enter into the decision to use computers, including the complexity of the legal and factual issues involved.[9]

The research system in the LEXIS Litigation Support Service is a slightly expanded version of the system used in the LEXIS Legal Research Service. The former contains all of the features of the latter, plus a few additional ones specifically designed for litigation support. A user familiar with the LEXIS Legal Research Service can master the Litigation Support Service quickly.

Its materials can be stored in many forms: the full, original source text, enriched sometimes with the lawyer's own comments and evaluations; digests or abstracts; excerpts or extracts; and highly coded, structured formats. The choice of format or formats for the materials in a litigation support data base or library is dependent upon the judgment of the lawyers who will use it. Every litigation support library is tailored to the case and the needs of its primary users.

Lawyers can search in their LEXIS litigation support library for ranges of dates and numbers, for example, or they can sort and rearrange retrieved items in a number of ways for more convenient review. In addition, it is possible to define as equivalent frequently occurring variations and abbreviations of names of persons, organizations, and things—and make a search for one variation a search for all.

This kind of flexibility with respect to function is one of the features of the service. Other services may impose limitations on the user because of the absence of functions in the litigation support system itself. Less obvious, but at least equally important, are limitations on the user's choice arising from performance restrictions. Many litigation support systems simply cannot respond reliably and swiftly if they must handle large volumes of materials (such as the full text or extensive extracts of millions of documents, rather than very brief summaries). LEXIS, on the other hand, imposes no limitations, either functionally or in performance, on the user's choice of the form, the mixture of forms, or the volume of the materials he or she chooses to store in the system.

With a powerful tool like LEXIS available for support, lawyers can prepare for litigation in ways that were not possible before. Experience has shown that the full-text approach is frequently no more expensive, and in many cases less expensive, than coding, indexing, abstracting, digesting, and extracting (generically, all summarizing).[10] Most importantly, the qualitative superiority of full text is overwhelming. The use of full text in a computer-assisted litigation support service permits the researcher with a question to have instantaneous access to the materials without having to rely on the judgment of intermediaries who prepared the summaries without knowledge or anticipation of that question.

For example, one subscriber to the LEXIS Litigation Support Service encountered this problem: after taking over a case that had been handled by another firm for two years, the litigation team was faced with preparing for trial in six weeks. The case file weighed over a ton. The documents produced during the one-year discovery period were neither indexed nor abstracted. The case itself involved a complex fact situation and was technical in nature, and deponents were scattered over two continents.

According to the lawyers, computer-assisted litigation support was the key to their success in the case. It allowed them to prepare for trial effectively by marshaling all of the evidence they needed (dates, meetings, technical subject matter, details of damages), and they were able to utilize fully the materials provided to them by the other firm and those arising from their own discovery to cover the points they needed to prove.

One of the lawyers commented, "LEXIS gives a litigator a simple way to look for the needle in the haystack. For example, to examine a key witness during a deposition, we had to find out—overnight—if the witness had ever seen a document (a purchase order) that would have made him aware of his company's purchase of a certain item. Without the purchase order number, all that we had to go on was the name of the item purchased, and the approximate date. We found the purchase order in the same amount of time that it took us to dial up the computer—a matter of seconds."

Conclusion

In the early days of computer-assisted research in legal source materials (cases and statutes), debates raged about the relative merits of digests and of full text. Today those debates have been laid to rest. Few lawyers question the overwhelming superiority of full text for computer-assisted research in legal source materials. Similarly sophisticated litigators have resolved a comparable debate about computer-assisted litigation support services. Services based on indexes and digests (because these are what the early computer systems and their descendants can handle) are giving way to services that have the features and the functions needed for full text. LEXIS is the most powerful and flexible service in existence today.

Mead Data Central has always attempted to anticipate the needs of the professions it serves and has continued to make both functional and performance improvements to the LEXIS legal research and litigation support services. Some improvements and enhancements have been suggested by users; others have been the result of MDC's own research and planning. MDC is confident that computer-assisted research, both in legal source materials and in litigation support materials, will become an increasingly important part of the daily research habits of lawyers and accountants.

Notes

1, For further discussion of the development of computer-assisted legal research in the United States, see J. S. Rubin, W. A. W. Krebs, and R. L. Woodard, "Computer-Assisted Legal Research—A Status Report," *International Bar Journal* (May 1973).

2. For further discussion of the accounting materials sponsored by the AICPA, see W. A. Leonardi and R. W. Neuman, "NAARS and LEXIS: Research Tools," *CPA Journal* (September 1977).

3. That is, in a type font that has been specially designed for preparing material to be read by optical scanning equipment, converting it directly to magnetic tape, which can then be loaded into the computer.

4. For additional information on the use of LEXIS in law firms, see F. H. Musselman, "Computers—A Boon to Legal Research," *Legal Economics* (Winter 1976).

5. The exclamation point appended to "util" instructs LEXIS to search for the root *util* and all of its suffixes—for example, utilize, utilization, and utility.

6. *In re Watson,* 415 F.2d 465, 186 U.S.P.Q. 577, 1975.

7. *In re Hartop, Jr.,* 311 F.2d 249, 135 U.S.P.Q. 419, December 1962.

8. For other examples of search requests and applications of LEXIS in legal research, see J. A. Sprowl, *A Manual for Computer-Assisted Legal Research* (Chicago: American Bar Foundation, 1976).

9. See J. S. Rubin, "The Application of Full-Text Retrieval to Litigation Support," *Forum* (Summer 1976).

10. For a cost comparison, see *Computer Assistance in Litigation: A Lawyer's Guide* (Mead Data Central, Inc., 1977).

10

THEODOR HERMAN

WESTLAW: Computerized Legal Research Program of West Publishing Company

WESTLAW is the only computerized legal research system that provides access to legal decisions of all state and federal courts; permits the user to frame a search request in natural language free of the restrictions of Boolean logic; incorporates the familiar West Key Number System; and ranks retrieved documents for relevancy.

WESTLAW is an online interactive system that enables the user to carry on a dialogue with a data base stored in a computer at West Publishing Company's offices in St. Paul, Minnesota. Seated at a terminal and entering a search request consisting of the words, numbers, phrase, or combination thereof that describe a legal problem, the user can retrieve documents containing such terms from any state or federal court. These documents can be examined at the terminal or copied on the printer.

Any search request can be modified by the user to include or exclude additional terms. This interaction between the user and the computer gives the user great freedom in framing and modifying search requests based on prior results.

The WESTLAW data base contains the full text and headnotes of all decisions of the United States Supreme Court starting with 1932 and the United States Courts of Appeals and District Courts starting with 1961. Starting with 1978[1] the full text and headnotes of all reported decisions of all state courts are in the WESTLAW data base. Additionally, the data base contains the headnotes of all reported state court decisions from 1967 and in the topics Drugs and Narcotics, Civil Rights, Products Liability, Public Contracts, and Securities Regulation, the data base contains headnotes dating back to the earliest reported cases. West has announced that the full text of all reported decisions of New York, California, and Texas starting with 1967 and Washington starting with 1965 and the headnotes back to 1957 for all reported decisions will be added to the data base. The data base is arranged in files in accordance with the National Reporter System.[2]

WESTLAW enables the user to frame a search request in several ways. The user may frame the search request in sentence form, as a question or statement, may use descriptive key words, may use Boolean logic, may require the presence of the terms in the same paragraph or sentence, and may require that retrieved documents not contain certain terms. Regardless of how the search request is formulated, the documents retrieved by the search will be ranked so that those containing a greater number of different search terms will be displayed before those containing fewer search terms. This WESTLAW ranking system effectively results in an initial display of the most relevant cases.

An important feature of the WESTLAW System is the presence of the West Key Number System as part of every document. A WESTLAW user notes the particular topics and key numbers appearing on relevant documents and may search such topics and key numbers. Topic and key number searches often produce relevant cases not otherwise retrieved because the court used terms different from the search request.[3]

Learning to use a computer terminal requires only brief training. The skill of the searcher in identifying and framing issues, however, plays the most significant role in determining the success of any computer search.[4]

An example will show how the system operates. A lawyer has analyzed the issues and framed the queries or problems that are to be the subject of a computer search. Turning to the computer terminal, he pulls the switch to activate the system. A display appears on the terminal screen, and the searcher uses the keyboard to transmit the assigned identification and any file identification selected for personal records.

After "sign-on," the terminal screen displays the available data bases for selection by the searcher. The user enters the identifying letters for a particular search file and then the query.

The Search

Hypothetical Problem: The Internal Revenue Service has served a subpoena on the attorney for a taxpayer whose tax returns are under investigation. The attorney has records belonging to the taxpayer and seeks to assert the taxpayer's privilege against self-incrimination.

Natural language query. The searcher may formulate a query as a question or statement using the same language as would be used to state the problem orally or in writing. The use of natural language may be modified to incorporate synonyms or antonyms.

Example: May an attorney lawyer counsel having possession of records documents belonging to a client assert claim the client's privilege right against self-incrimination fifth?

Descriptive or key word query. The searcher may formulate a query using only those terms that are descriptive of the problem being searched. Synonyms and antonyms of any term may be used.

Example: Attorney lawyer counsel client records documents assert claim privilege right incrimination fifth.

Special symbols used in framing search. The searcher may use special symbols to increase the likelihood of relevancy of the documents retrieved. One such symbol is the ampersand, which requires that one of the terms on each side of it be in the document.

Example: attorney counsel lawyer & client & records documents & assert claim & incrimination fifth.

For a document to be retrieved under this query, it would have to contain *attorney* or *counsel* or *lawyer* and *client* and *records* or *documents* and *assert* or *claim* and *incrimination* or *fifth.*

Another symbol is /p which requires that one of the terms on each side of it be in the same paragraph. (/s can be used for the same sentence.)

Example: attorney counsel lawyer /p client /p records documents /p assert claim /p incrimination fifth.

For a document to be retrieved by this query, it would have to have a paragraph which contained *attorney* or *counsel* or *lawyer* and *client* and *records* or *documents* and *assert* or *claim* and *incrimination* or *fifth* in the same paragraph.

Still another symbol is the "but not" (%), which directs the computer to retrieve the documents in which the relevant words occur as long as other words irrelevant to the search concept do not occur.

Phrase search. A search may consist of a phrase enclosed in quotes.

Example: "Privilege against self-incrimination"

Combination search. Any of the above search techniques may be combined in a single search.

Topic and key number search. A search can obtain a display of all documents in the selected data base file that are classified to a particular West digest topic and key number by entering the topic and key number.

Example: topic Witnesses (K217) or 410K217

Special searches. The searcher may use statutory or rule citations and name or citation of a case as search terms alone or in combination with other terms. A search may be limited to a particular jurisdiction or court within a jurisdiction. With full text a search may be limited to decisions by a particular judge. A search may be framed to retrieve decisions of a particular year or span of years and to require that one or more search terms be located in a particular segment of a document.

Modifying a search. The searcher may recall a query for the purpose of adding or deleting any terms or for entry and search of another data base.

Examining Retrieved Documents

The searcher may examine on the terminal screen the entire text or selected parts of documents retrieved by a search. The search terms contained in any retrieved document are highlighted. A hard copy of any document may be obtained. The searcher may skip forward and backward within the list of documents retrieved.

The searcher can ascertain the total number of documents retrieved by the query and the weight assigned to each document by the ranking algorithm. He or she need not examine all retrieved documents and can modify a query or start a new query at any time.

Special Functions

The computer retrieval special features system has functions to facilitate searching.

Root expansion. Placing an asterisk at the end of a word root will generate a listing of all words in the file that have the root. Words that are generated but irrelevant to the problem may be eliminated.

Dictionary. The correct spelling and frequency of occurrence of any term in the data base may be obtained.

Messages. Various messages have been designed to advise the searcher of mistakes in the spelling or formation of a search query.

Service. During the hours that the system is operating, personnel are available at West's computer center to assist in solving any problems.

Notes

1. 1948 to date for New Jersey.

2. *Supreme Court Reporter, Federal Reporter, Federal Supplement, Federal Rules Decisions, Atlantic Reporter, California Reporter, Northeastern Reporter, Northwestern Reporter, New York Supplement, Pacific Reporter, Southeastern Reporter, Southern Reporter, Southwestern Reporter.*

3. An initial computer search on the right of an indigent to appointed counsel did not retrieve an important case because the court used the term impecunious. A search of the key number of a retrieved document found the case.

4. Some references on WESTLAW are: Sprowl, *A Manual for Computer-Assisted Legal Research,* American Bar Foundation; Halladay, Legal Research with WESTLAW, 61 *A.B.A.J.* 1414; Orrin, Now There Are Two, *Legal Economics,* Winter 1976, pp. 27-29.

11

STANLEY O. CROYDON, JR.

JURIS: A Tool for Legal Research

The scene on the television set shows an impressive oaken door with a sign on it reading "Court Room 3." From behind the door a stern voice is heard admonishing someone that unless he returns after the luncheon recess with some cases to the contrary, the case will be thrown out in accordance with the motion just made by the defendant. The camera drops back, and a young attorney emerges from the courtroom muttering some unintelligible epithet under his breath.

This is not an old episode of *Perry Mason.* It is a scene in *An Introduction to JURIS,* a twenty-two-minute videotape shown to all JURIS trainees to familiarize them with the concepts of automated legal research. The situation that it depicts happens daily in courtrooms across the country. Lawyers need to find court cases supporting a client's position, and they usually head for libraries to find them. The star of the videotape, however, looks for his cases using a new legal research tool, the computer.

Hundreds of computer terminals currently service law firms, courts, government agencies, and law schools throughout the United States and Canada.[1] The computer has become an important element in the attorney's arsenal of legal research tools. JURIS, used by the U.S. Department of Justice, is one of them.

Background

Automated legal research (ALR) had its public debut in August 1960 when two working systems were shown to an American Bar Association meeting in Washington, D.C.[2] The legal research data banks used in the demonstration consisted of statutes relating to the field of health law and information pertinent to trademarks. Words to be searched for in the data banks were submitted by punched cards to an IBM 650 computer, and results showing the actual text of the words in the data banks were produced on a computer printout in a matter of minutes. The demonstration showed that the computer enabled the researcher to complete the assignment more rapidly and more thoroughly than by manual research.[3] Before such a tool could be used by the general legal community, however, a number of problems had to be addressed.

One major area that needed improvement at that time was the computer hardware. Data banks of federal court opinions, material searched by all attorneys and thousands of times larger than the health statute experiment, simply could not be searched quickly enough using the tape storage devices of early computers. The reliability of the computers was also very low. During the 1960s, advances in computer technology produced disk storage devices, transistorized components, and electronic circuitry with significantly improved reliability. The disks, in particular, made possible almost unlimited data banks of information.[4] The other innovations resulted in machines that run continuously without failure.

Another major problem that had to be overcome was the difficulty anyone unfamiliar with math or computers had in using an ALR system. Lawyers were not willing to use punched cards and the seemingly incomprehensible symbols understood by the computer to do legal research. Over a decade of modifications and refinements have produced search languages that use simple English and computer terminals that look like and are as easy to use as a television set.[5] The net result of the modifications is a tool simple to operate.

The History of JURIS

JURIS is a direct descendant of the 1960 systems. Its initial programming began in-house in 1970 on an IBM 360/40. At that time, the immediate objective was to provide Department of Justice attorneys with a pilot text-retrieval system that could easily be modified to meet changing or expanding research needs. Computer software and concepts from existing government computer programs were used wherever possible to speed its development.

The combination of old and new techniques results in a powerful research capability, modeled after sophisticated tools used by the National Aeronautics and Space Administration and the U.S. Air Force.[6] Researchers could use the tool by sitting down at a terminal, a television-like device with a keyboard attached, and talking directly with the computer over telephone lines. A test of the usefulness of the system was soon made using the U.S. Code as the searchable data bank, and an evaluation of the test recommended further development of JURIS.

The pilot system was not without its problems.[7] It was almost too powerful, and consequently too complicated, for legal research. The mathematical symbols of scientific research actually hindered legal research. The next generation of JURIS, completed in 1973, sought to remedy this situation.

The goal of the next generation was to simplify the language to only those commands essential for retrieving information, displaying it in a way that provided for easy analysis, and printing actual copies of the retrieved material. The second generation of JURIS was successful in meeting much of its goal. Complex commands were either done away with or streamlined, and implementation of commands was made easier with the addition of special command keys. Some of the language required to do searches still retained mathematical symbols, but the new version of JURIS was a tool that could be used by attorneys for practical legal research. The question that still remained was what kinds of data should be on the computer and available for research.

To determine the final data bank and final system, the Department of Justice embarked on a year-long study (from 1974 to 1975) encompassing over a thousand attorneys trained in the techniques of ALR.[8] The study used two different ALR systems; the department's own JURIS, and the commercial system, LEXIS, owned and operated by Mead Data Central. Each system contained different data: JURIS contained Department of Justice work products such as solicitor general briefs, and LEXIS contained federal case law. Twenty percent of the attorneys trained during the study were interviewed for their opinions and observations regarding the utility of ALR, the types of material needed for an ALR data bank, and how they personally used the system.

Some attorneys in the survey did only preliminary research via ALR, and others used the systems for virtually all research. Different attorneys developed their own ways of searching, some staying almost exclusively to citation searching (looking for recent references to earlier cases) and others to searches for cases directly on point. A composite picture of an ALR user was impossible. Of the eight to ten different research methods documented in the department evaluation, any one attorney was likely to use only two or three to any great extent.

The responses in the first two areas were simple and to the point. The consensus of the interviewees was that ALR was a useful research tool. The most important data were federal case law, and the more timely the opinions, the more useful the data.

Following the evaluation in late 1975, three decisions were made concerning the future of JURIS. First, programming would be undertaken to refine the search language and display and print capabilities one final time. Second, requirements would be defined and procurement actions would be initiated to acquire a custom-tailored terminal for use exclusively by JURIS (general multipurpose equipment had been used until this time). Third, a data bank of case law would be built to provide for the department's research needs. The efforts made over the next year as a result of those decisions produced the final system, which now runs on an IBM 370/168 to support its growing number of users and data banks.

JURIS Today

The JURIS training literature outlines three fundamental steps to doing legal research by computer: deciding where to do research, formulating a search expression, and examining documents found by the computer. The first step is a function of the type of terminal used by the researcher. The second step depends on the legal question that needs answering. And the third step is basic to all research done on JURIS.

Searching

Every word, number, or phrase in the JURIS data bank (except for very common words like *and, of,* and *the*) can be used by a researcher to find court cases and statutes that bear on a particular legal question. JURIS stores the location of each word—document, sentence, position within a sentence—in its memory and is able to locate the word quickly once it and its relationships to other words are spelled out. The words are given to JURIS in a search expression, and connectors are used to indicate the desired relationships.[9] The types of connectors available on JURIS follow:

Document Connectors

or finds documents containing either the word before or after the connector. Example: house *or* home.

and finds documents containing both the words in front of and after the connector. Example: automobile *and* accident.

but not finds documents with the word preceding the connector, and then eliminates any of those documents containing the second word. Example: cocaine *but not* marijuana.

Proximity (Sentence) Connectors

p/n finds documents where the word appearing before *p/* precedes the word after it, by no more than *n* words, where *n* is a number. Example: statute *p/2* limitations.

w/sen finds documents where words on each side of the *w/* appear *anywhere in* the same sentence. Example: president *w/sen* authority.

w/n is the same as *w/sen* but allows a narrower refinement by specifying the precise range of words to be scanned *(n)*. Example: homicide *w/5* weapon.

Accomplishing a search is simple. Once the search command has been indicated to JURIS, the researcher types the requested search expression and sends it to the computer. A typical search might read "marijuana and automobile and search warrant" or "cost of living index and inflation." The number of words that can be used is theoretically unlimited, and the only possible problem that could be encountered is JURIS misinterpreting which words should be searched for first.[10]

Theory, however, is often different from reality, and that is especially true for ALR systems. Every word of every search request must be searched for in every document of the data bank being used. Many JURIS files (a file is a specific portion of the data bank) contain up to a hundred thousand documents. Some words, such as *court* or *circuit,* may appear in virtually all of them. The more times a word occurs in the data base, the longer it takes JURIS or any other system to find a result. Therefore strategies must be developed to use an ALR system like JURIS efficiently and effectively.

One research strategy advocates writing down prospective search terms before actually searching and analyzing the words for their significance. Significant or unique words are the best words for search expressions, and they improve the possibilities for a successful search. The phrase *United States House of Representatives* is an acceptable search expression, but the documents containing it can be found much more quickly with the expression *states p/3 representatives.*

Another strategy taught JURIS trainees involves the reuse of search expressions, a technique that can result in shorter search times and greater flexibility in solving a problem. JURIS provides this capability in the way it produces search results. Any documents meeting the criteria of a search expression are placed in a set, a group of documents whose locations and description are put aside in the computer's memory. An example illustrates the technique.

A researcher's first search produces set 1, his second search, set 2, and so on. The sets are unrelated unless the researcher asks JURIS to make them related. All sets can easily be reviewed at any time by calling on the JURIS search history, which lists the sets in the order of their creation. For example,

SET/	DOC	POI	DESCRIPTION
1	870	1933	ARREST
2	487	804	MARIJUANA
3	162	391	SET/1 AND SET/2
4	31	42	SET/1 W/SEN SEN/2

The headings of the search history indicate the number of the search, the number of documents in the set, the number of points of interest (or times the words occur in the document), and the actual search expression. The sets shown in the example are searches involving the words *arrest* and *marijuana.* Sets 1 and 2 are typical searches for individual words. Each word appears a number of times in the data bank being searched. Set 3 is equivalent to the search expression *arrest and marijuana* (sets 1 and 2). If the search expression containing both words had been entered, 162 documents and 391 points of interest still would have been found.

If the researcher decides that the answer in set 3 contains too many documents and wants to try the same words in a sentence, the use of the set terminology permits him to shift quickly to proximity searching without having to waste unnecessary search time looking for the search words again. The set *arrest w/sen marijuana* is identical to set 4 but requires JURIS to look in its data bank an additional time for the two words rather than checking its search history for sets already created. *Arrest* and *warrant* were searched for separately in sets 1 and 2 to provide for this possibility.

There are other search features on JURIS. Universal characters enable a user to look simultaneously for multiple endings of root words using only one search term. Segments permit quick searches for very particular kinds of information. A special keep set allows manipulation and editing of retrieved data. However, the basic formula for successful research consists of understanding sets and connectors and utilizing the search history to narrow search results.

Looking at Documents

Once a set is created, the user's task is to examine the documents JURIS found. A researcher can display documents on the terminal in one of three ways: viewing the full text of any of the retrieved documents, looking at just the citations or descriptions of the documents within each set, and examining only the KWIC (Key-Word-In-Context) sentences of each of the documents. Each format fulfills a particular examination need for the legal researcher.

The full-text format permits viewers to examine a case or statute in the same way as they would manually. Every word or number in the entire text is available by pushing the appropriate paging keys on the terminal. Use of the full format is reserved primarily for situations where a result is desired immediately or when the material to be examined is not readily available. It is an expensive way to look at the material when the costs of computer time and long-distance telephone lines are considered. The law library is generally considered more economical for full-text reading.

The citation display is a format designed for use in conjunction with manual materials. A list of cases or statutes giving a brief description of the documents found by a JURIS search is handy to have when returning to a library to continue research.

The JURIS format that represents a significant departure from normal manual research reading is the KWIC format. At the push of a button, the researcher can see just those portions of a document that use the search words. The user can control the number of sentences he views around the sentence containing the words and can switch back to full format at any time he desires. Another command key in the full format lets the reader jump between pages containing only key words. KWIC enables the attorney to determine quickly which cases are irrelevant and which should be read in more detail.

Printouts of any of the formats are available either through the local printer (limited to one screen of information at a time) or the remote printer located with the JURIS computer (virtually unlimited printout capability with overnight mailings of material). A number of JURIS users have employed the system and the remote print facility to save dozens and even hundreds of hours of manual work. Just before President Carter's cabinet was confirmed, the Library of Congress searched the JURIS data bank for all of the court opinions written by Judge Griffin Bell.[11] It took the researcher about an hour to find the five hundred or so cases and another hour to issue all of the appropriate commands to obtain a full-text printout of the cases, which was delivered to the House Judiciary Committee the next day.

The Training Film

Communicating with JURIS is not shown on the videotape because it is used for training with a number of different terminal configurations. Any teletype compatible terminal can be used to access JURIS, as well as ones manufactured by Sanders Technology, Hazeltine and Bunker-Ramo. A number of different telephone options are also available.

The usual steps of communication are dialing the appropriate JURIS telephone number, making the connection on the telephone device, and finally identifying oneself to the computer. Each user has a unique number in order to provide a means for saving research results throughout the week.

After the attorney in the film leaves the courtroom, the narrator of the tape sets the scene by telling us that JURIS is a new tool, available to Department of Justice attorneys for legal research, and now we, the audience, will see if it can help.

The attorney describes his problem to the JURIS expert. The defendant was stopped for speeding and could not produce a valid driver's license. In the process of taking the defendant to the police station, the police officer discovered a gun sticking out of a brown paper bag, an item that the prosecutor seems to be having trouble introducing into evidence. What he needs are cases showing that the gun can be introduced as evidence.

The JURIS expert quickly takes control of the situation. She suggests that the attorney look at the CASELAW file group, one of a number of research areas available, which contains a number of individual files of full-text opinions from the Supreme Court, Court of Appeals, and Court of Claims. She selects the HOTCASES file because it combines the most recent cases from all of the files.

The expert questions the prosecutor as to the significant words in his problem. He explains that the problem concerned a search of an auto, incident to a lawful arrest. Keeping the usefulness of searching by sets in the back of her mind, the expert generates the following search history:

SET/		DESCRIPTION
1	. . .	AUTO OR CAR OR AUTOMOBILE OR VEHICLE
2	. . .	INCIDENT W/SEN ARREST
3	. . .	SET/1 AND SET/2

The search expression in set 1 was suggested to pick up needed synonyms for *auto.* The set contains a very large number of documents, as might be expected. Set 2 contains the unique words necessary to find cases with the phrase *incident to a lawful arrest.* Set 3 combines the first two sets, so that both concepts will appear in the same cases. It also narrows the results to a manageable number of documents.

At some point in the creation of sets, it is useful to survey some of the retrieved cases to see if you are on the right track. The expert encourages the prosecutor to look at his documents in KWIC. He does and finds that the first document is a civil rights case, the wrong area of law.

Some more significant words are needed. The search of the auto could be considered an investigatory stop. Prompted again by the expert, who appreciates the fact that different authors use different sets of vocabulary, some more synonyms are added. New documents are found and sets combined, resulting in the following:

SET/		DESCRIPTION
4	. . .	INVESTIGATORY or FIELD or TRAFFIC p/3 STOP
5	. . .	SET/4 and SET/3

Now the prosecutor has only a half-dozen cases to work with. An examination of the cases in KWIC and then in full format reveals the case needed. After the prosecutor gets a printed copy of some of the text and the cites to them, the videotape returns to the narrator.

The narrator reviews the techniques just shown: set searching, looking for synonyms, using the various formats, and using the local printer. Then the narrator describes the data bases available on JURIS, detailing the files containing statutes, regulations, U.S. Attorney office briefs, and the Court of Military Review. She particularly mentions the DIGEST file group, containing the *Modern Federal Practice Digest* and *Eighth Decennial Digest* from the West Publishing Company.[12]

JURIS differs from most other ALR systems in the types of data it has available for searching. Some of its early efforts involving support of specific Department of Justice litigation used data banks that contained both full-text and indexed or abstracted material. The various analyses of the JURIS project indicated that the combination of the two types of data would result in a more comprehensive research tool.[13] The digest of the West Publishing Company, the same data that exist in the WESTLAW system but in a different form, are available back to back with the full text file. The second half of the videotape demonstrates how the DIGEST files can supplement a full text search.

The JURIS expert takes one of the six cases found in the CASELAW file and finds in it the corresponding DIGEST file. The West headnote of interest is listed under "Arrest 71.1 (1)." Next to that topic and key number, in parentheses, is another number, 35K71.1.1.[14] It is the computer designation for the same topic and key number. Using it as a search expression, the JURIS expert searches the entire *Modern Federal Practice Digest,* over 150,000 cases, for similar topics and key numbers.

JURIS as a tool for legal research is gaining acceptance by government attorneys who are in need of quick and comprehensive answers to legal problems. ALR is its own best promotional device, for the JURIS user soon realizes that the terminal provides instant access to standard research sources and provides the option of using his or someone else's analyses to find cases.

Notes

1. The three major legal research terminal networks in operation in the United States are JURIS (U.S. Department of Justice), LEXIS (Mead Data Central of Dayton, Ohio), and WESTLAW (West Publishing Company of Minneapolis, Minnesota). In Canada, the QUIC/LAW system of Queen's University, Kingston, Ontario, is used.

2. See Lawlor, Historical Perspective and Future Prospects, American Bar Association, *Sense and Systems in Automated Legal Research* (1975) (papers presented at the Second National Conference on Automated Legal Research 1973), for a detailed discussion of the early history of ALR.

3. James Sprowl in "Computer-Assisted Legal Research—An Analysis of Full-Text Document Retrieval Systems, particularly the LEXIS System," *AB Foundation Research Journal* (1976): 177-179, points out a number of research applications,

including statutory searches, where he feels the computer is an indispensable tool. Not all applications, however, will result in so dramatic a time savings or thorough a search.

4. The size of the JURIS data base, for example, has surpassed six billion characters. A character is a letter or number, and a typical court reporter volume contains two to three million characters.

5. The search languages are based on Boolean logic. English words such as *and* and *or* represent the concepts of *union* and *intersection.*

6. The Air Force programs came from project LITE (now FLITE), a text retrieval system that was a by-product of the ABA experiment. JURIS has a working agreement with FLITE, which permits the Department of Justice to use FLITE's extensive data bases covering nearly all federal court opinions since 1800.

7. "JURIS: Justice Retrieval and Inquiry System," B. W. Basheer, American Bar Association Standing Committee on Law and Technology (collection of presentations delivered at the First National Conference on Automated Law Research, 1973).

8. "Automated Legal Research, an Evaluation Report," U.S. Department of Justice, Information Systems Staff, Legal and Management Systems and Procedures, May 1975.

9. For a general discussion of connectors and the mechanics of searching, see Sprowl, *A Manual for Computer-Assisted Legal Research* (Chicago: American Bar Foundation, 1976).

10. The problem is best illustrated by the mathematical equation: $2 \times 4 + 5$. Is the answer 13 or 18? JURIS has a connector hierarchy which resolves proximity connectors, *or, and,* and *but not* in that order.

11. Kathleen E. Shea, "JURIS," *Library of Congress Professional Association Newsletter* 8(March 1977).

12. JURIS, under a contractual arrangement with the West Publishing Company, receives weekly updates of both full text and digest material for its federal and digest data banks.

13. The West Publishing Company appears to have arrived at the same conclusion, since they started supplementing the WESTLAW digests with full-text material in 1978. Ejan MacKay in "Designing Datum II," Society for Computers and Law, Ltd., (September 1976), describes similar conclusions reached by another Canadian project.

14. The number, similar to one used in the WESTLAW system, represents the topic ("35" stands for "arrest") and key number (71.1.1 is equivalent to 71.1 (1)). The special number 35K71.1.1 represents just one search word to JURIS, while "arrest 71.1 (1)" represents three. Using the special number results in shorter search times.

Part IV

LITIGATION, THE COURTS AND COMPUTERS

This part provides a view of how courts have been affected by the computer. To this effect, Lawrence Berul, Michael Stern, and James Keane and Robert McCormick and Steven Rosen concern themselves with the use of computers as a litigation tool, Larry Polansky discusses the effect of computers on the courts, and William Fenwick and Gordon Davidson look at the introduction of computer evidentiary data.

The two chapters on litigation information management stress that at times a manual system is sufficient, but at other times computer support is necessary. Factors to be analyzed in considering which to use include size of documentary evidence, complexity of case, number of parties and sites involved, cost-benefit review, time scale, anticipated data-base reuse, and the need for detailed document analysis. Berul, Stern, and Keane detail the methods by which an exhaustive data base can be created, and McCormick and Rosen describe the different requirements of a computer litigation support system at the strategic points of litigation.

Polansky explains how the courts themselves have begun to value the use of computers. In addition to the handling of day-to-day operations, computers are being used for docketing, calendars, notices, scheduling, and jury management. In addition, prosecutors' offices are utilizing the computer to aid in the management and operation of their offices. The defense, the prosecution, and the courts are also all benefiting from the positive effect of automated transcription service on court reporting.

Fenwick and Davidson describe the unique legal issues facing the courts today with regard to the admissibility and use of computer-generated evidence. As such, they discuss the evidentiary problems encountered, printouts as objects of proof, whether a printout can be considered best evidence, and other timely and critical issues. They cite legal precedents for the use of computer evidence and hypothesize possible future legal developments.

12

LAWRENCE H. BERUL,
MICHAEL P. STERN, and
JAMES KEANE

The Need for Computer-Managed Litigation Files

Increasingly attorneys have been using the computer as an aid to the practice of law. Nowhere has its impact been greater than on the practice of litigation attorneys and, indeed, on the shape of major litigation. The expansion of the discovery process, particularly in federal courts, the growth of product liability suits, antitrust and regulatory cases, and the increase in the willingness of individuals and corporations to go to court has added immeasurably to this effect.

The history of successful application of the computer to litigation has made attorneys amenable to its future application. As more trial lawyers have successful encounters with computers, they no longer seem to be awed or intimidated by information technology. There is an increasing realization that the computer can be used as a lever to multiply the effects of their intellectual efforts. Automated litigation support is no longer in its adolescence; it has grown up, matured, and is fully operational.[1]

The computer can contribute to more effective litigation in many ways. Statistical analyses and computer-created econometric models are in use. Major certified public accounting firms are using the computer to provide a form of litigation support; they can create, summarize, and evaluate extensive cost and other financial evidence, particularly in the area of accounting reports. The species of computer-assisted litigation support we shall discuss here pertains to textual data, files consisting of large masses of documents and transcripts.

Manual Approaches

Most computer functions can be duplicated by massive numbers of people over large periods of time.[2] However, comparing the time required and effort spent in creating and using a large manual system with that of a computer-managed litigation system shows greater benefit for less cost and effort in the computerized approach. The traditional method of indexing a document collection is for an attorney, perhaps with the aid of paralegals, to create card files. Shortages of time and manpower generally dictate that the attorney will only catalog his file to create a set of cards that will allow the identification of documents by date, author, recipient, and other easily captured objective criteria. Cataloging does not classify documents based on any of the information contained in them. The document may thus be found by author name but not by subject matter.

If time permits, attorneys may attempt to create a subject matter scheme to be applied to the documents. The attorney or paralegals will then read the documents and produce a separate index card for each important subject mentioned. One document may require ten or fifteen cards, which are filed alphabetically. Attorneys rarely are versed in information science and have been content with rudimentary subject classification schedules. All too often these fail when additional matters of subject interest are discovered. There is usually no consistent way to revise the scheme or to index documents that have already been scanned by paralegals at this time without reprocessing most or all of the documents.

Computerized System

A well-designed litigation information system will permit the creation of the equivalent of forty or fifty different index cards for each document by cataloging, abstracting, and indexing the documents in one or two steps using specially trained paralegals.[3] Not only is the capture of information done efficiently at relatively low cost, but the uses to which the information may be put and the ways it may be correlated and compared are far beyond the capabilities of even the most complicated manual systems. Further, the possible correlations that may be desired need not all be preplanned, as in the manual system. The computer allows the attorney to use his ingenuity in exploring the document files.

Computerized litigation support is necessary when the file is too large to manage manually. Some basic considerations are the number of documents, complexity of issues and evidence, number of parties and witnesses, cost-benefit factors, and time.[4] These are judgment factors required by all large cases, but they are frequently not faced until the trial team has attempted to manage it by hand. This was in fact the experience of the Select Committee on Presidential Campaign Activities of the U.S. Senate, which compiled ten thousand index cards in the initial weeks of the Watergate investigation, before turning to automation.[5] In that case, the change came early enough. Those who supply litigation file management are accustomed to having clients request computerized file control at the last moment, often after the clients have already read every file document several times.

A litigation system can be established very quickly but only at high cost. The most expensive and time-consuming component in the creation of an automated litigation file is not computer processing. It is the design of the system, the capture of the information by paralegals, and the creation of the data base itself, which takes the major amount of effort and money. Estimates go as high as 80 percent for these activities.[6] The elapsed time required for the effort can be compressed, but costs rise as the number of coders or document analysts increases. Rushed vocabulary development, the training of additional people, and the lowered productivity due to the impact of learning curves only raise costs. The stakes involved in the type of litigation that requires computerized support are quite large; the marginal cost of a quick start-up may not be a significant proportion of the stakes.

Litigation is an adversary procedure, a contest; somebody wins and somebody loses. A win may not even be a favorable judgment but merely be a reasonable settlement. Litigation attorneys are in the business of winning cases for their clients. They have a duty to do their best and to employ those techniques, skills, and tools that are necessary for the furtherance of their clients' rights. Computerized litigation support is such a tool.

A computer-managed file may be created for offensive, defensive, or joint reasons. If used offensively, it serves as an intimidation to the defense. It may encourage them either to settle or to, themselves, establish a computerized system. Under the Federal Court Manual for Complex Litigation, a common document depository may be created.[7] At least partial joint access to this file and the computerized access to it may result.

The need for such computerized support becomes most obvious when there are large numbers of documents and, perhaps, testimony. Manual control may become impossible to implement and ineffective to use. The whole purpose of a computerized control system is to pinpoint specific documents and correlative groups of documents that fulfill requirements. These needs clearly rise as the collection increases in size.

During pretrial and trial, large amounts of transcript may be produced. Attorneys preparing for further testimony have little time to analyze that which has already been spoken. The computer can, with almost no effort on the attorneys' part, dramatically reduce the amount of time they must spend in performing that analysis. The computer will not perform the intellectual analysis but will create information products that allow the attorneys to devote their time to analysis rather than to the drudgery of poring over the transcripts.

Many large litigation matters involve attorneys and clients located in multiple sites across the United States and, even, internationally. Simultaneous access to the document collection by the allied attorneys, perhaps even for different purposes, may be a requirement. The computer with on-line telecommunications access to a large searchable data base supports such a requirement. Microfilm, microfiche, and ultrafiche addresses can be linked with the computer to permit instantaneous display of a document located by a search. The creation of a microfilm document collection is often the first step in the implementation of a multisite document and index system. Copies of the entire microfilm collection are provided for each attorney. The attorneys may have computer terminals that provide access to a central data base index economically. Additionally, it has proven economical to use computer-supplied desk reference printouts, which may be produced in multiple copies. Thus, attorneys in many locations may have complete and quick bibliographic or subject access to the entire document collection, as well as the ability to read the text of the documents they need. In a computerized system, this multilocation capability is a relatively small addition to the cost of the system. This shared collection concept also applies to a common document depository. With a suitcase-size computer terminal and a briefcase containing a viewer and the entire document collection on microfilm, an attorney may indeed walk into a courtroom with a major document library and the tools to use it.

The Trial Document Collection

Litigation file management is more dependent on information science than on electronic data processing. A litigation support system is a document file management system, not a data-processing system. It must capture a dynamically expanding flow of data, allow access to issues that may not become apparent until trial, and yet avoid endless reprocessing of irrelevant documents. A carefully and responsively designed information system will require the application of some mental process on each document passing through it. A document collection to which no intellectual operation has been applied will result in a needlessly large and expensive data base, which will not permit the precise and timely document location power required by complex litigation.

Collecting the Documents

The first process in the creation of the information system is to establish a controlled central document collection. This collection will exist throughout the litigation and should contain all documents and potential exhibits pertinent to the case, whether found internally or as a result of discovery.

Because of the use of copying machines and the resulting proliferation of paper, the discovery team will retrieve many copies of even trivial documents. Thus, the elimination of duplicates is an important task. It is here that eventual cost savings through information systems design are first realized. It is obvious that each document going through the system will require handling and processing. The goal is to reduce the number of documents passing through the system and to reduce the average amount of processing per document. Duplicate elimination is a high-priority item; a typical document collection will consist of 15 to 40 percent duplicates. If these are eliminated inexpensively and early in the flow of the processing, great savings will result.[8]

Screening

Another step that gives direction to the flow of information is screening: drawing important documents into the system and eliminating totally or restricting the level of treatment (money and time) applied to less important documents. It may be sufficient to catalog these by capturing information pertaining to the document's identity, its title, date of creation, author, and other readily found information. It might be important to know of the existence of such documents but not to index or abstract them.

The attorneys may perform the screening function, or they may be able to provide objective criteria for paralegals by which classes of documents may be eliminated or their level of treatment reduced. As simple examples, they may decide to eliminate all brochures and to give less treatment to bills of lading more than five years old. These standards may be easily applied by persons not intimately familiar with the contents of the document.[9]

Accessioning

Prior to processing, the documents may have been arranged by the attorneys chronologically, by author, by subject matter, or in no way at all. Since they will be computerized, there is no reason to arrange the central collection by any such catalog devices at this point in the system. All that is necessary is that each document have a unique identity, such as a log or accession number. The computer will arrange the collection in any way necessary or desired. There is no reason to stack the physical file chronologically when the computer can create a printout of documents listed by date, by author, or by subject ranked by author in chronological sequences. The varieties are endless and can all be created, each providing access to the document collection by the accession number.[10]

As the central collection is established and a unique accession number is assigned to each document, it is possible to photocopy or microfilm segments of the collection. Hard copy can be created by using microfilm to provide full-sized paper copies. Microfilm technology is coming into increased use, and its many advantages for large document collections are being recognized. Computer-Output-Microfilm (COM) is another economical application of information technologies. Instead of bulky index printouts, COM can create multiple miniaturized libraries directly from the data in the computer.

Bibliographic Surrogation

Establishing procedures and developing detailed training manuals for paralegals and abstractors are the next steps in creating the abbreviated data, or a surrogate of the document, which will go into the data base.[11] A surrogate is a representation that captures all information in and about the document deemed pertinent and useful.

The cataloging or bibliographic surrogation process has the aim of capturing objective information from the documents. In many cases the objective information may be sufficient for control purposes. The attorneys can use it to have the computer locate all documents authored by a particular party, sent to a party, from whose files the document originated, within a chronological span, of a certain type, or any combination of these and similar factors.

Document Analysis

Following bibliographic surrogation, documents that have been identified for further processing during the screening process will proceed to document analysis: the capture of subjective information. This process may take a number of forms, and it is here that the greatest amount of intellectual energy is applied to each of the documents. A number of alternative information science techniques may be applied at this point. The one most familiar to practicing attorneys is that of creating an abstract or an extract.

An abstract may be indicative or informative. The former does not represent all of the information contained but merely serves as an indication of what is in the document so that the document itself must be consulted. An informative abstract contains all of the essential information from the document in condensed form. An extract, the most quickly produced of these three, is merely a capture of portions of the actual text of the document, perhaps marked by the attorney.

Vocabulary Control

To aid in retrieval of the documents, a standardized indexing language will ameliorate the weaknesses of full-text retrieval.[12] This is commonly in the form of either a hierarchical taxonomy, a list of uniformly applied key words, or a complete thesaurus. The purpose of any of these three tools is to counteract the vagaries of natural language. For example, document 007 contains the word *hound* but not the word *dog* or *dogs.* In a full-text system, if you are seeking all documents that include the word *dogs,* the computer will not retrieve 007. Or perhaps you are seeking documents dealing with harassment. One of the creative and synonymous search terms you use is *hound.* To your surprise, you retrieve a treatise dealing with hunting dogs.

If you had a hierarchical taxonomy, a key word list, or a thesaurus, these problems would be ameliorated. A paralegal would read the documents and determine that the one at hand dealt with hunting dogs and would apply the preferred word or a selected code from a taxonomy to the information capture form. Thus if you were trying to retrieve documents aimed at a specific subject, you would have a standard term or code upon which to retrieve.

Data Base Creation

In the next stage of work, following quality control review of the work performed by paralegals, the form used for information capture would be converted to computer-readable form. It may be keyboarded on an office word-processing machine, which will store the information on a magnetic tape; it may be typed on a key-to-disk machine, which writes directly onto a computer disk or diskette; it may be entered by a keypunch machine on punchcards for input; or it may be recorded-typed on a piece of paper using a type font that may be read by an optical character reader (OCR) to produce a computer tape. With a raw data listing, the information in the computer can be proofread and corrected, and a clean master data base created. At this point the data base is usable for the creation of printed indexes and directories but is not yet ready for complex or efficient computer searches. Searches run on this first-stage data base are relatively expensive and inefficient in computer terms.

To obtain high retrieval value, it is necessary to create a searchable data base, which requires some computer preprocessing. The computer will arrange the data in a manner amenable to searching; it will create a concordance. It in effect creates an internal index of all significant words in the file in the mass memory of the computer; this is called an inverted file. It is this index, rather than the entire data base, that the computer uses for its basic searching. File inversion results in a considerable saving of computer time during searching and of actual elapsed time as well.

Updating

A litigation information system is rarely a static library. Additional documents come in as a result of subpoenas, interrogatories, and actual trial testimony. The data base must be regularly supplemented to be effective. Additionally, as litigation proceeds, the attorneys and others utilizing the documents may wish to make some record of their use of the documents, noting who has seen them, their importance, and other information. These tracking and interpretive data have proven quite useful when added to the prime data base.[13]

Uses of the System

The most frequent and widest use of the litigation information system is likely to occur during pretrial. A system that is planned and implemented at the last minute will still be in the process of creation during this critical period and will be of less than optimal utility. In any potentially complex case, the lawyers should, at a minimum, start with a manual information system that is amenable to transfer to a computer. Good management dictates such a course.[14]

Generally the central document collection will initially be composed from the documents that the attorneys and their client have in their possession. The establishment of a computerized central document system requires the attorneys to do that which they must do anyway: determine which documents are applicable to the case and collect them. By compiling and evaluating the documents, the attorneys prepare for discovery from the other party and at an early date are able to establish the quality of documents that they possess. By being familiar with their collection, they are also better able to determine what additional documents or types of documents they should seek from the opponent during discovery. By establishing and applying criteria of relevance, they can better limit the number of documents that they must supply to their opponent.

Discovery response time and comprehensiveness are improved substantially through the simple process of automatically sorting relevant documents into lists that correspond with the interrogatory in question, the specific request for document production, or subpoena duces tecum. Attorneys will be better able to evaluate the response, after having examined all relevant sources.

Document production requests or interrogatories can also be translated into very precise queries and the data base searched specifically for each question or request. This capability to respond directly to specific questions posed by an opponent during discovery may serve to limit inordinate "fishing expeditions" by making it unnecessary to allow opponents to rummage through files. It is possible, for example, to identify all documents dealing with a particular subject, in a specified period, relating to the costs of a particular item. Some litigators prefer, nevertheless, to saddle their opponents with large masses of unsorted documents. By such a production with an automated system, counsel could deny themselves the knowledge they can gain by adding to the computer record of each produced document a simple code indicating to whom, in a multiple-party suit, they had provided a specific critical document. In a similar manner the computer can enhance the preparation of witnesses for deposition or trial. Using the computer, it is possible to retrieve all documents with which the person had contact—as author, recipient, or a person mentioned in the document—or to retrieve all documents dealing with the subject area competence of the witness. The witness may then be prepared with a realistic appreciation of the areas in which the opposition will expect him to testify, and a strategy may be planned for defending the witness against the introduction of harmful documentary or testimonial evidence.[15] The enhanced ability of an attorney to impeach a witness at trial is clear. The greater the degree of control over past testimony, the greater the ability to impeach. This is particularly true in dealing with expert witnesses who may have testified at a series of related matters.

In preparation for trial, counsel may write pretrial briefs, which will set forth the points to be proven and the means by which they will be proven. With computer control over the document collection, the attorney will know with some certainty which documents and testimony he may expect to produce at trial in support of his points. A taxonomy that classifies by subject the factual underpinnings of the expected points of proof and that forms the basis of the overall index to the subject matter of the litigation will aid in sorting the document collection to this end.

At trial and in preparation for trial, the most important functions a computer can perform are in the preparation of witnesses and in laying a foundation for the introduction of evidence. Since much evidence will be documentary, the use of the computer in establishing who had contact with the document in what context is extremely useful in maintaining the chain of custody, a prerequisite for introduction.

Online search capability is generally appropriate at trial time. Any document may be identified in a search by specifying a wide range of qualifying and limiting criteria. The ability of the computer to process an extremely complex query and come up with a small and specific list of documents is vital at this time. The use of portable computer terminals allows attorneys to query the computer from anywhere: a hotel room, court anterooms, or, one day, the courtroom itself.[16] Trial teams have successfully employed the telephone to instruct paralegals to search and retrieve documents from the data base and hard-copy collection. The creation of computer output microform allows attorneys to carry with them to the courtroom lengthy computerized indexes to the document collection.

The ability to search the document collection in minutes for past statements of a witness or a related witness at trial is invaluable. Small points made during trial can be quickly formulated into computer queries. Lingering doubts of vulnerability and notions of the existence of favorable evidence may be quickly confirmed. The psychological value of one side's knowing the other has a computerized system is, of course, not to be dismissed lightly. An attorney's credibility with the court or jury will be enhanced by an ability to produce documents on point quickly through a search required by the trial judge.

Witnesses' testimony can be entered into the data base as a trial progresses for comparison with other documents. By typing transcripts onto magnetic tape overnight, court reporters have successfully placed testimony into machine-readable form. Special type fonts are typically used for creating optically scannable pages, which are read by an optical character reader. Recently there has also been experimentation with computer stenotype translation systems, which translate the court reporter's shorthand into English automatically.

The computer can serve a critical function in speeding up counsel's ability to evaluate his status before the close of the case. After a year of trial, as in some antitrust cases, an automated checklist of evidence submitted against proposed points of proof will quickly highlight omissions or unexpected directions that the evidence as a whole has taken. The final summation, for which the rigors of trial leave scant time to prepare, can be enriched by quickly grouping related documents, exhibits, and points of testimony together in one place for quick review. Thoroughness is not a virtue in jury arguments. The computer can speed up the process of sorting the most important material, allowing counsel to weave the strongest elements of documented proof together.

A central computerized collection provides an incidental benefit by aiding in continuity. Many cases go on for five or more years. During that time government attorneys, and to a lesser extent private attorneys, are very likely to have been replaced. The knowledge they possessed of the documentary evidence would be lost with them. However, the central computer file allows an attorney to come into a case and to have control over documents with relative ease.[17]

A computerized legal research library often will be most appreciated during the appeal phase. The statement of facts in an appellate brief is frequently the cutting edge of an appeal. The computer's ability to display and modify different combinations of proof, or simply to create a total integrated index of the entire record, dissolves two of the greatest problems when it is time to read the transcripts. Instead of taking elaborate notes or serving as a scribe, the appellate attorney can use automation to study the record in depth. A text-processing computer could also be used to draft, revise, and index the brief; the index would serve a function that is not currently required but would be welcomed by appellate judges.

Litigation support systems have reached a clear level of cost-effectiveness in cases large enough or complicated enough to warrant a trial team. As memory costs and machine speed improve, computer and information science will streamline the design, creation, and expense of building the trial data base. Modular systems for classes of cases, ranging from malpractice to insurance fraud, with online access to thesauri and specialized automated libraries will expand the use of automation in litigation.

Although the focus here has been on the organizational power of the computer, trial lawyers will be faced with electronic data as a standard form of evidence. Expert witnesses will use computer models or analytical programs as a basis for forming their opinions. Mere organization will not be enough. The bar, aided by consultants and contractors, will use the analytical powers of the computer to marshal evidence, subject it to profile analyses, or even conduct statistical runs against the file. Computer graphics will be used as another form of demonstrative evidence. On the investigative and strategy ends, the computer will and has been used to find inflated or fraudulent patterns or to develop alternative theories of proof. It is a significant and powerful tool in sorting out the masses of facts and law needed to render justice.

Notes

1. See H. Halladay, "Anatomy of an Automated Law Suit," *Litigation* 3 (Spring 1977), for a description of Honeywell v. Sperry Rand.
2. Ibid., p. 16.
3. James T. Halverson, "Coping with the Fruits of Discovery in the Complex Case—The Systems Approach to Litigation Support," *Antitrust Law Journal* 44 (1975): 48-99.
4. Ronald Rust and John Rome, "The Combination of a Manual and an Automated Approach to Trial Preparation," *Forum* 2 (1975-1976): 817-18. See also David Gold, "Pretrial Management of the Big Case," *Litigation* 3 (Spring 1977): 8-9, for a discussion of several cases.
5. U.S. Senate, Select Committee on Presidential Campaign Activities, *Final Report* (Washington, D.C.: Government Printing Office, 1974), p. 1087.
6. See Steven Olson and Leon Goodrich, "Litigation Support Systems—Present Status and Future Use," *Forum* 2 (1975-1976): 850.
7. See Gold, "Pretrial Management," p. 11.
8. See Lewis Vovakis, "Litigation File Management: Preparation for Trial," *Forum* 2 (1975-1976): 823-824. Duplicates with marginalia are not completely screened out. Comments of this nature are linked to the document citation, and the extra copy with note is preserved.
9. See Rust and Rome, "Combination," pp. 814-815.
10. Ibid., pp. 813-815.
11. See Halverson, "Coping," pp. 48-49. As director of the Bureau of Competition, Federal Trade Commission, which has pioneered in litigation support

systems, Halverson rated paralegals with a B.A. degree as utilized most effectively at this level of document processing. Our subjective experience is that the paralegals are most effective when they are treated as part of the investigative and trial staff, posted on new developments and encouraged to flag hot documents that seem relevant.

12. See B. W. Basheer, "Systems Support for Lawyers," *Law and Computer Technology* 6 (1973): 115.

13. Ibid., p. 116.

14. See Rust and Rome, "Combination," p. 816.

15. See Halladay, "Anatomy," p. 15. In Honeywell v. Sperry Rand the trial judge specifically found a key witness's testimony to have credibility and "tenacious consistency" though it ranged over thirty years of computer systems development. The witness had been briefed on his entire professional life by a printout from the litigation file.

16. Lawrence Berul, "Legal and Legislative Information Processing in the United States," *Encyclopedia of Information Science* (Fall 1974): 194; See also Olsen and Goodrich, "Litigation Support Systems," pp. 861-862; Berul, "Computerized Litigation Research," *Computer Law Service* 3 (1977): sec. 5-4.3, art. 1; Berul, "Computerized Files, a Powerful Weapon," *New York Law Journal,* August 16, 1977.

17. See Rust and Rome, "Combination," p. 814.

13

ROBERT S. McCORMICK and
STEVEN E. ROSEN

The Computer as an Aid to Litigators

The massive amount of data that confronts modern lawyers, scientists, businessmen, and bureaucrats has led to the dominance of the digital electronic computer among contemporary technological developments. Unaided, the human brain must ignore most of the data presented to it or else be paralyzed by the onslaught. As a tool that extends human information processing capability, the computer reduces the inhibiting effects of massive data. Just as modern transportation technology dramatically increases man's capacity for travel through physical space, so the computer has magnified man's ability to function in his unique inner space: the mental processes required to extract information from random data. Lawyers, who experience keenly the demands of the information explosion, may be expected to place increasing reliance on modern technology to manipulate data.

Early computer usage centered around numerical calculation and quantitative record keeping, thus offering only tangential assistance to most litigants. In recent years, however, the computer has become useful to store, retrieve, and manipulate large amounts of documentary information, primarily because of the development of faster, large-capacity memory devices. In addition, the development of user-oriented computer systems has enabled lawyers to interact dynamically with their data and thereby obtain continuous feedback as an adjunct to the thought process. The advent of English-language retrieval systems has brought the computer across the threshold of the legal profession, where needed information is customarily nonnumerical in nature.

Since the mid-1960s, the computer has begun to assist lawyers in tasks central to their profession. In both legal research (access to statutes, regulations, and opinions) and fact research (access to private confidential files specific to a particular controversy), computer assistance has expanded greatly lawyers' ability to acquire, manipulate, and present both precedent and evidence. Freedom from investigative drudgery, which the computer now offers, will enable attorneys to concentrate on the discretionary and judgmental tasks constituting the essence and value of their profession.

The computer can be used to organize and recall the factual material needed to develop and execute litigation strategy. The goal in using it to support modern complex litigation is to remove the impediments of scale, thereby permitting counsel to apply effectively their skills of advocacy, despite a large or complex body of evidence. If these impediments of scale are not resolved, they will impede effective advocacy, regardless of the amount of legal talent that is brought to bear.

The Challenges of Voluminous or Complex Evidentiary Data

Very often, files relating to complex litigation may run to tens or hundreds of thousands of pages that need to be readily accessible by many engaged in the litigation process. Procedures must be developed to provide for:

1. A controlled chain of custody for evidentiary documents.
2. Access to a complete document collection at all times for authorized research.
3. Avoidance of misfilings, misappropriations, or losses, which make documents inaccessible, in the face of heavy use over a long period.
4. Security against unauthorized research or file alteration.
5. Access to the documents, or a copy of the documents, at more than one geographical site (for multidistrict and multicase litigations).
6. Organization of the data into reports and sequences as required to analyze patterns and trends.
7. Access to the data in timely fashion to meet deadlines imposed by the court or procedural rules.
8. Maintenance of file currency by adding new information and disseminating it to those who might otherwise rely upon incomplete, inaccurate, or obsolete information.
9. Document indexing to permit rapid identification of documents based upon relevance to diverse search criteria.

The resistance of these conceptually simple tasks to facile implementation is learned through concrete experience in establishing document control and indexing systems. These requirements are most fully appreciated by attorneys who have had prior responsibility for managing large evidentiary collections, thereby learning firsthand the degree of commitment to precision and diligence required.

The duration of most complex litigation makes it likely that substantial turnover of staff will occur, including key employees of the law firm and its client. Even where there is no turnover, one cannot rely upon the frailties of human memory to provide the continuity of procedure necessary to protect the consistency and reliability of litigation files. Thus, a central goal of all preparation in the litigation must be the documentation and transmittal of acquired knowledge and procedures developed to ensure consistency in the files, the data, and the indexing strategy.

The outcome of major litigation frequently depends upon nonlegal tasks aimed at gaining and keeping control over the information in the case. Attorneys typically receive little or no training in management or information science, so it is not surprising that they increasingly seek assistance in imposing a systematic approach on large evidentiary collections. Although any litigation requires an information flow, it is in large-scale litigations that the potential for mishap can most easily jeopardize the outcome. Judicious use of management tools can ensure that evidentiary complexity and volume have no undesirable repercussions. The well-planned computer system is a useful tool and can enhance litigant's chances that the result will be at least as good as the theory and facts warrant.

The Computer and Litigation

Consider the following idealized scenario for the introduction and utilizational of technology in the litigation effort. Near the outset of the litigation, counsel analyzes the information requirements of the case. These include the nature and extent of the document population, expected growth of the population, ways in which the evidence will be searched, scheduling constraints, and requirements for information dissemination, special reports, and statistical analysis. From the outset, and at various stages thereafter, he inquires whether a manual information system will suffice or whether his information needs can be met best by automation. Counsel will be sensitive to the following factors, which point to the need for automation:

1. Sizeable evidentiary collection, including documents, transcripts, and derived materials.
2. Factual complexity, which requires an examination of the case from many perspectives.
3. Dependence of litigation strategy on the contents of documents that have not been or cannot be fully read or recalled in all pertinent particulars by counsel.
4. Complex deposition or trial situation involving many witnesses or exhibits.
5. Dependence of the case on the detection of trends or patterns in primary materials.

6. Probable involvement of several attorneys or firms.
7. Multiple geographical litigation sites.
8. Probable protracted duration of the litigation.
9. Relatively inflexible litigation schedule.
10. Anticipated reuse of the same document collection for many cases.

Unless the law firm or litigant has sufficient expertise in the analysis of information system requirements, it will need to acquire outside resources to evaluate whether automation is feasible and warranted. The primary goal of such a study is to define the benefits and costs of establishing a computerized information system. It must also consider alternative combinations of automated and manual procedures. If, in the early stages of litigation, it is thought that computerization is not yet warranted, initial manual procedures should be flexible and compatible with later automation. Planning the manual system in this way is essential if unpleasant surprises and unnecessary costs are to be avoided. The design of such procedures should include provisions for document security; document control; information flow; compilation, control, and growth of indexes; file organization; a methodology for use of the system; and the documentation of all system procedures.

Often the systematic planning of these items occurs only when a lawsuit is automated, although it is needed for a complex manual system as well. In one sense, planning is more crucial for a manual system than for a computerized system. The compilation of manual indexes to a large body of data may normally not be accomplished within the scheduling constraints of trial, whereas a new index to computerized files may be rapidly generated (by some systems). Thus, a poorly planned manual system will likely not be able to respond to many questions that arise later in the litigation. Of course, not all questions can be anticipated, but proper planning can go far toward minimizing this natural drawback of manual systems. This is why it is wise to seek assistance from experienced information systems professionals, whether or not computerization is intended.

The Computer Data Base

The inquiry about what materials should be included in the data base is really two questions: first, what types of documents require organization and searching by the computer? Second, for each qualifying document type, which items of information need to be obtained from each document? These questions ultimately depend on the information retrieval needs of counsel. Retrieval is the act of locating portions of the document collection related to logical criteria, such as one or more personal or organizational names, subjects, locations, or dates, or combinations thereof. This retrieval may be accomplished with the aid of a computer. It can search its memory for relevant documents, which it then organizes, sorts, displays, prints, and condenses in a useful format. These activities are performed in response to specific needs of counsel to locate references to a given person, firm, date, place, thing, or concept, to identify patterns of activity reflected in the evidence, or to prepare briefs and other materials.

The criteria for computerization to satisfy the needs at each stage of the case should reflect certain general principles. First, the goal of a computer system is to facilitate retrieval; it is not best used primarily to provide a vehicle for reading documents or transcripts. It is much more efficient and less costly to use the computer system to select only relevant portions of text and provide the researcher with locating information, such as microfilm or file number. The full text may be obtained easily from a document archive on paper or on microfilm.

Second, only those portions of each document that are of probable value ion discovery, deposition, or trial should be included. Irrelevant portions should be screened out of the computer system. However, an exception to this guideline exists for some computer systems that lack the ability to add new information to the data base quickly and inexpensively. In such cases, the lawyer should err liberally on the side of inclusion, despite correspondingly higher costs.

Third, different approaches are normally required for different types of documents, depending on the uses to which they will be put. For example, some documents may need to be inventoried only by date, author, recipient, and persons and organizations mentioned, with a pointer to the file location. Others may require subjective analysis such as subject terms, index codes, attorney comments, or informative abstracts. A final group may require the extraction of key words, or even inclusion of part or all of the actual language used. The precise complement of techniques used varies with each case. It is important that the attorney select a computer system capable of handling all methods deemed potentially desirable.

Fourth, the list of data elements to be obtained from each document class should correspond to the retrieval requirements for the class. These should be determined in advance. The elements may be numeric quantities upon which statistical operations are required; nonnumeric elements identifying subject matter, persons, locations, organizations, or dates referenced; bibliographic data such as document date, author, recipient, deponent, or witness; marginal notations; textual abstracts; or any combination of these or other elements.

Fifth, whatever types of data are deemed important to capture must be controlled and verified. No matter which approach is used, there are several ways in which errors may be introduced. In the process of converting the information on paper to a form readable by the computer, typographical errors are generated. Material prepared by a paralegal, indexer or coder, may have been erroneously conceived or written down. In the event that the material is taken directly from the document or transcript (full text), it may have been originally misspoken or transcribed in error.

If these errors remain uncorrected, the use of the computer system may be substantially less beneficial because the computer will not be able to find all references of concern to counsel. In addition, some references identified by the computer will lead down blind alleys. For example, if the date 1978 is mistakenly typed as 1973, an inquiry for all documents with a date of 1978 will miss the document in error; an inquiry for 1973 documents, on the other hand, will mistakenly obtain the error document. This principle extends to errors of varying degrees of complexity, subtlety, and harmful effect.

Some types of data are more susceptible to error correction than others. Detection of some types of errors may be accomplished automatically by the computer system as the data are processed; other errors must be manually identified. Corrections are made to the data base after its creation through an update procedure if the computer system has such a capability. If it does not, the entire data base may need to be recreated, at substantial cost.

The error correction process depends not only on the computer system but also on the structure of the data. For example, verifications are not performed well on full-text documents. The computer systems currently available cannot detect nonsense words or examine the contextual validity of language. As a further example, words in full text may not be validated automatically. In addition, the computer currently has no way of knowing whether a number in text is representative of a date or some other numeric quantity such as tons, miles, or dollars. In the case of full text, then, error detection and correction is largely a manual process.

These guidelines and principles should be considered by counsel in determining which data to include from documents obtained at various stages of the litigation. Other rules and procedures may be recommended by litigation support professionals, depending on the nature of the litigation, the data, and the needs of counsel. However, the question of which documents to include in the computer system in preparation for each strategic point is a matter largely for determination by counsel. The decision for inclusion is based on the anticipated use and value of each type of document and whether it can be managed effectively without computer assistance.

Uses of Computers in Lawsuits

Initial Assessment of the Case

Normally, at the outset of litigation, client personnel and other friendly sources of information are interviewed, under conditions of varying formality. Documents and other information believed relevant are collected from the client. The transcript or notes of such interviews and the voluntarily produced files are among the first items that may be included in the information system. They will provide an initial assessment of the merits of the case, unfolding promising directions for both offensive and defensive strategy.

Client Discovery

Based upon examination of this internal information, the first round of discovery may be planned to expand the document collection with material from the opposing side. The data received may be entered into the system after being screened for relevance and duplication. A minimal level of information may be entered from all documents to assist in document management and in the identification of duplicate or missing documents. More detailed commentary and analysis, such as abstracting or subject coding, may be applied to significant documents at this time by counsel, paralegal assistants, or trained analysts, or it may be added at a later time.

The rapid absorption of all relevant discovered material will permit the effective use of a second round of discovery aimed at areas of inadequate or evasive response, or claims of privilege. This is particularly true with respect to interrogatories, where answers are often casual or superficial in the first instance. A clear signal that responses have been carefully scrutinized for accuracy and completeness may result in greater cooperation on a second round of interrogatories.

Response to Opponent's Discovery and Production Orders

When planning a response to discovery demands and interrogatories, counsel faces a key decision concerning revelation of the use of automation. From the outset, the decision may be made to project to opposing counsel one of a variety of images:

- Absolute control over the litigation and the intention to make things difficult. This approach is particularly useful with respect to legitimate claims of privilege.
- The desire and ability to cooperate due to confidence that quick evaluation of the evidence by opposing counsel will lead to abandoning excessive claims or unmeritorious contentions.
- Lack of control over the evidentiary material, or lack of desire to assist in its evaluation, forcing opposing counsel to perform all screening and analysis. This so-called truckload approach has one significant drawback: prudence dictates that every document turned over to opposing counsel be controlled. Otherwise, counsel will be unaware of exactly which documents have been produced and what they say.

Although establishing early control over the document collection represents a substantial initial investment in the litigation, whether the investment is justified must be judged in the context of the entire course of the proceeding. Counsel's avoidance of redundant document processing, the hallmark of most manual systems, is a significant cost savings. Additionally, early document control can signal a serious intention to press a claim or defense, which may lead to a favorable settlement. By enabling a focused approach to discovery, it increases the readiness with which the attorney can approach the deposition stage. In fact, the ultimate expense of early computerization may be far less than the cumulative cost of an early manual approach followed by belated automation. The reason is that computerization promotes the planning of a cohesive, flexible system, which will not require redoing or undoing previous efforts. Frequently counsel have expended large sums in an attempt to support an inadequate manual system prior to the ultimate establishment of a computerized system.

Deposition Stage

With the advent of the deposition stage, the overall cost of litigation typically escalates, and scheduling normally becomes more complex. As a result, the use of the computer to manage the litigation efficiently takes on increased importance. As each deposition approaches, the attorney may retrieve the documents deemed relevant to the examination based on fact or issue information, or on the names of individuals responsible for the authorship or receipt of the documents or having knowledge of their contents. It is normally useful for the computer to produce witness kits or subject packets, which consist of documents authored or received by, mentioning, or within the knowledge of the witness, and related prior testimony of, or concerning, the witness. Reliance by counsel on such materials to plan deposition efforts will lead to a more informative deposition, with effective scheduling and lower cost. As the depositions proceed, the transcripts may be entered into the system, including subject coding, digests, full text, or a combination of these. Each exhibit used during the deposition stage should be added to the data base if it has not been previously. Exhibits and depositions should be linked together for cross-referencing.

The Pretrial Brief

The information entered during the discovery stage can be reorganized with ease by the computer to assist in the preparation of the pretrial brief. The computerized data may be obtained in sequence by issue, date, witness, or any other criterion provided for in the design of the system. This use of the computer permits compelling arguments to be discovered and patterns of activity over time to be discerned. It also shows the lack of supporting facts for a particular thread of an argument. The computer file may be tested for hundreds of alternative approaches and may display many alternative arrangements of the evidence. The attorney may avoid time-consuming and costly duplication and manual sorting of the physical file. Unlike a manual system, exploration of this type creates no risk of document misfiling. Information can be obtained in minutes at a desk-top terminal.

Records of productive arrangements may be saved; unproductive arrangements may be easily recognized and discarded. The result of this process will be a stronger pretrial brief. All exhibits, deposition testimony, and other material may be cross-referenced to the appropriate paragraphs of the pretrial brief, providing all of the evidence to support any contention. Effective requests for admission may also be formulated, based upon early knowledge of the structure of the trial presentation.

Opponent's Pretrial Brief

A similar process of matching available documents and deposition testimony against the opponent's pretrial brief can lead to a realistic assessment of the strengths and weaknesses of his case. Such a comprehensive analysis of both briefs may lead to key settlement discussions. The degree to which the detailed knowledge developed through the computer should be shared with opposing counsel will vary on a case-by-case basis, depending on counsel's assessment of the impact on the opposite of laying out the probable presentation structure for both sides. Whether or not settlement is pursued, the computer analysis of the opponents' brief will be quite helpful in the preparation of contravening arguments for trial.

Scheduling and Planning for Trial

Once trial preparation shifts into its final stages, the data base may be used to assist in drafting subpoenas and to prepare arrangements of the evidence most useful for witness preparation and examination. The computer system may be used to print lists for each witness of the exhibits and other documents to be used to lay foundation, present affirmative or rebuttal evidence, and impeach by prior inconsistent statement or otherwise.

The computer may be invaluable in locating documents related to ongoing testimony, even though the attorney who recalls the substance of the documents cannot remember their identifying numbers. Surprise testimony may also require quick access to deposition testimony, pleadings or other materials through the agency of computer searching.

A potential application of the computer not yet fully exploited for trial preparation involves trial strategy planning through the use of mathematical optimization techniques. If the computer is provided with certain information about witnesses and evidence, it could assist in this effort. For example, the computer could be given credibility ratings for witnesses, information about witness availability, logical order of foundation and evidence, and witness utility for laying foundation or introducing evidence. Through ranking and tabulating algorithms drawn from statistics, the computer could test alternate presentation strategies to determine the degree to which logical flow or persuasiveness is improved by a change in strategy. Fallback scenarios could be developed to cope with witness unavailability or other unforeseen circumstances. The attorney's ability to respond rapidly and effectively to scheduling changes could have a demoralizing effect on the opponent.

The development of such an application would involve the creation of refined algorithms based on modeling of the process of litigation strategy. To our knowledge, no operational system currently provides such assistance, although computer modeling is being used by some litigants for other purposes, such as developing econometric analyses to support expert testimony.

Computer-generated Evidence

The uses of the computer for litigation support primarily contemplate computerization as a method for organizing, maintaining, controlling, and providing access to evidence that already exists and that is obtained through traditional means. The attorney may use the computer system to build a case, but in court the presentation is made from the documents and testimony itself.

Computer products may themselves be used as evidence. For example, computerized business records of a corporation may be directly introduced. If useful to compare with other documentary evidence, such files may be incorporated in the litigation support data base. This is frequently a relatively inexpensive way to build a litigation file, since the incorporated records are already in magnetic form. Of course, expert analysis is required to assess the significance of the data obtained, the coding structure and conventions used in their development, and the standardization and controls required to incorporate the new data into the litigation data base.

The computer may also derive new evidence through simple or sophisticated analysis of information in the case by using standard quantitative techniques. With appropriate foundation by expert witnesses, establishing the methods and theory underlying preparation of the material, computer-generated products may be used in trial to support or refute factual contentions. Although the utility of any particular method of presentation depends upon the nature of the litigation, computers have been used to produce maps, statistical reports, graphs, simulations, correlations, and many other types of information display. If prepared carefully, these products are normally well received by the finder of fact.

The Trial

During trial, a trial support facility is normally established near the trial site. It provides online computer access to the data base and a full set of the documents and transcripts either in hard copy or on microform. After each day of trial, the transcript can be keyed for inclusion in the data base, or an abstracted or coded summary of the trial proceedings may be entered. Each section of transcript may be cross-referenced to pretrial brief sentence numbers, exhibit numbers, or other key materials. These links allow verification that each exhibit has a sound introduction and that each issue is adequately developed. The presentation of evidence by both sides should be analyzed. Necessary motions and closing statements can be planned and assimilated into the litigation strategy.

The computer may also assist in reacting to unforeseen events of the trial. It may, for example:

Find unexpected contradictions in past testimony.

Find documents in the data base not previously thought to be material.

Cope with reorientation in trial strategy caused by unavailability of a key witness or readjustment of schedules due to unexpected events.

Produce information desired by the court either in an ad hoc fashion or in the form of trial briefs. The computer can provide all of the raw material for such a brief and even display such information in a selected sequence. The actual synthesis into a brief will require human analysis and intervention, but this effort is greatly facilitated by the computer printout.

Research issues brought to the fore by the trial judge.

The ability of counsel to react quickly to judicial requests through the agency of the computer may lead to the formation of a bond of reliance and trust between counsel and the court.

The Trial Closing and the Appeal

At the end of testimony, the closing arguments and the more formal posttrial brief may be prepared. With the assistance of the computer, the orderly flow of proof promised in the pretrial brief may be confirmed and documented in the posttrial brief. Errors in laying foundation may be similarly cataloged. A properly prepared and compelling posttrial brief may be adopted by the court in its opinion, in whole or in part. Should the conclusion of the legal action be less than satisfactory, counsel may need to marshal factual information in support of an appeal. Computerized selection and organization of material from the trial to frame and document appeal issues is of great assistance in the analysis and preparation of the appellate brief and arguments.

Visibility of the Computer

To decide the appropriate level of visibility for the computer system, counsel should carefully evaluate the effect of computers on jury, judge, and opposing counsel.

The effect of computer usage on a jury may not be easily predicted and depends on the circumstances of the case. In defense of a consumer class action or products liability suit, an argument might be made that its profile should be low, lest it arouse an image of wealth or unfair advantage, and thereby create an unsympathetic jury reaction. On the other hand, the opposite conclusion may be reached on the ground that knowledge of computer use may instill confidence in the contentions of counsel. This is especially true in cases involving large institutional entities and complex subject matter.

The effect of computer use on the court also depends on the circumstances. The favorable bond of reliance that may be formed by quick and accurate response to information needs of the court has already been mentioned. Moreover, jurists, inclined to promote an early end to a difficult factual battle and extended encumbrance of the trial calendar, may rely heavily on a computer system that could facilitate the trial.

As to the visibility of the computer to opposing counsel, secrecy seems to be the rule rather than the exception in present uses. Since critical portions of the data base should be privileged as attorney work product, if properly prepared and maintained, this secrecy may represent excessive caution. However, the privilege has not yet been definitively established and is subject to growing attack, and caution has been exercised to date.

Given the security precautions that are normally taken in limiting access to litigation data bases, it should even be possible for both parties to share the same data base. Access to certain classes of information can be strictly limited to the authorized users. Although we know of only one instance of cooperation between opposing parties, there are increasing tendencies toward this phenomenon among partially adverse coparties. This cooperation may be particularly sensible when the litigation is expected to center upon a legal issue to be resolved on appeal and for which both parties desire resolution. In these instances it is often in the parties' interest to cooperate in data-base generation and maintenance. Substantial cost savings could result, since the alternative is independent preparation by both parties. A data base system can easily protect access to portions of each document for private materials, such as attorney comments, relevance codes, and other privileged components (although not all systems provide such a capability).

Fairness and the Computer

If only one party has access to sufficient resources, the computer can serve to widen the gap of power. Because of the tremendous advantage it gives the litigant—independent of legal merit—computerization can sharply distort bargaining positions. Obviously it is a significant means by which money and effort can alter litigation prospects. Consider, for example, a litigation in which twenty attorneys from a prominent law firm were pitted against two junior attorneys with less than ten years of total experience. In this instance political restrictions on hiring new personnel made the computer system the only way of altering the balance. Thus in some cases a litigation support system can help to equalize the strength of adversaries.

It is technologically feasible for a jurisdiction to offer the advice and facilities for computerization of cases to be tried in its courts, at cost. Although this would require a substantial initial investment, it could improve the administration of justice. Many cases that require litigation support involve matters of widespread importance. Antitrust and trade regulation matters, construction suits, class actions, and major product liability cases can clog courts for a decade. Enactment of legislation, or judicial announcement of a legal doctrine, when there are not adequate means to try controversies arising from that law or doctrine, may lead to disparities between public law and practice. An investment in resolving these claims, which often affects interests of thousands of stockholders, executives, taxpayers, injured parties, and the development of entire industries or communities, could well serve the needs of private, public, and institutional interests.

At the present time, however, litigation support rarely raises the issue of fairness. Currently computerization of evidence occurs most frequently in cases in which power is nearly evenly distributed among the litigants. Such litigation normally involves large corporate interests that are engaged in disputes with other large corporations, institutions, or the federal government. Usually there is adequate wealth at hand on both sides to commit to litigation support. Nevertheless an imbalance of power may result. For example, for years governments have made notably weak commitments to support systems for certain antitrust litigations. Only recently has this trend been reversed. And in some cases, powerful institutions failed to apply their resources to litigation support and were outmatched by corporate general counsel or law firms more aware of technological tools. Perhaps the greatest unfairness in these cases is in the greater willingness of counsel for one litigant to institute needed procedures, combined with the resistance of other counsel to new methods. In some cases, litigants have attempted to support their own cases internally and failed; in a few others, vendors have produced systems of poor quality. Thus, in most cases the question is not one of wealth and power but one of good judgment.

Assumptions Revisited

Against the backdrop of our assumption that the support system is available early in the litigation stands a contravening reality. The decision to develop a computer system, or even an upward compatible manual system, is frequently deferred until the crisis of impending deposition or trial. Usually thousands of dollars have already been spent on the manual processing of documents. In these instances, systems frequently must be created under crisis conditions. Attempts are made to salvage the prior manual work regardless of quality, and heavy premiums in cost are incurred. Yet a system implemented at the eleventh hour may be used only during the twelfth and by personnel who may not have adequate time to benefit fully from the availability of information provided by the computer system.

At the very least, attorneys in major litigations should: ensure that a system study is conducted near the outset, ensure that all manual document processing is compatible with later conversion to more powerful methods, keep the client fully informed as to the availability and potential need for computerization, and periodically forecast future support needs. Given evolving doctrines on legal responsibility, it is probable that in some situations failure to use such tools or at least to propose them to a client for evaluation could invite action against counsel by a client dissatisfied with litigation results. A very real risk is the loss of a valuable client because of the failure to manage the evidence properly in a major litigation. Despite these negative inducements, however, the focus of general counsel and law firm alike should be primarily on the positive results of litigation support: better, more professional service; clearer, more certain determination of the facts underlying the controversy; the potential for more favorable, more timely settlements; greater confidence on the part of the finder of fact; greater client satisfaction; and greater leverage of the legal staff to larger case loads and higher levels of productivity.

14

LARRY P. POLANSKY

Computer Technology in the Courts

The introduction of computer techniques into the administration of the courts has not been as sure and as swift as many hoped. The courts have not yet reduced their continuance rates or ensured the appearance of all parties at trial or eliminated backlogs, with or without computers. The state of the art of computers in the court is, relatively, that of the Stone Age. The courts are learning to count and, even more slowly, what to count. Whereas science began its heavy use of computers in the 1950s, industry in the 1960s, government, in general, in the mid-1960s, the courts began their use in the early 1970s. But even then there were very few people who could articulate the needs of the courts and none who could translate those needs into effective computer projects.

Court Operations

The most effective use of automation in the courts has been in the assistance of their day-to-day operations. A typical system starts with the capture of data on each case at the time of its original filing. In some jurisdictions, only the criminal cases are recorded and in others civil cases have been the top priority, but it appears that the only logical method is to capture both for any court that has jurisdiction over both because of the daily interaction of parties and resources.

The extent of the data captured at filing time will very often dictate the eventual effectiveness of any automated system. Much care must be given to determining the data to be captured and evaluating the costs to capture data against the benefits that are expected to be derived. It is as easy to decide to capture valueless data at excessive costs as it is to neglect to collect relatively cheap data, which later may prove to have been vital to a good information system.

The way to collect the greatest number of useful items without just collecting everything at huge costs and great waste is to involve top court management and all professionals on the court staff in the development of the information system. If the court wants a good system, which will be of use to it and its operation, it must articulate to the people who will design and implement it what it wants and needs. If the court has done its job well in determining what, where, and how to collect its data, the benefits to be derived begin almost immediately.

Indexing

The first fruit of an automated system is the virtually limitless indexing capabilities. The first step in most systems has been the creation of defendant (criminal cases) and litigant (civil cases) indexes, which are effortlessly prepared on demand. These indexes are not semi-alphabetic or partially ordered, as most manual systems inevitably are; they are fully and correctly alphabetized indexes.

Depending on the frequency and volume of the activity and upon the need for up-to-date status, these indexes may be on paper or, if the time constraints are critical, on computer terminals, available to an operator at the touch of a key. Many systems have incorporated automated name-searching techniques into their index search computer programs, and it is thus possible to retrieve names even when partially misspelled inquiries are made.

Names of litigants, however, are not the only indexes available in an automated file. Once the information is in machine-readable form, it is possible to index any data item in the record. It is, of course, impractical to index all data, but many courts have indexed specific information, to the advantage of their operation. For example, many systems create listings or online indexes by attorney, type of case or charge, year of action, and many other characteristics to aid in managing an operation or reaching information needed for a particular case or situation.

Perhaps the greatest value in indexing available to the court today is in the automation of the indexes for judgments and liens. The historic practices for the maintenance of these data are both expensive and impractical. The data, on the other hand, are an integral part of the commercial activity in the community, and it is vitally important that they be accurate, timely, and available. The operation is simple to automate and to operate. The major problem is that of converting the existing manual files to automated form. In many cases this step is virtually (if not actually) impossible. This deficit should not stop the court from acting prospectively in this area, however. It is far better to have a good modern system from some fixed date forward than to perpetuate a bad one.

Docketing

There is no more tedious function in any court than the posting of each substantive action affecting a case to a book in the form of a case log. In some jurisdictions this is called *docketing* or *making docket entries;* it also has a variety of other names. Dockets that have been maintained by hand are often difficult to read. Frequently dockets are far behind in their postings.

In jurisdictions with an automated system, it is generally necessary to post every substantive action relating to a case to the computer file in order to keep the automated case record up to date. Retaining these traditional postings within the machine to provide an up-to-date complete docket is not difficult. The major obstacle to this use of the automated system, until recently, has been its cost. But the price of randomly accessible computer data storage units continues to decline, and some computer installations believe that the cost-use ratio, plus the value of the expected improvement to the court's operation, can support an investment in the automated docket to replace the practice of laborious entries in hard-copy docket books. The advantages and savings in manpower and space are obvious, but along with this, the user gets a standardized and readable product.

Calendars

The need for the preparation of the lists of cases to be heard in court on a specific date is one that every automated court system appears to have recognized and answered. These lists range from a simple list of defendant names to a complex report showing name, case number, physical characteristics, attorney(s), bond data, jail status, charges, previous hearing and trial disposition, and, in some lists, a criminal history of the defendant. Almost any data item in the file can be relevant, and the limitations on what to include on the list appear to lie with the users.

One problem frequently encountered is the need for multiple copies of the calendar—sometimes as many as a hundred—for distribution each day. One court, recognizing the high cost of multiple copy list preparation by computer, has utilized a technique of producing a Ditto master on the computer and then running its copies on a Ditto machine.

Another problem frequently encountered is the timing of the preparation of the lists. Sometimes the trial list is needed several weeks ahead, and at others, it is most desirable for the list to be run at the last moment so that it contains the latest information. The most typical compromise is the production of early lists as far in advance as is practical, as well as an official trial list as close as possible to the actual trial date.

Notices

The preparation of notices appears to be a universal function of the systems analyzed and reviewed. The notices range from the automated preparation of the summons resulting from the filing of a civil complaint to the reminder of failure to pay restitution or court fees. Almost every system provides subpoenas for defendants and witnesses and notices to counsel of their assigned dates for court action. Some systems provide notes to defendants reminding them of their trial date and that they must be represented by counsel at trial. Others produce notices to attorneys of their court appointment as counsel in a case. Notice to police officers of their trial commitments and to sureties of the failure of their client to appear when required (thereby placing a bail bond amount in jeopardy) are also frequently seen as by-products of automated court information systems.

Attorney Reports

One valuable tool that is readily available in most systems is the individual attorney work load, or inventory, report. Lists that identify all cases for which an attorney is recorded as counsel of record are invaluable to the operation of the court and the scheduling of cases and are even more desirable to the attorneys themselves.

Philadelphia's civil court, for example, has found that attorneys rely heavily on the monthly report (distributed to each one) to plan their monthly trial preparation and to review the current status of their caseloads in court. A by-product of this report has been the ability of counsel to identify any cases that may have been inadvertently neglected in the law office or in the court system.

On the management side, reports on case load, as well as disposition activity by counsel, enable the court to determine whether counsel has more cases than can be properly handled and, if records are maintained by firm, whether a firm has sufficient trial counsel to handle its work load. The reports show the quantity and age of the cases pending for every attorney.

Other jurisdictions have been able to analyze various attributes of attorneys and firms to see which ones are prone to settle, to go to trial, to file numerous delaying motions, or to appeal an inordinate percentage of the time. In some jurisdictions where the information is legally available, the same analysis is done of insurance company practices.

Scheduling

From a theoretical standpoint, the greatest advantage to be derived from an automated system is the utilization of automated scheduling algorithms, which will provide optimum utilization of all parties, resources, and facilities. The state of the electronic art is ready for this, but due to the great number of variables no jurisdiction, no matter how far advanced in the use of technology, has been able to implement successfully a fully automated schedule. The proposed system for the criminal court of New York holds great promise for success.[1] More important is the most recent and extensive work of the Institute for Law and Social Research in this area.[2]

Statistical Reporting

Computers have excellent summarization capabilities to provide statistical reports. Most typical are the pure counting-type of reports, which determine the number of cases entering and leaving the system and perhaps break them down further by type of case and type of court action required to effect a disposition. Other reports enable administrators to count their inventory of cases on hand and, perhaps, to break these down by the type of case and type of court action involved. Good use has been made of automated systems to identify the causes and the responsibilities for case continuances, probably the largest single deterrent to the completion of the court's daily work.

Courts are beginning to realize that more can be done. Some are seriously considering weighting cases so that one can compare the work effort required to handle case loads. Serious attention is also being paid to the analysis of the time it takes a case to progress through each stage of the court process. From a management standpoint, calculated averages are an excellent method of periodically checking the "vital signs" of a court system. The same data can be used to identify, by comparison to these norms, which cases may require individual attention of the operating staff because they deviate from those statistically identified norms.

A very sensitive area in which these statistics are being utilized is that of the analysis of dispositions by judge or by attorney or perhaps of the sentencing propensities by charge, by judge, or even by race or sex. Care must be taken in this area, for cases are not interchangeable, as industrial units of production are. One case is not the same as every other case with a similar charge, nor is one defendant and his or her background the same as every other defendant charged, tried, and convicted of a particular crime. Until one can adequately weigh each case for its difficulty and also scientifically weigh each defandant's prior history and rehabilitative probability, it is practically meaningless to make these sensitive evaluations of judge disposition rates and sentencing propensities.

Another danger, identified by Ernie Friesen while directing the Institute for Court Management, is the problem of court personnel doing only whatever court management gathers statistics for. If the need for meeting statistical goals is the ultimate one, then the workers in the system will put all their efforts to those tasks that will count toward the statistical goal and ignore the work that does not add to their count. The message here is to be sure that what the court counts is a proper reflection of the real purposes of the organization.

Jury Management

Selection

A vast number of jurisdictions have successfully tackled the automation of the selection of prospective jurors. The largest problem encountered has been the source of the eligible juror list. The most frequent solution is the use of the registered voter lists for the jurisdiction, but there are all kinds of variations. They range from combining voter lists with property owner lists, telephone directories, and vehicle registration to the most costly approach of a complete periodic census. No matter what the source, if the original lists can be put into or, preferably, are in machine-readable form, the court is well on its way to the most cost-effective application available in the courts area. An added benefit is that the court will no longer be troubled by challenges to the make-up of its machine-selected jury panels.

The methods for fair selection from the eligible list range from very simple random selection techniques to some very sophisticated techniques. One provided for the Harris County, Texas (Houston), courts by NASA space systems specialists utilizes a computerized random number generator for selection.[3]

Questionnaires and Notices

Following selection is the preparation of questionnaires for the prospective jurors and, in jurisdictions that use interviews, notices for interview. Once the machine has captured the name and address for selection, it can provide simple and inexpensive subsequent mailings.

Additional savings have been effected by using special forms, generated by the computer, with message, questionnaire, and a stamped return envelope. Several jurisdictions have developed this combination computer and special form system to the extent that there is no need for a single act of intervention by a human from the point where selection starts until the items reach the post office for distribution. (The same techniques can be used for the preparation of the summons to appear and any other required notices.)

Further benefits are being realized in improved utilization of those jurors summoned for duty. In Cuyahoga County, Ohio (Cleveland), simulated computer runs showed that annual savings of $200,000 were possible, in this county of approximately two million people, by a simple study of the number of jurors called versus the number actually used.[4] Not only have a vast number of dollars been saved by this project, but juror satisfaction (an unquantifiable factor) has been tremendously improved. Most encouraging is the report that the costs of running such a monitoring program are very low and the system is simple to implement.

The use of automated techniques to provide the court with the optimum number of jurors to call for service and to allot to panels for voir dire, which will result in the lowest dollar cost and still provide jurors when needed with little or no wait, and, at the same time, will lead to better juror satisfaction, is the most successful use of the computer in the courts area today. It is well documented in a series of Law Enforcement Assistance Administration publications authored by Bird Engineering Associates.[5]

Traffic Violation Systems

Automated traffic violation systems have been in operation the longest of all systems in the courts. As early as 1964, the city of New Orleans implemented a system for handling moving and parking violations by keypunching the tickets and feeding the records to a computer. Later, disposition data were fed to the computer by paper tapes produced by the cash registers in the traffic court. The system provided moving violation driver-history records for all cases set in traffic court, reviewed all unpaid tickets against the motor vehicle registration file, and then printed a defendant notice of court arraignment. Another feature of the system enabled computer inquiry, tied in to the six-month vehicle inspection, which showed outstanding parking violations and denied owners an inspection sticker until the tickets were disposed. San Diego, California; Chicago, Illinois; Phoenix, Arizona, and Orange County, California, among many others, all feature excellent inquiry capability traffic systems. Other major cities appear to have entered the computer arena early.

The major needs in this area are for creating a record of all traffic cases and bail deposits. The recording of all payments, adjudications, and bail forfeitures must subsequently be posted to the file and, upon failure to close the case prior to trial or failure to appear at trial, various notices and postings must be recorded. Indexes, available either through inquiry terminals or by printed listings, also appear to be of critical value. Finally, because of the large flow of cash, almost all of the systems have extensive audit control features and reports to ensure the continuing integrity of the system.

Administrative Systems

One administrative application that shows great promise is the combined payroll-personnel system. For courts responsible for their own payroll operation the possibilities are obvious and the available experience almost unlimited. Personnel systems are somewhat less frequently seen but nevertheless are fairly common. Systems that keep track of open positions, annual increment, and retirement dates are commonplace in local governments today. A by-product of personnel control is, normally, standard classification and salary structure, both of which are missing in many court systems.

Attendance reporting and leave balance control is another area where the computer can be used to serve the needs of modern court management. Once management has put into machine-readable form the absence of its employees, it is able to review for pattern absences, (such as the employee who often misses work on Fridays and Mondays), and it can quickly identify units suffering from chronic absentee rates. Typical exception reporting techniques will bring to the attention of management many unusual leave-taking activities that normally go unnoticed in the manual system.

Good management principles require solid control of facilities and resources. An automated real and personal property inventory system can keep track of every item and area under court control, can keep management up to date on the condition of its property, and can alert to the need for replacement or repair. Most importantly, this is an easy system to design and maintain, and the effort required to set it up will enable management to learn a great deal about their resources and facilities. An immediate by-product of some of these systems has been the assignment of responsibility to supervisory personnel for specific property and the resultant improvement in its care and continued existence.

The Prosecutor's Office

In the past few years prosecutors' offices have displayed interest in the use of computers to aid in the operation and management of their offices. By far the most advanced effort to date in this area is PROMIS (Prosecutor's Management Information System), developed in the District of Columbia for the U.S. Attorney's Office by the District of Columbia Government Office of Crime Analysis; it is continually under modification and improvement by the Institute for Law and Social Research in Washington, D.C.[6]

Clerk of Court

In addition to benefits provided to the clerk of court in docketing, calendaring, and indexing, there are other areas where work is needed and has been done strictly for the clerk's office operation. The automated control of file location is particularly important. The typical projects that have been successfully implemented have been those relating to fee and fine accounting and the control of escrow deposits. Many clerks' offices have ventured quite successfully into the field of microfilming, and some have combined microfilming with computer indexing of the microfilm files to provide the capability of fast retrieval of filmed data.

The Juvenile Courts

Typical juvenile information systems in many respects parallel the adult court systems. A system designed for the St. Louis, Missouri, area juvenile courts appears to have satisfied all of the normal court administrative needs and has ventured into at least two other areas. The first is a counselor evaluation module, which appears to service the need for self-analysis of the effectiveness of staff. The second is the Correctional Probability Aid Module, which purports to evaluate the juvenile's behavior profile against available treatment alternatives and to select the treatment program or programs that will most likely lead to successful rehabilitation of a particular child.[7]

An area deserving of special attention in the juvenile area is that of security, privacy, and confidentiality of data. Although the entire criminal justice information area requires special attention to these matters, the juvenile data area is especially sensitive and requires added effort to protect and control the access and use of the information. Most computer systems enabling inquiry into data files guarantee restricted access, but they can no more guarantee the total confidentiality of data than we can with manual systems.[8]

Corrections

The control of prisoners and the knowledge of their status and location during and after the life of their court case is an integral part of effective court operation. Many courts have found that the introduction of an automated prisoner inventory has resulted in a decided improvement in case flow as it relates to committed defendants. Similar advantages accrue from automated probation and parole information systems to which the court may have access. There are obvious advantages to the court system of being constantly alert to the current criminal justice status of their clientele. Several court systems have found the corrections area information so valuable to them that they are working toward the implementation of automated systems for these related agencies.

Domestic Relations

One court or court-related area where automation has been effective and where extensive use of computer capabilities has been made is that of support payments. The problem here is the typical business-accounting one of many items of similar activity and a great number of highly repetitive processes.

The typical domestic relations system provides court order and payment history data, as well as current status-of-account information. It produces checks for the dependents after receipt of payments from the supporting party. At least one of these systems implements court policies by having the computer hold up the issuance of checks for large amounts for several days to insure the sufficiency of funds in the payor's account and also has the computer distribute, in accordance with court policy, the payments received from payors who have multiple payees for whose support they are responsible. In conjunction with automated banks, it is possible to set up a system of automated check reconciliation and bank account balancing as well.

Transcription and Other Court Reporting

The latest area to feel the presence of the electronic age is that of court reporting. Several excellent studies and projects undertaken by the National Center for State Courts have provided state-of-the-art reports covering the most recent advances in this field. They show that computer-assisted transcription is technologically feasible.[9]

Work on multichannel audio equipment continues, with several jurisdictions utilizing these tape recorders almost exclusively. One product provides "flip-flop" taping capability on one unit (to avoid all tape-changing interruptions) and also provides for the monitoring clerk to listen to the tape (with about a four second delay) so that he or she can recognize unrecorded activity and have the court repeat it for the record. Videotaping for depositions has saved many dollars and provided a much better document for the jurors or jurist.

Perhaps the most dramatic advance has been the work done by Judge James L. McCrystal in Erie County, Ohio, where in November 1971, the civil case of *McCall* vs. *Clemens* was tried before a jury. All proceedings except the impaneling of the jury, opening statements, and closing arguments were presented by videotape. All testimony in this case was recorded on videotape one to two weeks prior to trial and reviewed by the judge and the attorneys involved. For all objected statements, the judge ruled on all their objections and an edited videotape was utilized for the actual trial. (Recent state appellate court decisions have restricted the use of this approach in many jurisdictions.)

Just as dramatic in its effect, but perhaps less spectacular in its operation, has been the use (by Judge Leon Emerson in a municipal court in Downey, California) of a telephone, with speaker attachments, in the courtroom to allow busy and/or out-of-jurisdiction witnesses to be heard and cross-examined during trial. The availability of videophone service in several U.S. locations seems to indicate that further extensions of Judge Emerson's innovative thinking are on the horizon.

Conclusions

The progress from an early 1960s tab card effort in Pittsburgh, Pennsylvania's civil court to the online systems of today has been excellent. But even the best court systems leave much room for improvement. Furthermore too few courts are using these modern management tools. It is time for the courts to begin implementing the best programs and ideas that have emerged during the electronic revolution in the courts.

Notes

1. Programming Methods, Inc., "A Report on the Development of a Criminal Court Calendar Scheduling Technique" (Unpublished report, 1970).
2. Institute for Law and Social Research, *Guide to Court Scheduling: A Framework for Criminal and Civil Courts* (Washington, D.C.: INSLAW, 1976).
3. Sidney W. Frost et al., *A Jury Selection System as Designed and Implemented for Harris County, Texas* (October 1969).
4. Larry P. Polansky, "Jury Management in Cuyahoga County," *Cleveland Bar Journal* (February 1973).
5. National Institute of Law Enforcement and Criminal Justice, *A Guide to Juror Usage* (December 1974), and *A Guide to Jury System Management* (December 1975).
6. Institute for Law and Social Research, *PROMIS (Prosecutor's Management Information System) Briefing Series* (Washington, D.C.: INSLAW, 1974).
7. Larry A. Boxerman and Norman J. Heying, *The Practical and Effective Use of Computers in Social Sciences and Social Services,* Proceedings of the First International Symposium on Criminal Justice Information and Statistics, October 1972.
8. Robert R. J. Gallati et al., *Project Search Security and Privacy Publications* (May 1973). A number of subsequent publications have been produced by this organization, which is generally recognized as the national expert on security and privacy of criminal justice information.
9. J. Michael Greenwood and Jerry R. Tollar, *Users' Guidebook to Computer Aided Transcription* (National Center for State Courts, April 1977); J. Michael Greenwood and Douglas C. Dodge, *Management of Court Reporting Services* (National Center for State Courts, August 1976); and J. Michael Greenwood and Jerry R. Tollar, *Evaluation Guidebook to Computer Aided Transcription* (National Center for State Courts, May 1975).

15

WILLIAM A. FENWICK and
GORDON K. DAVIDSON

Use of Computerized Business Records as Evidence

With the explosive growth in the use of computers in automated record-keeping systems and the gradual education of the legal profession in computer technology, novel legal issues relating to the use of computers have emerged in the courtroom during the last decade. The most common computer problem that a trial attorney is likely to face is moving (or opposing) the admission into evidence of a computer printout of a routine business record to prove a fact recorded by an automated data processing system. Now that such systems are so widely used, it may be surprising that the first reported appellate decision to address the legal questions raised by the use of computer-produced evidence did not appear until 1965. More surprising is that appellate courts in many jurisdictions have not yet faced these issues.

Today, of course, the use of computer evidence is pervasive. It is not by any means limited to commercial litigation. The admissibility of computer records kept by both businesses and law enforcement agencies has frequently been contested in criminal cases. Computer records have been offered, for example, to prove that a bill was or was not paid, to prove that a person had no criminal record, and to prove a person's whereabouts on a critical date. This chapter reviews the principal evidentiary questions that have been

This chapter is adapted from an article published in 14 American Jurisprudence Proof of Facts 2d and is reprinted with the permission of Lawyers Co-operative Publishing Company, Rochester, New York, and Bancroft-Whitney Company, San Francisco, California.

considered by the courts thus far and highlights some of the recent developments in the use of computers in litigation.

Although most of the cases discussed in this chapter address the computerized business record problem in the context of a courtroom contest over their admissibility at trial, it is by far the better practice to raise and resolve such issues during the pretrial proceedings. Counsel should exchange the computer documents they intend to introduce, or at least lists of such documents, and make every effort to reach stipulations as to their admissibility to expedite the trial and avoid unnecessary excursions into such peripheral foundational matters at trial. Where counsel cannot reach agreement, they should move to have the court determine the admissibility of the contested documents by pretrial order. Not all issues of admissibility will be resolved before trial, of course, and counsel must still be prepared to lay or attack the foundation of critical computer evidence and, if admitted, to support or impeach its credibility.

Evidentiary Problems

The litigator who wants to introduce into evidence printouts of computerized business records faces two fundamental hurdles presented by the law of evidence: the best-evidence rule, which generally requires original documents, rather than copies, to be used as evidence, and the hearsay rule, which generally excludes from evidence statements made other than by a witness testifying in court from personal knowledge. Two time-honored evidentiary principles—the voluminous-writings exception to the best evidence rule and the business-records exception to the hearsay rule—make those hurdles surmountable, however.

A related problem for introducing computer printouts into evidence is that of laying the proper foundation to authenticate the printout and establish the foundational predicates for the voluminous-writings and business-records exceptions. The reported cases strongly indicate that laying the foundation is the most common difficulty encountered by lawyers in attempting to introduce computer evidence.

Perhaps the most crucial aspect of laying the foundation is convincing the trial judge of the reliability of the computer. Judge Van Graafeiland of the U.S. Second Circuit Court of Appeals has pointedly cautioned, "As one of the many who have received computerized bills and dunning letters for accounts long since paid, I am not prepared to accept the product of a computer as the equivalent of Holy Writ."[1] In another case, involving an action by a gas company on an open account, the Wyoming Supreme Court noted, "It is a frightening prospect to think that a person could be sued for services rendered and have the plaintiff base its claim solely upon a recapitulation of computer printout sheets."[2] And in yet another case, where

Sears Roebuck & Co. attempted to prove an amount due on a customer's charge account by a computer printout (the original invoices had been destroyed), the trial judge expressed a disdain for computer technology, ruled that he would not accept the printout as evidence, and dismissed Sears's complaint. On appeal, however, the court ruled the evidence admissible, noting that "the business records exception is intended to bring the realities of the business world into the courtroom" and thus that "a record kept on computer in the ordinary course of business qualifies as competent evidence."[3]

The current judicial attitude toward computers is reflected in the comments made in a recent case by Judge Vincent Biunno of the U.S. District Court for the District of New Jersey:

> The computer is a marvelous device that can perform countless tasks at high speed and low cost, but it must be used with care. This is because it can also make errors at high speed. Those who use computers for record and accounting purposes, including the government, are accordingly obliged to operate them with suitable controls to safeguard the reliability and accuracy of the information.[4]

Objects of Proof

Computer-kept business records have been introduced to prove an astonishingly wide variety of facts. Most common is the use of computer accounting statements to prove the amount owed to a merchant on a charge or trade account.[5] Computerized bank records have been introduced to prove the criminal misappropriation of funds by a fiduciary.[6] Computerized insurance records have been introduced in a mail fraud prosecution to prove that a doctor defrauded an insurance company by filing bogus claims seeking payment for medical treatments that were not performed[7] and in a tax evasion case to prove that an insurance agent fraudulently collected commissions on sham insurance policies.[8] Computerized credit card accounts have been used to prove theft.[9] In other criminal prosecutions, computerized telephone bills have been introduced to prove communication between co-conspirators[10] and computerized airline reservations information has been introduced to prove that a defendant was in a certain city on a critical date and thereby negate his alibi.[11]

One of the more resourceful uses of computerized records was that by a New York taxpayer in challenging a real property assessment using computer printouts showing the statistical data collected by the State Board of Equalization in establishing the applicable equalization rate (designed to facilitate uniform state aid to localities). His aim was to prove that his individual property was overassessed by the city and county taxing authorities. The New York Court of Appeals upheld the admission of the printouts as business records regularly collected in the routine course of the state board's work.[12]

One of the most difficult objects of proof is the use of computer records to prove a negative: the absence of an event. National Crime Information Center computer printouts have been offered to prove that a victim did not have a criminal record, but rejected by the court for want of proof that the arrest records in question would customarily have been entered on the computer.[13] A similar issue has arisen in criminal actions for willful failure to file tax returns where the government has sought to introduce Internal Revenue Service printouts indicating that the defendant did not file a tax return. In such cases, the printouts are generally held admissible, but the defendant must be given a reasonable opportunity to impeach the accuracy of the IRS's data-processing system, if the defendant makes a timely request for such discovery.[14] In one case, testimony based on computerized Hertz rental car records was introduced to prove that the allegedly stolen car had not been rented (thus tending to support the allegation that it was stolen).[15] The court admitted the testimony as proof of nonrental, but one judge stressed that in admitting such evidence, the courts must be satisfied with all reasonable certainty that both the machine and those who supplied its information had performed their functions with utmost accuracy.[16]

Computer Printouts as the Best Evidence

It is a well-established rule of evidence that a party wishing to prove the contents of a writing must produce the original writing, if available, as the best evidence of what the writing says. Computer printouts thus present an interesting conceptual problem in defining what constitutes the original writing.

Certainly the ribbon copy of a computer printout is the original of the printout. But if the printout merely represents a copy of information electronically or magnetically recorded in computer memory or on computer tape, it might be argued that the printout is not the best evidence of what is actually in memory or on tape. As the courts have recognized, this argument is specious, since without the printout, it is virtually impossible for humans to make sense of the recorded data.[17]

If the information stored in memory or on tape was derived from invoices or other paper records, it might also be argued that the paper records constitute the best evidence. But if those paper records were destroyed in the ordinary course of business, the computerized records are the best available evidence, and the courts have uniformly so held. Where the computer printout is not a complete copy but rather an extracted summary of vast amounts of computer-kept data, the best-evidence rule becomes a more formidable problem, but most jurisdictions recognize the practical voluminous-writings exception, which permits the introduction of the summary, provided that the underlying voluminous data are available for inspection.[18] The best-evidence rule, like other evidentiary objections, may be waived if not timely raised at trial by the opponent of the evidence.[19]

The reported cases show that proponents of computer-produced evidence occasionally flounder on the best-evidence rule by presenting oral testimony based on the witness's review of computer printouts without actually introducing the printouts themselves into evidence. For example, in one criminal case, the prosecution fell into this trap.[20] To prove that the defendant had stolen a credit card, the prosecution had a bank investigator testify that a computer printout showed that a certain card that was reported missing had been used seventy-three times in twenty-two cities in a two-month period. The court said that the printout itself would have been admissible upon a proper foundation but ruled that the witness's testimony as to the contents of the printout was inadmissible under the best-evidence rule.[21]

Computer Printouts as Business Records

Computer printouts, like other written documents, are perforce hearsay and cannot be admitted into evidence to prove the truth of the matters asserted in them unless they fit within a recognized exception to the hearsay rule. All jurisdictions, however, recognize some sort of exception for records maintained and relied upon in the regular course of business. The rationale is that it would be impractical (and probably not even helpful) to summon as a witness every employee of the business necessary to establish the matters through personal knowledge and direct testimony and that if the records were used in the ordinary course of business for purposes other than the litigation, there is little reason to doubt their reliability.[22] Gradually by statute and by judicial decision in several states and federal courts, the business-records exception has been recognized or extended to include computer business records—largely by necessity because business records now are often kept only by computer.

The Uniform Business Records as Evidence Act provides:

> A record of an act, condition or event, shall, insofar as relevant, be competent evidence if the custodian or other qualified witness testifies to its identity and the mode of its preparation, and if it was made in the regular course of business, at or near the time of the act, condition or event, and if, in the opinion of the court, the sources of information, method and time of preparation were such as to justify its admission.[23]

In the landmark case of *Transport Indemnity Co.* v. *Seib* decided in 1965, the court observed that this statutory provision was intended to bring the realities of business and professional practice into the courtroom.[24] It concluded that the statute was broad enough to authorize the admission of computer printouts in evidence, noting that to interpret the statute narrowly and hold otherwise would destroy its obvious usefulness.

In *Seib,* the plaintiff insurance company introduced a computer printout to prove the amount of premiums due on a retrospective insurance policy. The plaintiff's director of accounting gave foundational testimony showing that the printout was prepared for trial under his supervision from computer records stored on tape. The tape records showed the premiums due, which had been calculated in the usual course of business by the computer according to an established formula on the basis of the defendant's past claims, which had been fed into the computer in the usual course of business. The witness also testified that he had manually verified each of the calculations and reconciled the amounts shown as due on the printout. His foundational testimony stretched across 141 pages of the record. Over defendant's objection, the printout was admitted. On appeal the court held that the foundational testimony met the requirements of the statute and that it was not necessary to identify and produce the persons who had originally supplied the information as to past claims recorded on the tape.

Even absent a statutory business-records exception, however, the courts have admitted computerized business records under the common-law shop book rule. For example, in *King* v. *State ex rel. Murdock Acceptance Corp.,* the Mississippi Supreme Court held in 1969 that printout sheets of business records stored on electronic computing equipment are admissible in evidence if relevant and material, without the necessity of identifying, locating, and producing as witnesses the individuals who made the entries in the regular course of business if it is shown that the electronic computing equipment is standard equipment, the entries are made in the regular course of business at or reasonably near the time of the happening of the event recorded, and the foundation testimony satisfies the court that the sources of information, method, and time of preparation were such as to indicate its trustworthiness and justify its admission.[25] This formulation has been adopted by several of the courts that have since considered the question.[26]

Courts in Alabama, Arizona, Georgia, Louisiana, Missouri, Mississippi, Nebraska, New Jersey, New York, North Carolina, North Dakota, Pennsylvania, Tennessee, and Washington[27] and several federal courts[28] have approved the introduction into evidence of computer output under the business-record exception. Courts in a lesser number of jurisdictions have excluded such evidence on the grounds that one or more of the foundational predicates were not satisfied.[29]

One of the ways the proponent of computerized business records may stumble in introducing such evidence is by failing to show that the raw data on which the computer printout is based were entered into the computer in the normal course of business at or near the time of the happening of the event recorded. For example, the proponent may fail to prove that persons at remote terminals regularly logged information into the computer system. In a Texas murder case, the prosecution was precluded from introducing a printout from the National Crime Information Center (NCIC) computer showing that the murder victim had no criminal record because the prosecution failed to show that law enforcement agencies in the cities where the victim was allegedly arrested customarily entered arrest information in the NCIC computer.[30]

Another pitfall revealed by the cases is attempting to introduce summaries manually extracted from computer printouts made in the ordinary course of business without also introducing the printouts. While the printouts themselves should be admissible, the summaries of such antecedent records may not be deemed made "in the regular course of business."[31] However, annual statistical summaries and computer surveys of data that were entered in the usual course of business in a timely manner have been held to qualify as business records where such summaries and surveys were customarily prepared for business purposes.[32]

That the computer printout offered in evidence was prepared for use in the litigation will not preclude its admission if the data it represents were entered and stored in the computer in the normal course of business. As the court stated in *Seib,*

> This argument [that a computer printout is inadmissible because it was prepared for use in litigation] exalts the form over the substance. The retrieval from the taped record . . . was made for the purposes of the trial. But, the taped record and the information and calculations thereon were made in the usual course of business and for the purpose of the business alone.[33]

If, however, the data recorded on tape or other medium are summarized or serve as the basis for calculations made especially for trial, copies of the recorded data, as well as the summary or results of the calculations, should be introduced (or at least made available).

The Requirement of a Foundation to Show Trustworthiness

The most common reason that courts have rejected computerized evidence is that the proponent of the evidence failed to establish a sufficient foundation to show the accuracy and trustworthiness of the evidence.[34] To preserve the issue for appeal, however, the opponent of proffered computer evidence must object to an insufficient foundation in order to give its proponent an opportunity to lay the proper foundation.[35] Examples of carefully laid proper foundations may be found in the cases of *Transport Indemnity Co.*

v. *Seib*,[36] *King* v. *State ex rel. Murdock Acceptance Corp.*[37] and *United States* v. *Russo.*[38]

The foundation for admitting a computer printout as a business record should establish, through the testimony of the custodian of the computer-kept records or other person familiar with the manner in which the records were processed and maintained, the following:

1. The reliability of the data-processing equipment used to keep the records and produce the printout.
2. The manner in which the basic data were initially entered into the system (cards or teletype, for instance).
3. That the data were so entered in the regular course of business.
4. That the data were entered within a reasonable time after the events recorded by persons having personal knowledge of the events.
5. The measures taken to insure the accuracy of the data as entered.
6. The method of storing the data and the safety precautions taken to prevent loss of the data while in storage.
7. The reliability of the computer programs and formulas used to process the data.
8. The measures taken to verify the proper operation and accuracy of these programs and formulas.
9. The time and mode of preparation of the printouts.

The witness need not necessarily have personal knowledge of the basic data as input to the system or personal knowledge of the actual physical operation of the data-processing equipment, as long as he or she is generally familiar with the methods employed by the company in processing the business records.[39] Indeed, the courts seem to be reluctant to require the proponent of computer evidence to call more than one foundational witness. In an antitrust action by an auto-parts jobber against Ford, for example, Ford introduced (over the jobber's objection) a computer printout of monthly sales to the jobber. Ford used its assistant controller, who was in charge of Ford's field accounting department, as the authenticating witness and did not produce the head of its data-processing department or any of its computer people. The court held the printout admissible even though Ford failed to use a witness familiar with its data-processing department to lay the foundation.[40] But, of course, the foundational testimony will be all the more persuasive if the custodian can, as the witness did in the landmark *Seib* case, testify that he or she has manually checked some or all of the computer calculations.[41] And it may still be a worthwhile precaution for the proponent of computer evidence to provide expert testimony as to the accuracy of the computer system.[42] At least one court has held that a witness who was neither the custodian of the computer records nor able to testify as to the legitimacy and accuracy of the printouts was not qualified to lay the necessary foundation for admission of the printouts.[43]

Credibility

In view of the overwhelming trend toward computerization of business records and the steady acceptance by the courts of printouts under the business-records exception, in most cases the proponent of computer-produced evidence who takes the care to have the witness touch all of the foundational bases will succeed in having the evidence admitted into evidence. Indeed, the court in *Seib* was impressed that the foundational testimony took 141 pages of transcript, perhaps suggesting that stamina may suffice where substance is lacking. In any event, the advocate's job does not end when the evidence is admitted. Whatever weaknesses in the foundational testimony the opponent of the evidence may have elicited on voir dire becomes the basis for later cross-examination and a credibility attack—arguing against the weight of the evidence.[44]

The court may be willing to give the proponent the benefit of the doubt where a computer record is the only evidence available and presume that it was accurately derived from reliable data for purposes of admitting it, leaving its persuasiveness to be weighed by the jury. But there are so many opportunities for error, most of them human, in any data-processing system that the skillful opponent may be able to exploit the inevitable uncertainties and diminish the impact of the computer evidence on the jury. It is particularly important to do so because, once the printout is admitted, the trier of fact may be beguiled by its neat tabulations or the apparent precision of its numbers. And, of course, the proponent of the evidence must be ready to defend the printout against the assault on its credibility.

In mounting the assault, the opponent of the computer evidence should take the same approach, but perhaps in more depth than was used to resist introduction of the evidence in the first instance. The potential weaknesses in the evidence may be divided into four categories: integrity of the input data, integrity of the computer equipment and programs, security of the data-processing system, and integrity of the output.[45]

Humans have the most significant role in the input process, and their intervention makes this stage the most likely source of error. Source information such as orders, bills, and invoices may be incomplete, lost, or inadvertently duplicated; keystroke transfers of their contents to computer records may contain errors that go undetected; the wrong tape may be entered into the computer; or data might be intentionally altered.

Malfunctions in the computer equipment may occur, but these are likely to manifest themselves immediately (warning lights flash and the computer may stop running) and are not often the source of subtle errors. Minor hardware errors might, however, result in the loss of data on one segment of a magnetic tape or disk and, absent back-up data, thereby significantly impair the validity of any computer analysis of the remaining data.

Program errors, on the other hand, do not often manifest themselves so dramatically. It is possible, for example, for a program to apply the wrong discount factor to an invoice price, and such an error might not be discovered until after a large number of invoices had been processed. Furthermore, programs, being written by humans, share the biases and assumptions of their authors. If the programmer did not anticipate that an invoice might contain more than ten items, the program may just ignore the eleventh item on each invoice. The advocate, therefore, should probe carefully the procedures used in designing, coding, documenting, and testing the programs for the possibility of error, bias, or faulty assumptions.

An interesting issue that arises in this context is whether the absence of complaints about errors in a program is probative of its accuracy and reliability. In personal injury cases, for example, the absence of complaints about a dangerous physical condition has sometimes been excluded from evidence as not being probative of the safety of the premises under the particular conditions in issue.[46] One commentator argues that since the conditions of a computer program are not subject to deterioration, the absence of complaints about a computer program ought to be admissible.[47] Unfortunately, however, the conditions under which a program operates do sometimes change, and the volume and special characteristics of the data being processed may cause malfunctions that other data have not caused. Similarly the interaction of different programs may reveal otherwise undetected errors. Finally, virtually all programs are in a constant state of evolution. They are continually being modified, enhanced, and expanded, and each change is a potential source of error. Thus, it is difficult to say categorically that an absence of past complaints is persuasive evidence of the absence of errors. Past complaints, on the other hand, are probative of the existence of errors.[48]

The security of the data-processing system from unauthorized use also bears directly on the reliability of computer-produced evidence. If unauthorized persons have access to the physical computer records, such as the tape or disk pack library, the records might be destroyed by vandals. More troublesome is the danger of unauthorized access to the data through the computer. Someone familiar with the system could gain access to selected data items and change or delete them or even create bogus new items. Counsel should therefore explore what precautions are taken against tampering.

Finally, there is the question of the integrity of the output. The advocate should investigate whether the particular printout introduced in evidence is the one produced in the manner described by the authenticating witness, because computer outputs are easily reproduced by the computer and appear interchangeable. The proponent of the printout should have the witness sign and date the printout when it is produced to avoid any such question.

In addition, the opponent of the printout should investigate whether the output was produced in a biased or self-serving way. For example, the printout might contain only selected records carefully chosen to cast the statistical results in favor of the party producing the evidence.[49]

While a skilled cross-examiner might be able to uncover such weaknesses in a data-processing system by chance, it is far preferable for the opponent of the evidence to investigate these matters in advance by discovery, aided by data-processing professionals, to prepare effective cross-examination, and to avoid unnecessarily emphasizing the precautions that were taken in preparation of the computer evidence.

Use of Computer-Created Evidence

Since *Seib,* computer-kept business records have been regularly admitted into evidence upon the laying of a proper foundation. Where the raw data recorded on computer tapes are not organized in a useful way, the courts have had little problem in admitting printouts of data culled from tapes and concurrently tabulated in a printout. If, however, extracts or summaries of computer-kept records are introduced, the underlying raw data should be introduced, or at least made available to the court and adversary. But some proponents of computer evidence have gone one step further and enhanced the raw data by performing calculations based on the data or, further yet, by creating computer simulation models to project the possible outcomes of different hypotheses.[50] Such computer-generated evidence should, upon proper foundation, also be admissible but not, of course, under the business-records exception. Rather it should be admissible as the basis of expert testimony, provided that the reliability of the evidence and means used to produce it are adequately established. The use of the computer in this way, effectively as an expert, raises another range of problems, which courts and practitioners are just beginning to face.

Perma Research and Development v. *Singer Co.* is an interesting case in point.[51] It involved an alleged breach of an agreement by Singer to use its best efforts to perfect and market a patented automotive antiskid device. To prove its case, plaintiff introduced expert testimony, based on the results of a computer simulation, that the device was indeed perfectible. Singer objected to the use of the computer simulation on the grounds that it did not have an adequate basis on which to cross-examine plaintiff's experts. The trial court nonetheless allowed the experts to testify as to the computer simulation as the basis for the conclusions and, largely on that evidence, held Singer liable for $7 million in damages. A divided Second Circuit panel affirmed the ruling and decision as within the trial judge's discretion, noting only that "it might have been better practice for opposing counsel to arrange for the delivery of all details of the underlying data and theorems employed in these simulations in advance of trial to both avoid unnecessarily belabored discussion of highly technical, tangential issues at trial . . . and protect truly proprietary aspects of the programs."[52]

Judge Van Graafeiland filed a lengthy dissent, stating:

> Proof that plaintiff's defective and dangerous device could be transformed in some way to accomplish [its antiskid function] required more than the running of some figures through a computer which involved calculation of a theoretical series of stops, following the assumed installation of a hypothetical or simulated antiskid device on a 1968 Thunderbird.[53]

After reviewing a number of authorities on computer simulation, he criticized the trial judge's acceptance of the simulation results without supporting feasibility studies involving actual prototypes and further criticized the trial judge's refusal to require plaintiff to disclose to Singer the manner in which the computer was programmed to create the evidence used at trial. Recognizing the decisions upholding the admission of computerized business records, Judge Van Graafeiland noted the different considerations present where a computer is programmed to produce information specifically for purposes of litigation and argued that a court should not permit a witness to state the results of a computer's operation without having the program available for the scrutiny of opposing counsel and his use on cross-examination.

In *Pearl Brewing Co.* v. *Jos. Schlitz Co.,* the court gave opposing counsel such an opportunity to scrutinize computer programs used to support expert testimony.[54] There, the plaintiff in an antitrust action retained an economics expert and two computer experts to develop a highly sophisticated computerized econometric model to simulate local beer market conditions and to make calculations of estimated damages based on the simulated results, all to serve as the basis of the economist's expert testimony at trial. During discovery, plaintiff produced printouts of the programs used in the model but refused Schlitz's requests for explanatory documentation of the model and damage assessment programs, to depose the two computer experts who authored the programs, and for the alternative computer models developed but rejected by plaintiff. On motion to compel such discovery, the court granted Schlitz's first two requests, recognizing that Schlitz needed the information to understand the workings of the programs and to prepare a meaningful cross-examination of the economist, but the court refused discovery of the alternative models as being in the nature of nontrial experts whose reports are not normally discoverable under the Federal Rules of Civil Procedure absent "exceptional circumstances."

It seems clear that if complex computer simulations are to be used to support controverted expert testimony, the adversary must be given a reasonable, meaningful opportunity to probe the assumptions, biases, and accuracy of the computer programs used to perform the simulation. As the court recognized in *Pearl,* a source code listing of the programs will probably not be sufficient because it would take even a computer expert an inordinate amount of time to understand the programs without the assistance of a map (the documentation) and a guide (the author of the program). The discovery order in *Pearl* seems amply justified on these grounds, and the decision in *Perma Research* seems unduly restrictive.

Future Developments

Following the landmark decision in *Seib,* one commentator predicted that as business records kept electronically became increasingly prevalent, the legal problems regarding their use in evidence would resolve themselves into whether the proof offered met the preelectronics requirements for admission of business records.[55] That prophecy was fulfilled in 1969 when it was quoted and endorsed by the court in *King.* Ever since, the courts have followed the traditional course of the common law in adapting and applying old rules to new circumstances by analogy. But that is not the only course open to the law. Recent statutes have included explicit references to accommodate the advent of automated data processing.

Yet another alternative is to draft comprehensive statutes and write new rules governing computer-generated evidence. An interesting attempt at this has been essayed in South Australia and may portend future developments in the United States.[56] It provides that computer output is admissible in civil cases if the court is satisfied:

1. That the computer is correctly programmed and regularly used to produce output of the same kind as that tendered in evidence.
2. That the data from which the output is produced is systematically prepared upon the basis of information that would normally be acceptable in court as evidence of the statements represented by the output.
3. That there is no reasonable cause to suspect any departure from the system or any error in the data.
4. That the computer has not been subject to a malfunction that might reasonably be expected to affect the accuracy of the output.
5. That there have been no alterations to the processes of the computer that might reasonably be expected to affect the output adversely.
6. That the records have been kept by a responsible person in charge of the computer operations.
7. That there is no reasonable cause to believe that the accuracy or validity of the output has been adversely affected by the use of any improper process or procedure or by inadequate safeguards in the use of the computer.

Although the statute contains the same sorts of provisions as are applied by the American courts, it is a far more precise articulation of them than the courts have provided and appears to be more demanding of the proof required for admission. Nonetheless, it should serve as a useful guide to American advocates and courts alike.

Once the computer business-records problem is solved, the focus of attention may move to other intriguing questions. For example, perhaps a computer record of a party opponent is admissible, though hearsay, as an admission against interest.[57] Or, as the computer simulation cases and some commentators suggest, computer-created evidence may be accepted as scientific evidence much like the results of chemical blood tests, radar speed-trap measurements, and X-rays.[58] Finally, there is the thought-provoking possibility that with the advent of electronic funds transfer systems, the computer record may not be hearsay at all because it will be the operational event itself.[59] Inevitably the computer will provide lawyers new types of evidence, and the courts will be challenged to evolve new rules to cope with it.

Notes

1. Perma Research and Development v. Singer Co., 542 F.2d 111, 121 (2d Cir. 1976) (dissenting opinion).

2. Harned v. Credit Bureau of Gillette, 513 P.2d 650, 5 CLSR 394 (Wyo. 1973). Throughout this chapter, parallel citations of cases are given to CLSR, the *Computer Law Service Reporter* written by Robert P. Bigelow.

3. Sears Roebuck & Co. v. Merla, 142 N.J. Super. 205, 361 A. 2d 68, 5 CLSR 1370 (1976) (reversing the trial court.)

4. Neal v. United States, 402 F. Supp 678, 680 (D.N.J. 1975).

5. *E.g.,* Cotton v. John W. Eshelman & Sons, Inc., 137 Ga. App. 360, 223 S.E. 2d 757, 5 CLSR 1287 (1976) (computer ledger printouts of information stored on tape showing feed and grain purchases); Sears Roebuck & Co. v. Merla, 142 N.J. Super. 205, 361 A.2d 68, 5 CLSR 1370 (1976) (printout of charge account where original invoice had been destroyed in regular course of business); Union Elec. Co. v. Mansion House Center North Redevelopment Co., 494 S.W.2d 309, 5 CLSR 929 (Mo. 1973) (printouts of unpaid utility bills). *Compare* Harned v. Credit Bureau of Gillette, 513 P.2d 650, 5 CLSR 394 (Wyo. 1973) (rejecting admission of summaries not made in regular course of business).

6. State v. Smith, 16 Wash. App. 425, 558 P.2d 265 (1976) (abstracts prepared from printouts of guardian's bank accounts).

7. United States v. Russo, 480 F. 2d 1228, 5 CLSR 687 (6th Cir. 1973).

8. United States v. Fendley, 522 F.2d 181 (5th Cir. 1975).

9. North Carolina v. Springer, Jr., 283 N.C. 627, 197 S.E.2d 530, 5 CLSR 432 (1973).

10. State v. Hodgeson, 305 So. 2d 421 (La. 1974).

11. State v. Stapleton, 29 N.C. App. 363, 224 S.E.2d 204 (1976).

12. Ed Guth Realty, Inc. v. Gingold, 34 N.Y.2d 440, 358 N.Y.S.2d 367, 5 CLSR 880 (1974).

13. Gassett v. State, 532 S.W.2d 328, 5 CLSR 1309 (Tex. Crim. App. 1976).

14. *Compare,* United States v. Liebert, 383 F. Supp. 1060 (E.D. Pa. 1974) (dismissing prosecution on government's refusal to permit discovery of data processing system), *vacated and remanded,* 519 F.2d 542, 5 CLSR 952 (3d Cir. 1975) (on government's offer to permit defendant to run tests on system to analyze its reliability) *with* United States v. Greenlee, 380 F. Supp. 652, 5 CLSR 949 (E.D. Pa. 1974), *aff'd,* 517 F.2d 899 (3d Cir. 1975) (defendant's request for access to IRS computers three days before trial, absent a prima facie showing that return was filed and possibly lost by IRS, was not timely), decided a month earlier.

15. United States v. DeGeorgia, 420 F.2d 889, 2 CLSR 479 (9th Cir. 1969).

16. Rule 803(7) of the Federal Rules of Evidence expressly authorizes the use of evidence of the absence of an entry in a "data compilation" maintained in the regular course of business to prove the nonoccurrence of a fact unless the circumstances indicate a lack of trustworthiness.

17. *E.g.,* King v. State ex rel. Murdock Acceptance Corp., 222 So. 2d 393, 2 CLSR 180, 185 (Miss.1969) ("Records stored on magnetic tape by data processing machines are unavailable and useless except by means of the printout sheets such as those admitted to evidence in this case"). Rule 1001(3) of the Federal Rules of Evidence has solved this problem by defining the printout to be an original copy of the record.

18. A typical voluminous writings exception is that stated in Rule 1006 of the Federal Rules of Evidence: "The contents of voluminous writings, recordings, or photographs which cannot conveniently be examined in court may be presented in the form of a chart, summary, or calculation. The originals, or duplicates, shall be made available for examination or copying, or both, by other parties at a reasonable time and place. The court may order that they be produced in court."

19. United States v. DeGeorgia, 420 F.2d 889, 2 CLSR 479 (9th Cir. 1969).

20. North Carolina v. Springer, 283 N.C. 627, 197 S.E.2d 530, 5 CLSR 432 (1973). The same error was made in United States v. DeGeorgia, 420 F.2d 889, 2 CLSR 479 (9th Cir. 1969) (computer record maintained by Hertz car rental agency indicating that car had not been rented and therefore was stolen), but the defendant failed to raise the best-evidence rule at trial and thereby waived the objection.

21. For a criticism of *Springer,* see Sprowl, *Evaluating the Credibility of Computer-Generated Evidence,* 52 Chicago-Kent L. Rev. 547, 561 (1976), arguing that the witness should be allowed to state the results of the printout without having to bring the printout into court.

22. *See, e.g.,* United States v. DeGeorgia, 420 F.2d 889, 2 CLSR 479, 484 (9th Cir. 1969).

23. There are several other similar business-records exceptions. For example, the ALI Model Code of Evidence, Rule 514(1) provides: "A writing offered as a memorandum or record of an act, event or condition is admissible as tending to prove the occurrence of the act or event or the existence of the condition if the judge finds that it was made in the regular course of business and that it was the regular course of that business for one with personal knowledge of such an act, event or condition

to make such a memorandum or record or to transmit information thereof to be included in such a memorandum or record, and for the memorandum or record to be made at or about the time of act, event or condition or within a reasonable time thereafter."

Rule 803(6) of the Federal Rules of Evidence excepts from the hearsay rule "a memorandum, report, record, or data compilation, in any form, of acts, events, conditions, opinions or diagnoses, made at or near the time by, or from information transmitted by, a person with knowledge, if kept in the course of a regularly conducted business activity, and if it was the regular practice of that business activity to make the memorandum, report, record, or data compilation, all as shown by the testimony of the custodian or other qualified witness, unless the source of information or the method or circumstances of preparation indicate lack of trustworthiness. The term "business" as used in this paragraph includes business, institution, association, profession, occupation, and calling of every kind, whether or not conducted for profit."

24. 178 Neb. 253, 132 N.W.2d 871, 1 CLSR 368 (1965).

25. 222 So. 2d 393, 2 CLSR 180 (Miss. 1969).

26. Dept. of Mental Health v. Beil, 44 Ill. App. 3d 402, 2 Ill. Dec. 655, 357 N.E.2d 875 (1976); City of Seattle v. Heath, 10 Wash. App. 949, 520 P.2d 1392 (1974); State v. Hodgeson, 305 So. 2d 421 (La. 1974).

27. Nelson Weaver Mortgage Co. v. Dover, 216 So. 2d 716 (Ala. 1968); Rumage v. Dry Dock Sav. Bank, 179 So. 2d 277 (Ala. 1965); State v. Veres, 7 Ariz. App. 117, 436 P.2d 629, 1 CLSR 918 (1968); Merrick v. U.S. Rubber Co., 7 Ariz. App. 433, 440 P.2d 314, 1 CLSR 995 (1968); Cotton v. John W. Eshelman & Sons, Inc., 137 Ga. App. 360, 223 S.E. 2d 757, 5 CLSR 1287 (1976); State v. Hodgeson, 305 So. 2d 421 (La. 1974); Union Elec. Co. v. Mansion House Center North Redevelopment Co., 494 S.W.2d 309, 5 CLSR 929 (Mo. 1973); King v. State ex rel. Murdock Acceptance Corp., 222 So. 2d 393, 2 CLSR 180 (Miss. 1969); Transport Indemnity Co. v. Seib, 178, Neb. 253, 132, N.W.2d 871, 1 CLSR 368 (1965); State v. Watson, 192 Neb. 44, 218 N.W. 2d 904 (1974); Sears Roebuck & Co. v. Merla, 142 N.J. Super. 205, 361 A.2d 68, 5 CLSR 1370 (1976); Ed Guth Realty, Inc. v. Gingold, 34 N.Y.2d 440, 358 N.Y.S.2d 367, 5 CLSR 880 (1974); State v. Stapleton, 29 N.C. App. 363, 224 S.E.2d 204 (1976); Endicott Johnson Corp. v. Golde, 190 N.W.2d 752 (N.D. 1971); *In re* Matthews, 47 Pa. D. & C. 2d 529 (1969); Wheeler v. Cain, 459 S.W.2d 618 (Tenn. App. 1970); State v. Smith, 16 Wash. App. 425, 558 P.2d 265 (1976); City of Seatttle v. Heath, 10 Wash. App. 943, 520 P.2d 1392 (1974).

28. *E.g.,* United States v. Fendley, 522 F.2d 181 (5th Cir. 1975); United States v. Russo, 480 F.2d 1228, 5 CLSR 687 (6th Cir. 1973); Olympic Insurance Co. v. Harrison, Inc., 418 F.2d 669 (5th Cir. 1969); United States v. DeGeorgia, 420 F.2d 889, 2 CLSR 479 (9th Cir. 1969); D & H Auto Parts, Inc. v. Ford Marketing Corp., 3 CLSR 856 (E.D.N.Y. 1973). *See also* Manual for Complex Litigation sec. 2.716 (1973) ("Computer maintained records kept in the regular course of business should be admitted when it has been shown that the criteria for the admission of non-computer maintained business records have been met and there is no reason for the Court to find the material unreliable or of no substantial probative value").

29. Dept. of Mental Health v. Beil, 44 Ill. App. 3d 402, 2 Ill. Dec. 655, 357 N.E.

2d 875 (1976); People v. Gauer, 7 Ill. App. 3d 512, 288 N.E.2d 24, 4 CLSR 477 (1972); North Carolina v. Springer, Jr., 283 N.C. 627, 197 S.E.2d 530, 5 CLSR 432 (1973); Gassett v. State, 532 S.W.2d 328, 5 CLSR 1309 (Tex. Crim. App. 1976); Kamen & Co. v. Young, 466 S.W.2d 381, 4 CLSR 444 (Tex. Civ. App. 1971).

30. Gassett v. State, 532 S.W.2d 328, 5 CLSR 1309 (Tex. Crim. App. 1976).

31. *See* Harned v. Credit Bureau of Gillette, 513 P.2d 650, 5 CLSR 394 (Wyo. 1973).

32. United States v. Russo, 480 F.2d 1228, 5 CLSR 687 (6th Cir. 1973) (summary of medical insurance claims made during the year was prepared eleven months after close of the year).

33. Transport Indemnity v. Seib, 178 Neb. 253, 132 N.W.2d 871, 1 CLSR 368, 373 (1965).

34. *E.g.,* People v. Gauer, 7 Ill. App. 3d 512, 288 N.E.2d, 24, 4 CLSR 477 (1972) (no testimony as to reliability and accuracy of telephone tracing equipment); North Carolina v. Springer, Jr., 283 N.C. 627. 197 S.E.2d 530, 5 CLSR 432 (1973) (no testimony as to methods under which computer printout of credit card account was made).

35. *See, e.g.* United States v. Fendley, 522 F.2d 181 (5th Cir. 1975); United States v. DeGeorgia, 420 F.2d 889, 2 CLSR 479 (9th Cir. 1969).

36. 178 Neb. 253, 132 N.W.2d 871, 1 CLSR 368 (1965).

37. 222 So. 2d 393, 2 CLSR 180 (Miss. 1969).

38. 480 F.2d 1228, 5 CLSR 687 (6th Cir. 1973).

39. *See, e.g.,* Endicott Johnson Corp. v. Golde, 190 N.W.2d 752 (N.D. 1971) (where witness had no personal knowledge of operation of computer system or information contained on original orders input to computer but was generally familiar with method of processing orders and copies of original orders were available to cross-check, court admitted computerized invoices, stating its reluctance to require company to incur cost of more qualified person to lay foundation); State v. Veres, 7 Ariz. App. 117, 436 P.2d 629, 1 CLSR 918 (1968) (court had discretion to admit printout even though bank officer was not aware of mechanical operation of machine); Merrick v. U.S. Rubber Co., 7 Ariz. App. 433, 440 P.2d 314, 1 CLSR 995 (1968) (court had discretion to admit printout even though witness had no personal knowledge of operation of computer but was generally familiar with accounting records). *But see* Kamen & Co. v. Young, 466 S.W.2d 381, 4 CLSR 444 (Tex. Civ. App. 1971) (computer printouts inadmissible because there was "no proof that the person who prepared [the data on which the printouts were based] had personal knowledge of the data or information allegedly printed into the cards"). The *Kamen & Co.* decision was criticized in 24 Baylor L. Rev. 161 (1972) on the grounds that the Texas statute does not require such a showing.

40. D & H Auto Parts, Inc. v. Ford Marketing Corp., 3 CLSR 856 (E.D.N.Y. 1973) (one factor influencing the court's decision was that the jobber had had copies of the printouts for six months and had failed to point out any inaccuracies during that period).

41. Transport Indemnity v. Seib, 178 Neb. 253, N.W.2d 871, 1 CLSR 368, 371 (1965).

42. *See* United States v. DeGeorgia, 420 F.2d 889, 2 CLSR 479, 485 n. 11 (9th Cir. 1969).

43. Railroad Commission v. Southern Pacific Co., 468 S.W.2d 125, 3 CLSR 720 (Tex. Civ. App. 1971).

44. *See generally Law and Technology Symposium: Coping with Computer-Generated Evidence in Litigation,* 52 Chi.-Kent L. Rev. 545 (1976).

45. *See* Sprowl, *Evaluating the Credibility of Computer-Generated Evidence,* 52 Chi.-Kent L.Rev. 547, 557-62 (1976).

46. *See* C. McCormick, *Evidence* sec. 200 at 476 (2d ed. 1972).

47. Sprowl, *supra* at 559-60 n. 23.

48. *See, e.g.,* United States v. Liebert, 519 F.2d 542, 5 CLSR 952 (3d Cir. 1975) (in prosecution for failure to file income tax returns errors on IRS nonfiling lists would cast doubt on accuracy and reliability on list showing defendant as nonfiler).

49. For an argument that the data were so slanted in United States v. Russo, 480 F.2d 1228, 5 CLSR 687 (6th Cir. 1973), see Sprowl, *supra* at 563-65.

50. For a discussion of computer simulation models, see Eastin, *The Use of Models in Litigation: Concise or Contrived?* 52 Chi.-Kent L. Rev. 610 (1976).

51. 542 F.2d 111 (2d Cir. 1976), *cert. denied,* 97 S. Ct. 507 (1976).

52. 542 F.2d at 115.

53. 542 F.2d at 121.

54. 415 F. Supp. 1122 (S.D. Tex. 1976).

55. Anno., *Proof of Business Records Kept or Stored on Electronic Computing Equipment,* 11 ALR 3d 1368, 1378 (1967).

56. South Australia Evidence Act, reproduced in 5 Computer Law Service App. 6-4.1a No. 4 (1977) and discussed at length in Tapper, *Evidence from Computers,* 8 Ga. L. Rev. 562 (1974).

57. Freed, *Computer Records and the Law—Retrospect and Prospect,* 15 Jurimetrics J. 207, 209 (1975).

58. Abelle, *Evidentiary Problems Relevant to Checks and Computers,* 5 J. of Computers and Law 323, 358-65 (1976); Jenkins, *Computer-Generated Evidence Specially Prepared for Use at Trial,* 52 Chi.-Kent L. Rev. 600, 608 (1976).

59. Abelle, *supra* at 344-45.

Bibliography

Abelle, *Evidentiary Problems Relevant to Checks and Computers,* 5 J. Computers and Law 323 (1976).

Bernacchi and Larsen, *Philosophy, Data Processing and the Rules of Evidence,* 10 ABA Law Notes No. 1 (1974) and 48 Los Angeles B. Bull. 374 (1973).

Comment, *Admissibility of Computer Print-Outs Under the Business Records Exception in Texas,* 12 S. Tex. L.J. 291 (1970).

Comment, *Computer Print-Outs of Business Records and Their Admissibility in New York,* 31 Albany L. Rev. 61 (1967).

DeHetre, *Data Processing Evidence—Is It Different?,* 52 Chi.-Kent L. Rev. 567 (1976).

Eastin, *The Use of Models in Litigation: Concise or Contrived?* 52 Chi.-Kent L. Rev. 610 (1976).

Freed, *Computer Print-outs as Evidence,* 16 Proof of Facts 273.

Freed, *Computer Technology and Trial Technique,* 1962 Trial Lawyer's Guide 113.

Freed, Fenwick, and McGonigal, *Mock Trial: Admissibility of Computerized Business Records Problem,* 15 Jurimetrics J. 206 (1975).

Jacobson, *The Use of Computer Printouts as Evidence in Commercial Litigation,* 82 Com. L.J. 14 (1977).

Jenkins, *Computer-Generated Evidence Specially Prepared for Use at Trial,* 52 Chi.-Kent L. Rev. 600 (1976).

Note, *Admissibility of Computer Business Records as an Exception to the Hearsay Rule,* 48 N.C.L. Rev. 687 (1970).

Note, *Admissibility of Computer-Kept Business Records,* 55 Cornell L. Rev. 1033 (1970).

Note, *Admissibility of Computer Print-Outs in Kansas,* 8 Washburn L.J. 330 (1969).

Roberts, *A Practitioner's Primer on Computer-Generated Evidence,* 41 U. Chi.-Kent L. Rev. 254 (1974).

Sprowl, *Evaluating the Credibility of Computer-Generated Evidence,* 52 Chi.-Kent L. Rev. 547 (1976).

Tapper, *Evidence from Computers,* 8 Ga. L. Rev. 562 (1974).

Younger, *Computer Printouts in Evidence; Ten Objections and How to Overcome Them,* 2 Litigation 28 (1975).

Part V

OTHER APPLICATIONS OF COMPUTERS TO THE LAW

The previous parts of this book have examined the use of information-processing techniques by legislatures, for legal research, and for litigation and court management. But the effect of computers on the legal profession has been even broader, encompassing such areas as criminal detection and law enforcement (including, but not limited to, fingerprint identification, traffic violations, and drug enforcement). The U.S. Patent Office and the Internal Revenue Service use sophisticated information-processing techniques, as does the Environmental Protection Agency and the Copyright Office. The three chapters in this part describe three very different computer applications: the Treasury Enforcement Communications System (TECS), computer management of environmental law, and the Responsa Project.

TECS, described by Patricia Coss, is a modern online communications network developed and maintained by the U.S. Customs Service of the Treasury Department and used by various other agencies, including INTERPOL and the IRS. Coss explains how this system evolved, who uses it, and for what purposes. In the next chapter, Victor J. Yannacone, jr., discusses the need for better collection, organization, and analysis of environmental data in order to create a more effective data base for enforcing environmentally related laws. And in the final chapter of this book, Yaacov Choueka, Aaron Schreiber, and Menachem Slae explain a computerized information-retrieval system con-

cerned with the traditional Jewish law called the Responsa. After explaining the Responsa literature, they describe the computer system developed for handling it, provide examples of typical legal-issue searches that have been run, and discuss future developments.

16

PATRICIA COSS

The Treasury Enforcement Communications System

From the earliest days of this country, U.S. Customs officers have been manning the ports of entry into the United States in line with their broad range of enforcement responsibilities. Smuggling and fraud involving every conceivable commodity fall under Customs jurisdiction, as do currency and neutrality violations, endangered species and foreign art treasures, unquarantined parrots, and air-polluting imported autos. In all, the service has been entrusted with the enforcement of over four hundred laws for more than forty federal agencies.

The United States has roughly ninety-six thousand miles of land, air, and sea border. International travel and trade continue to soar. In fiscal year 1977 (October 1, 1976, through September 30, 1977) more than 270 million people, 78 million carried, and $150 billion in imported goods entered this nation. These figures give some idea of the enormous law enforcement challenges faced by the Department of the Treasury, U.S. Customs Service.

To meet the challenges, Customs has turned to sophisticated technology. A custom-built chase aircraft, night vision devices, closed-circuit television systems, and ground sensors are prime examples. The need for up-to-the-minute enforcement information has been met with the Treasury Enforcement Communications System (TECS), an integrated, computerized information system with three primary components: the online (queriable) Enforcement Lookout Systems, the Customs Law Enforcement Activity

Reporting (CLEAR) System, and an automated index to Customs central enforcement files.

The Treasury Enforcement Communications System

Using TECS, Customs officers have apprehended murderers, smugglers, fugitives, and thieves; they have recovered stolen vehicles, firearms, vessels, and aircraft; and they have unearthed frauds and conspiracies. Operated by U.S. Customs, TECS serves the Bureau of Alcohol, Tobacco and Firearms (ATF) and INTERPOL Washington, and it also supports the Internal Revenue Service (IRS), the Drug Enforcement Administration (DEA), the Coast Guard, the Department of State, and the U.S. Immigration and Naturalization Service (INS).

At the heart of the TECS system is a data base with over 800,000 records. Most of these provide information on known and suspected violators of federal law—businesses as well as individuals—and the vehicles, vessels, and aircraft associated with them. A small percentage give details on lost, stolen, and recovered firearms and explosives. Because TECS contains information on individuals, the system is operated in compliance with the Privacy Act of 1974.

TECS is an invaluable component in the enforcement of federal law. Interfacing with two other law enforcement systems maximize its potential. The first is the National Crime Information Center (NCIC) operated by the Federal Bureau of Investigation (FBI). In the systems are over 6 million records on wanted persons, identifiable stolen or missing property, and criminal histories. These records, entered by enforcement agencies across the country, are all quickly available to TECS users. The strategic location of Customs officers at all ports of entry into the United States provides them a unique opportunity to take advantage of the NCIC data. As a result of TECS-NCIC interaction in fiscal year 1978, Customs officers apprehended 1,386 fugitives wanted by state, local, and federal enforcement agencies.

TECS is also connected with the National Law Enforcement Telecommunications System, Inc. (NLETS), the computerized communications network that connects all states but Hawaii. This link enables TECS users to identify suspected individuals by querying state driver's license and vehicle registration files. NLETS is most important, though, as a near-instantaneous medium of communication with state and local enforcement agencies.

The Data Communications Network

Like NCIC, TECS has a data base. Like NLETS, TECS is a communications network, a large one. The network consists of roughly a thousand terminals hooked up to a modern, large-scale computer in San Diego. The computer has a memory size of three million bytes and almost a billion bytes of disc storage space. Each byte provides storage for one character (for example, the letter *a*).

Attached to the computer are communications lines ranging in speed from 11 to 960 characters per second (110 to 9600 baud), depending on the terminal(s) being connected. There are three main types of TECS terminals: secondary, land border primary, and airport primary. TECS secondary terminals—model 35 teletypewriters or cathode ray tubes (CRTs)—are linked to 110-baud lines. Land border primary terminals—plasma display tubes—also rely on 110-baud lines. Airport primary terminals—CRTs—are normally hooked up to 1200-baud lines. High-speed 2400-baud lines mesh TECS with the NCIC and NLETS computers. Computer programmers at the San Diego Data Center use terminals linked to lines ranging from 2400 to 9600 baud.

At land border primary terminals, only vehicle license plates can be queried. At airport primaries, only names and AIRPORT INTEL, a record with intelligence on smuggling by air passengers, can be queried. Great speed is the advantage of the primary terminals. Within seconds, the TECS user finds out if the person in question is a suspect.

Secondary TECS terminals share a response time of seconds but are much more versatile. Both names and license plate numbers can be queried at secondaries, along with much of the data in Customs central enforcement files. Other queries run the gamut from passport to case number. Records can be entered, modified, or cancelled at secondary terminals.

TECS terminals are located at more than three hundred sites in the United States and several outside the country. Nearly all Customs facilities along the Canadian and Mexican borders, at seaports, and at international airports are equipped with the terminals. Others have been installed in the National Central Bureau of INTERPOL and the headquarters and major field offices of Customs, ATF, and IRS. The Coast Guard currently has one TECS terminal; the State Department, INS, and DEA have several. Outside the continental United States, there are TECS terminals at U.S. Customs stations in San Juan, Puerto Rico, the Virgin Islands, and Honolulu and U.S. Customs preclearance facilities in Montreal, Toronto, Vancouver, Calgary, Winnipeg, Bermuda, and Nassau.

For the exchange of administrative enforcement information, TECS provides a message-switching capability linking all secondary terminals in the system. Messages can be sent instantaneously from one point to another, to a group of terminals, or simultaneously to all secondary TECS terminals. This capability is particularly useful for the broadcast of lookouts on suspected persons, vehicles, and new methods of smuggling.

How the System Began

Inspection facilities at every port of entry into the United States give the Customs Service a unique enforcement opportunity. But the country is too large and transportation too rapid to rely on manual communication of enforcement information. In the fall of 1969, Customs turned to computerization for rapid retrieval of up-to-date suspect data. The Customs Automatic Data Processing Intelligence Network (CADPIN) was born.

In a test phase, CADPIN relied on the California Department of Motor Vehicles computer and consisted of twenty terminals at the port of San Ysidro, California. When the test proved successful, Customs installed its own computer in San Diego. The CADPIN system, modeled on the Michigan State law enforcement system, was implemented in April 1970.

The system initially provided limited information on suspected vehicles and individuals. As terminals were added to Customs facilities along the Mexican border, CADPIN's message-switching feature met Customs need for rapid, simultaneous dissemination of lookout information. By 1972 CADPIN, operating smoothly, included nearly three hundred terminals around the nation. Other Treasury enforcement agencies shared Customs' need for rapid information retrieval and communications. To meet their need without duplicating expenditures, TECS was established in the fall of 1972. It began with the system, equipment, and facility that had been CADPIN's. Its first members were the Customs Service, ATF, and IRS. INTERPOL Washington joined the system in September 1973.

TECS Users

The three primary users of TECS are U.S. Customs, ATF, and the National Central Bureau of INTERPOL.

The U.S. Customs Service

The U.S. Customs Service has the unique mission of collecting import duties; preventing fraud and smuggling; and regulating carriers, individuals, and articles that enter and leave the United States. Because of the Customs presence at all ports of entry into the country, the service has also been charged with the enforcement of hundreds of laws on behalf of other federal agencies. Among them are laws protecting American agriculture, labor, business, public health, and environment.

Customs officers profit from TECS lookout records (perishable information), index records (to case files), and the following special files: the Vessel Violation Profile System (VVPS), the Private Aircraft Inspection Reporting System (PAIRS), the Currency and Monetary Instrument Reporting (CMIR) file, and INTEL. VVPS charts violations (when, where, and mode of concealment, if applicable) and penalties associated with commercial vessels, steamship companies, and vessel masters. PAIRS records list arrivals from foreign soil by private aircraft, valuable information when used in conjunction with TECS records on aircraft involved in suspect activity. PAIRS is not a suspect system; that is, the persons named on PAIRS records are not (necessarily) fugitives or suspected law breakers. CMIR charts compliance with the requirement that anyone taking out or bringing into the U.S. more than $5,000 in currency or bearer monetary instruments must file a report with Customs. CMIR, also, is not a suspect system.

For Customs, TECS provides the latest intelligence on smuggling trends and methods. The basic INTEL query elicits a response with several current intelligence messages. Another INTEL query, activated by key words, such as *cocaine, bomb, fraud, hangers, infant,* or *religious,* brings up-to-date information on the subject queried. A third, AIRPORT INTEL, provides data on smuggling techniques used by airline passengers and can be queried at airport primary terminals.

Queries can be directed to all of these systems. In addition, the TECS computer supports the Telephone Analysis system (TELAN), and the Customs Law Enforcement Activity Reporting (CLEAR) system. TELAN is a computerized program that charts data-participant patterns from subpoenaed telephone toll data. Customs furnishes TELAN services to its own investigators and to those of the Drug Enforcement Administration, the Internal Revenue Service, and the Bureau of Alcohol, Tobacco and Firearms. Investigators involved in conspiracy cases can frequently use toll data from long-distance telephone calls to identify previously unknown participants in a conspiracy, to discover a pattern of activity (such as calls to the same number at certain intervals), to substantiate testimony of an informer, and to provide other avenues for investigation.

The CLEAR system is another primary component of Customs's integrated, computerized information system. It was designed to document Customs enforcement results and pinpoint areas (types of cargo, for example, as well as geographical areas) needing intensified enforcement. This documentation is essential to Customs management, who must regularly justify existing levels of spending or the need for additional funds to the Department of the Treasury and the Office of Management and Budget. CLEAR information is equally important to management from the port to the national level faced with allocation-of-resources decisions.

The CLEAR system has four components: search/arrest/seizure; the investigative program analysis; the theft information system; and the fines, penalties, and forfeitures system. As the name implies, the search/arrest/seizure system furnishes statistics on arrests and seizures from the port to the national level. The source document for this system is also used in a variety of intelligence analyses. The investigative program analysis provides an inventory of investigative cases with statistics on man-hours expended and results (arrests, seizures, and penalties). The theft information system profiles theft from Customs custody—when, where, how and by whom, what, and in what quantity. From it, statistics will be compiled, and Customs will be able to determine where its antitheft efforts should be concentrated. The fines, penalties, and forfeitures system provides violations histories.

The U.S. National Central Bureau of INTERPOL

An international crime-fighting mission is the distinguishing feature of INTERPOL, the International Criminal Police Organization. INTERPOL is not an autonomous police force with search, arrest, and seizure powers. It is an organization of 126 member countries, headquartered near Paris, that is charged with fostering cooperation and communication among law enforcement agencies around the world.

Each INTERPOL member country has a National Central Bureau (NCB) through which the countries exchange information and channel investigative requests. The U.S. National Central Bureau—INTERPOL Washington—is a joint operation of the Departments of Justice and the Treasury.

For its primary constituency—U.S. law enforcement agencies—the U.S. NCB will coordinate criminal investigations in any of the INTERPOL member countries. Among the types of investigations are criminal history checks; license plate and driver's license checks; full investigations leading to arrest and extradition; locates of suspects, fugitives, and witnesses; and weapons and motor vehicle traces.

INTERPOL Washington uses TECS to enter intelligence on U.S. nationals convicted of crimes aboard. The system also serves as an index to case files, as a statistical inventory (for the number of murder cases handled per year, for example), and as a source of investigative leads. TECS-NLETS has proven invaluable for communication with the forty thousand federal, state, and local enforcement agencies in the United States that INTERPOL represents and serves.

The Bureau of Alcohol, Tobacco and Firearms

The Bureau of Alcohol, Tobacco and Firearms (ATF) is responsible for tax collection, industry regulation, and law enforcement in the alcohol, tobacco, firearms, and explosives industries. In line with its duties, ATF has entered into TECS records wanted persons, major criminals; persons granted or denied relief from legal prohibitions denying the right to own firearms or explosives; and lost, stolen and recovered explosives.

TECS is an invaluable communications medium for ATF, a source of investigative leads, and a central repository of investigative records. ATF uses NCIC for entry and retrieval of records on fugitives and firearms. NLETS automates communications with state and local law enforcement agencies; TELAN furnishes investigative leads.

Other Agencies

To promote cooperation, TECS terminals have been furnished to the State Department, IRS, DEA, and the Coast Guard. IRS enters fugitive records, uses the data base as a source of investigative leads, and analyzes CMIR data for applicability to tax investigations. TECS helps the State Department preserve the security of visiting diplomats. The Drug Enforcement Administration uses TECS to enter and retrieve information on narcotics suspects. Records on aliens not admissible to the U.S. are the most important TECS feature for Immigration and Naturalization Service officers.

On the high seas and in U.S. waters, the U.S. Coast Guard is responsible for enforcing all federal laws. TECS is a major source of intelligence on vessels engaged in drug smuggling.

TECS Uses

When speed is important, TECS is particularly useful. The police in Niagara Falls recently called the U.S. port of entry twenty miles north, requesting a lookout for three men who had just robbed a liquor store. Entry of a TECS lookout record was completed at 6:46 P.M. Just six minutes later, an Immigration and Naturalization Service inspector querying TECS got an affirmative response, which led to the arrest of all three suspects.

Distance is unimportant to the system. Customs inspectors in Blaine, Washington, have gotten positive results on records entered at Niagara Falls, New York; inspectors in El Paso have been alerted to violations by TECS records entered in Sumas, Washington. INTERPOL data from all over the world have been put into TECS. Customs in Norfolk discovered a hundred pounds of hashish, with a street value of over $4 million, as a result of INTERPOL information on a drug conviction in Morocco. In another cases, Customs in Chicago found $107,000 in unreported checks; TECS had revealed that the subject was of interest to the IRS.

Smugglers of heroin, cocaine, amphetamines, and marijuana have been captured with the help of TECS. Frequent input of information from the Drug Enforcement Administration makes TECS particularly valuable as a drug suspect detection system. Stolen aircraft, firearms, and vehicles have been identified through TECS, and recovered.

No one would deny that crime is a problem today, one that keeps increasing dramatically. Criminals are better armed—with firearms, radios, and other technology—and are more mobile. To counter their threat, law enforcement agencies have turned to computerized communications systems such as TECS. TECS will never replace the skill or judgment of experienced law enforcement officers. It can enhance their efforts.

17

VICTOR J. YANNACONE, JR.

The Electronic Barrister: Applications in Environmental Law

With the increasing tide of consumerism, there is significant public demand for objective measures of the performance of lawyers in addition to whether or not a particular case has been won or lost. Now that consumers have become increasingly vocal in complaining about services rendered by lawyers, many thoughtful citizens have challenged the raison d'être of the legal profession and attacked the judicial system for ignoring advances in science, engineering, and technology. The legal literature now contains articles by consultants clamoring for the opportunity to apply the methods and technology of computer science to the practice of law.

Litigation

It appears that in matters of public controversy, such as evaluation of the benefit/risk-cost/benefit relationships affecting continued use of certain environmental toxicants, allocation of limited natural resources, and the cost-effectiveness of public projects and certain administrative agency actions, litigation will furnish an increasingly effective and sophisticated means for delineation of issues and reduction of the data base prior to ultimate consideration by legislative bodies and regulatory agencies.

Litigation is essentially a dialectic process. In a criminal or quasi-criminal proceeding, the party charging that a crime has been committed (usually the People of the United States or the People of an individual state, acting as the sovereign) has the burden of proving that all of the elements of the crime have been committed by the party charged and that burden must be sustained by presenting evidence sufficient to establish "proof" beyond all reasonable doubt. In civil actions, or in the general run of administrative agency proceedings, the burden is on the parties seeking relief to establish their right to the relief sought by a fair preponderance of the substantial credible evidence.

One of the distinguishing characteristics of litigation in Anglo-American jurisdictions is the adversary nature of the process, which generally commences with service of a document setting forth a claim of right and seeking some legal remedy and concludes with a trial.

A trial is conducted in an essentially linear fashion. The party with the burden of proof generally presents, through the testimony of witnesses, data or other demonstrable evidence supporting the allegations of a complaint or petition. The representative of the adverse party then tests the testimony or evidence offered against three criteria:

1. Is the testimony or evidence relevant to the subject matter of the litigation?
2. Is the testimony or evidence a material contribution toward satisfying the burden of proof?
3. Is the witness competent to present the testimony or qualified to introduce the evidence?

Following the dialectic of direct and cross-examination by the advocates representing the adverse parties, the court rules, or in some cases the jury finds, for one party or another solely on the basis of that evidence offered that was deemed admissible: that is, relevant and material and presented by a competent witness.

The conclusion of any trial on the merits, as distinguished from a trial resolved on a procedural point of law, leaves a substantial body of well-edited and carefully tested information, which represents an often-overlooked source of thoroughly processed information.[1] Unfortunately, unless access to the data base developed during such litigation is improved, much of its value and utility will be lost.

Information from Litigation: the Example of Environmental Law

If information, by definition, includes only useful data, criteria for evaluating raw data must be either derived *a priori* from eternal truths or established *a posteriori* as a means of imposing order upon the random data accumulated by mankind. However, since information is only useful data, data-base management must begin with some kind of criteria for evaluating the data in the data base. Fortunately, the law of evidence, evolving as it did from the collective wisdom of human experience from the time trial in the courtroom replaced trial by combat, provides the following basic criteria for screening any mass of data: Are the data relevant? Are the data material? Is the source of the data competent?

Relevance depends in large measure upon the use to which the data are put and although the data base can be general and nonspecific, useful data—information—must be relevant to a specific concern of the data user, a particular issue that must be resolved. Materiality is a much subtler concept in the law of evidence and requires a determination of whether data that are otherwise relevant serve any useful purpose. Determining competence goes to the fundamental problem of evaluating the source of the data. In a courtroom, the process of *voir dire* tests the credentials of the author of any data through the dialectic of both direct examination by the party presenting the data and cross-examination by the adverse party.[2]

A great deal of data has been gathered, generated, and accumulated on environmental matters since the National Environmental Policy Act of 1969 (NEPA) took effect at the beginning of the 1970s.[3] Some of the data are irrelevant to all but the most esoteric concerns. Even when the data are relevant and material, the nuggets of information are often imbedded in a rich vein of trivia and misstatement.

To the legislator, lawyer, litigator, or other concerned citizen who needs environmental information, the answers to certain fundamental questions are crucial: Am I getting the information I want, as early as I need it, and without any misinformation? Am I paying as low a price as possible in the time required to consider and use the information as well as the actual cash cost of obtaining the information I need? Unfortunately, for most of those concerned with environmental matters the answer to both questions is probably no.[4]

One of the most obvious results of the environmental movement has been to demonstrate the enormous quantity of environmental information that exists and the continued proliferation of private and public processes that contribute to the generation of more environmental data, often without recognition of the inherently multidisciplinary rather than merely interdisciplinary nature of environmental law and environmental science.

One of the principal causes for the difficulty in obtaining, much less processing, environmental information from the data base is semantic. Although the dictionary definition of the word environment seems clear enough—"The aggregate of surrounding things, conditions, or influences, especially as affecting the existence or development of someone or something"—the definition that is of interest to those concerned with environmental law, environmental legislation, environmental litigation,[5] and environmental planning,[6] is more appropriately that which was developed by environmental systems scientists[7] and tested in the courtrooms since 1966.

Environment is that single word that represents the complex system established by the union (in the algebraic sense) of the set of resources—natural, social, societal, and economic—that exist in a region, together with the set of all the interactions among those resources and the natural, social, societal, and economic processes operative within the region of concern, or upon the resources of that region.

Generally five major subsets of the environment are recognized for ease in the classification of data: the physical (abiotic) environment; the natural (biotic) environment, which includes plants and animals other than humans; the human or social environment; the societal or institutional environment; and the economic environment.

Just as it is essentially impossible to practice environmental law without a substantial background in environmental science, it is equally futile to attempt to organize environmental science, or more particularly, classify the body of environmental information without a considered awareness of the concerns of society which demand the legal regulation of activities having environmental impact.

The Law as an Intellectual Discipline

One of the most significant areas of confusion limiting mutual understanding among those who practice law and those who process data is attributable to lack of precision in describing and defining the data base in the law. The misunderstandings are most obvious and costly particularly in those applications where legal research and the data base management on which it depends must be tested continuously during the course of real time litigation in the courtroom.

Litigation is the ultimate test of the effectiveness of legal research and data base management, but most computer-managed or computerized litigation support services are directed toward pretrial proceedings, such as depositions rather than actual trials, so that many of the existing applications of computer science to the law turn out to have illusory benefits at best. Litigation is civilization's alternative to revolution. The results of litigation determine whether legal research is correct, however the law considers correct in the pragmatic sense of persuasive.

One of the first steps in the process of mutual education of lawyers and computer scientists is to recognize that the law is a composite domain involving at least two distinctly different intellectual activities: (1) The acquisition, logical organization and literate presentation of information about particular matters; and (2) The analysis of that information in order to establish a publicly acceptable standard of conduct or alternatively to persuade, *ex post facto,* some arbiter—be it legislature, court, executive officer, administrative tribunal, or jury—that one particular course of conduct or one particular adjudication is more probably correct (and thereby socially acceptable) than others.

The first activity is called by many names: research, counseling, legal draftsmanship, legal writing, or just legal advice; the second is generally referred to as litigation.

Although each of the major areas within the entire domain of the law may be involved in adjudication of a controversy, there are dramatic differences in the content of each legal activity or operation. The place of computer science as a means of improving the administration of justice differs in the context of each legal operation.

Continued failure to consider the legal process as a system and the adjudicatory procedures for resolving disputes in terms of their systems characteristics has left the law to flounder outside the evolutionary mainstream of technology. The legal profession must widen the present narrow path that impedes its communication with computer scientists. It is up to the lawyers and judges to precisely define and describe the law as a "system" and the laws as the ordering program of civilization. Litigation is the means by which the legal system "debugs" its programs—the laws.

Legal Research

The data base that must be managed during the course of legal research consists of billions of words organized in two major areas: (1) the statutes, rules, and regulations that have been promulgated by legislative and executive order for the purpose of prospectively guiding human conduct; and (2) the common law which includes all the judicial and quasi-judicial adjudications of specific controversies between individual parties, the substance of which guides the retrospective determination of rights and liabilities based on facts that have already occurred or are presumed to be occurring or inevitably to occur as the result of existing circumstances in the light of the history of those circumstances.

The value of the common law rests on the principle of *stare decisis* which provides reasonable assurance that similar circumstances will lead to similar judicial determinations of the respective rights and liabilities of the parties.[8]

This enormous number of English words (estimated on the order of 10^{12}) distributed throughout thousands of independent volumes in hundreds of organized systems must be subject to both random access search and structured hierarchical search through indexes and annotated classification lists—all within a reasonable time and at reasonable cost.

Once the entire data base of the law has been searched with reference to a particular case or controversy and all of the materials which seem to be relevant have been assembled, the relations of all the elements of the data base—statutes, regulations, orders, judicial and administrative decisions—

to each other and among themselves must be determined. These relations must then be analyzed in light of the position to be advanced by the party performing the research effort and a comprehensive "rule" derived which can be supported by specific reference to the appropriate items drawn from the data base, whether statutes, regulations, executive orders, or "cases."

The ultimate test of whether the analysis is correct is whether in a particular case or controversy the judicial or executive authority accepts the rationale as the basis for the relief demanded.

Methods of Research

Within the Anglo-American system of jurisprudence, the bulk of the substantive law, (the area of the law not concerned with procedure) is contained in chronologically ordered, serially published reports of judicial opinions generally grouped for the purpose of bookbinding according to the individual court or judicial jurisdictional unit which renders the decision. The entire set of these published judicial opinions and decisions makes up the body of what is traditionally referred to as the common law. Over the last one hundred years several attempts have been made by private publishers and government agencies to index and abstract these decisions, and since great weight is placed upon the doctrine of *stare decisis* within the Anglo-American system of jurisprudence, the need to locate a particular precedent becomes more important and more difficult as the elements of the set of all judicial opinions and decisions increase in number.

The generally accepted indexing and abstracting services utilized by the legal profession to search the vast body of common law have been the results of the efforts of private enterprise and range from the straightforward Shepard's Citations through the Key Number System of the West Publishing Company and the Total Client Service Library of the Lawyers Cooperative Publishing Company.

Shepard's Citations system is a single source for ascertaining the history and present status of particular statutes or cases—federal, state, and local—and, to an increasing extent, administrative law materials. The method is to trace the history in the courts of all reported cases, of the various kinds of statutory materials, and of the decisions or orders of selected administrative agencies. With respect to statutes and administrative decisions, developments through subsequent legislative or administrative action are considered in addition to relevant case law.

The citations consist of tabular listings of references that indicate: (1) with respect to cases, all reported opinions involved in or connected with the case itself as it went through the litigation process; every subsequent case that has specifically referred to it in any way whatsoever; and to an increasing extent other basic sources of reference such as American Law Reports, attorney general opinions, and law review commentary; (2) with respect to statutory materials, subsequent amendments, or other legislative action, as well as case law and other sources of reference affecting or illuminating them; and (3) in the case of administrative decisions, subsequent administrative action, as well as case law and related information.

Through the use of special symbols, letters, and numbers, the citations indicate the specific manner in which the case or statute has been cited in later materials and for what purpose.

The basic limitation of the system is that its tables include only references that specifically cite the material being checked. Similarly the indication by a symbol of the matter or basis in and for which the citation was made simply has reference to an *express* statement in this regard in the citing material, and the statement is accepted at its face value. Thus, a later case in the same jurisdiction that overrules or modifies the case cited *sub silentio* (without expressly naming it) would not be indicated, unless the later case happened to be cited. Even then the actual effect might not be indicated. There is also no independent appraisal as to the accuracy of any statements made in the citing opinion with respect to its relationship to or effect upon cited cases. Likewise, a statute or administrative action changing the law as enunciated in a particular case would not be directly reported discovered by the system.

Although Shepard's is the one reference system that must always be consulted before a case or statute can be cited as authority, it must be supplemented by other research if a complete view of the law on a particular point is to be obtained.

The modern classification system for legal digests and encyclopedias is that pioneered in the American Digest with the adoption of the West Publishing Company Key Number System. Under this scheme the entire body of law is classified by reference to more than four hundred topic categories.

A West Digest is in effect a direct index to cases and their holdings summarized in the form of individual brief abstracts or precis of each point, factual and legal. In the American Digest System, the abstracts are originally prepared and printed by the editors of the West Publishing Company as unofficial headnotes to the opinions themselves when they are published in the National Reporter System maintained by the same publisher. Each headnote is given and is itself placed under a subject heading or headings, and also assigned a topical key number or numbers. These headnotes are then collected and arranged in the American Digest System according to subject matter. As a result the American Digest system is a master reference to the case law in this country from 1658 to date.

If during research a case in point is discovered, by noting the key number or numbers under which the particular point or issue is classified, the researcher can immediately check the abstracts of the other cases listed under the same key number in any or all jurisdictions. By conducting a key number search, frequently a researcher can quickly locate controlling case law.

Every ten years, the General Digest volumes for the preceding decade are consolidated into a permanent Decennial Digest. In the event a new topic has had to be created since the preceding Decennial—as was the case with "Workmen's Compensation" in the Fourth Decennial, "Administrative Law and Procedure" in the Fifth, and "Aviation" in the Sixth—the Decennial in which it first appears lists under the new topic headings and subheadings and key numbers all relevant cases covered in previous Decennials. This is also done within the decade between Decennials through the General Digest. The Eleventh General Digest, Third Series added "Zoning" as a new digest topic and the Sixteenth General Digest (1961) added "Trade Regulation."

The Digest System, like the headnotes on which it is based, is not authoritative. The topic classification was developed so long ago that it is a comparatively inefficient data base with respect to many topics of current importance in litigation. It is impossible for editors to identify correctly, to state accurately, and so to include in a digest, all of the legal issues involved in a case, particularly those not specifically identified or accurately summarized by the opinion itself.

Lawyers Cooperative Publishing Company has long specialized in annotated case law service reprints where the annotations in effect represent detailed memoranda of law on the subject matter of the leading case whose opinion is reported in full. The American Law Reports (ALR) are in their third series. Their predecessor, Lawyers Reports Annotated, began in 1888 and ran through three series and 146 volumes until 1918. ALR annotations are generally cross-referenced to the encyclopedic text *American Jurisprudence,* now in its third edition. Together ALR and *American Jurisprudence* most closely approximate the continental legal materials of the last century. They provide a good starting point for researchers and their use reduces considerably the amount of time needed to find the applicable law in many situations. Like all other secondary sources, however, the citations and analysis in the annotations must be verified.

Computers and Lawyers

No single simple cause can be blamed for the lamentable lack of computer sophistication among lawyers. The antipodal differences between research and litigation and between the law as that system that includes both computer science and mathematics are responsible for the many setbacks in the application of computer science to the practice of law. So familiar are lawyers with the distinction between research and litigation that they tend to disregard the importance of the differences when discussing the need for computer assistance. Lawyers often forget the importance of their own contribution to the logic of computer system design for legal applications and become mesmerized by what they do not understand: the hardware and software of the computer industry.

On the other hand, computer scientists or engineers or salespeople are generally unfamiliar with the basic logic and data of legal research or litigation, and can be awed by the mystique associated with the practice of law. They can not really be considered responsible for the difficulty because they are just not aware of much that is important in the legal system as a system. They often provide hardware and software in the hopes that the lawyers or their staff will ignore those elements of the computer system that are inappropriate.

The lawyers are not really responsible either since they have been told that their complex problems can be helped by computers, but they often make the false assumption that once they have hired a computer consultant there is no further need for any input from the legal profession.

During this brief period of collaboration both lawyers and computer scientists engage in the self-delusions that have created the major problems in bringing the fruits of the modern age of electronic data processing to the law. Instead of giving mutual attention to the logic and system of the law and the structure of the legal data base, the collaborators become obsessed with the number-crunching or paper-pushing capability of the hardware. The consequence of this *folie a deux* is a mutual misconception that the main targets of computer-assisted legal practice are word processing and random access Key-Word-In-Context data-base searches.

The Successful Attorney and the Computer

Practicing attorneys are successful in large measure to the extent that they can adapt to significant changes in social, economic, and political conditions. Successful attorneys are capable of planning just far enough ahead to examine and evaluate alternative courses of conduct open to them and their clients before the need to make irrevocable decisions is upon them.

If they are to be successful, attorneys learn how to classify and reclassify information, how to evaluate its reliability, how to move from the concrete to the abstract and back again, how to look at each problem constantly from new directions and how to teach themselves those things of interest to their clients.

The practice of clinical medicine has begun to take advantage of computer science with PROMIS (Problem Oriented Management Information System) and the practice of law is little more than an ancient version of that system. The famous English physician Sir William Osler once said,

> System, or as I shall term it, the virtue of method, is the harness without which only the horses of genius travel.
>
> Take away with you a profound conviction of the value of system in your work.
>
> If you have the good fortune to command . . . , remember one of your chief duties is the tabulation and analyses of carefully recorded experience.[9]

One of the most overlooked elements of legal practice to which the computer can add a new dimension and improve efficiency is the "file." The meaning of the word to lawyers and computer scientists is significantly different, however, and a further source of misunderstanding. In a law office, the file for any given client usually consists of a collection of separate problem- or case-oriented accumulations of documents. The maintenance of those files is the common bond among all the attorneys who may serve a particular client and among all the clients of a particular attorney who may have similar problems. If the records in that file are of poor quality, or if the data contained in the file cannot be retrieved quickly, any group legal practice may be inefficient, and could, even after much effort, deliver significantly less than the best available legal services.

Although word processing equipment has now become an accepted part of the office decor in even the most traditional conservative law firms, the continued lack of consideration of the legal process as a system and the judicial system for the resolution of disputes in terms of systems science has left the legal profession and (because of its monopolistic control of litigation) the public in the backwaters of modern technology. In spite of the proliferation of management consulting firms serving the legal profession and selling the latest in electronic gadgetry, the fundamental contribution of computer science to the legal profession—data-base management—has been ignored.

Lawyers have been slow to emerge from the era of drafting legal documents in longhand, dictating routine correspondence to human stenographers, and relying on scurrying clerks and messengers to transmit information. As recently as 1969, want-ads for legal secretaries included such inducements as electric typewriter and the special classification, IBM-typist.

Not only is there little or no economic incentive for lawyers and legislators to avail themselves of modern information science, there is an overt, although well-concealed animosity toward the scientific method that has become a part of legal education during this century. An illustrious law professor when asked why he had never taken any but the most trivial science courses during his academic career, succinctly revealed this intellectual bias when he replied, "I had better things to do in the afternoon than cut up frogs."

The economics of large law firms are such that there is no financial incentive to improve productivity and efficiency as long as the basic billing unit is time, and the time rates simply increase with the costs of other goods and services. In fact, as far as major litigation is concerned, there is an actual financial disincentive to efficiency and the use of sophisticated data-base management techniques.

Modern litigation conducted by attorneys who are being paid time-based fees for services rather than a contingent or fixed fee is quite similar to "cost-plus" procurement. There is no incentive to proceed more efficiently and minimize costs when the costs are reflected in additional time billable to the client.[10] Only in cases where immediate equitable relief such as injunction is sought and counsel for at least one party to the litigation has a vested interest in minimizing the time spent in litigation and the costs of litigation does the legal profession begin to look toward efficient methods of information processing.

This is not to say that the modern law firm has not discovered data processing—just that data processing is seen by many attorneys as the equivalent of data-base management, and most certainly data processing is not data-base management, unless the data base is nothing more than time and activity records, and the only output of interest is invoices, bills, statements, and checks.

Data and Data-Base Management in Environmental Law

Since litigation is the ultimate means for the resolution of human controversy short of war, revolution, or other violent physical confrontation, the exigencies of the Anglo-American system of adversary jurisprudence are the ultimate determinant and constraint upon the usefulness and value of information processing in matters of environmental concern.

Although the more liberal rules of discovery adopted by most courts have eliminated much of the element of surprise that once made litigation such a "sporting" endeavor, and the courts have defined the elements of proof required by the parties in most litigation, occasions arise during every trial on the merits when additional evidence must be presented to support specific offers of proof that may be required to meet the exigencies of the adversary process but which were not necessarily contemplated by the parties prior to that point in the trial. Even if all of the information contained in the world's libraries were in machine-readable form and accessible to anyone with a computer terminal, accessing the information would still represent a significant problem during active litigation. The need is obvious. It has already been identified.

For example, the data base in environmental law (which includes the products liability aspects of toxic substances) must include the full text of all the laws and regulations, both enacted and pending, at all federal, state and local levels, together with their legislative history, and the opinions of all the courts and administrative agencies, attorneys general, and legal scholars construing, interpreting, and criticizing those laws and regulations. The data base must be maintained in a form subject to search and retrieval at the state-of-the-art level in computer information retrieval technology. To that extent the data base in environmental law is not unlike the data base in any other area of the law, except, however, that the data base in environmental law must also include the relevant scientific information in a form accessible by legislators, regulatory agencies, the bench, the bar, business, industry, and the public.

Over the centuries, libraries and librarians have developed search and access procedures dictated by the exigencies of storing the printed word in bound volumes, periodicals, and other page-limited formats. However, limitations on the size of permanent collections and the need to maintain current information in rapidly emerging disciplines brought us first to the vertical file and then numerous proposals for electronic publishing and editorial processing centers.

There is also a substantial need to protect the diversity of editorial viewpoint represented by private enterprise in the area of environmental information processing and a similar need to encourage the continued concern of public benefit, nonprofit corporations in the area of interdisciplinary cooperation in environmental science. The federal government and to a more limited but nonetheless important extent, state and local governments must be encouraged to improve accessibility to government-generated or government-sponsored data, information, and publications. At the same time we must improve the access of legislators and regulatory agency personnel to available data in the private sector.

It must be assumed now that most printed materials are being created through some form of electronic typesetting and therefore that the information can be accessed by computer. Improvements in optical character recognition have made it possible to convert existing printed works into machine-readable form and permit electronic access to the data. Recently attempts have been made to reduce the data base of the common law—the reported decisions of the courts and other judicial bodies—to machine-readable form and then offer users some form of full-text search and retrieval with human evaluation of key words in context.

Yet before the problems of accessing and retrieving the information contained in the data base that now exists can be addressed, the fundamental problem of data storage must be solved. With the cost of data storage space increasing each year, the problem of storage has become economically significant. Computer-Output-Microfilm (COM) has significantly reduced the problem of storing the enormous output of modern data-processing systems, but in most cases the data being generated by those computer systems are suitable for serial processing in some kind of batch mode rather than random access in real time.

The techniques available to process information from such a data base, however, are little more than the application of electronic brute force that require ever larger central processing units and memories and take ever longer to provide useful information. Serial search of a large data base is inefficient where the probability of the demand for recall of any individual item of data is the same of that of recalling any other item of data. Nevertheless, from the earliest days of judicial reporting, the legal profession has stored its data in chronological order and relied upon indexes, and hierarchic subject matter abstract systems of limited taxonomy to enter this data base and process the useful information it contains.

If information processing and data-base management are ever to attain their full potential in the process of promulgating ecologically sophisticated, environmentally responsible, socially relevant, economically viable, and politically feasible legislation, the information contained in the data base must be accessible to the user in real time, recoverable on demand, and amenable to reformatting. Unless information is readily accessible and easily retrieved, the continuity of human experience will be lost.

Notes

1. Victor John Yannacone, jr., "Environmental Litigation as a Source of Environmental Information," in *Environmental Science,* pp. 124-28; and *National Environmental Information Symposium: An Agenda for Progress,* NTIS: PB-219 071, pp. 340-50.

2. *Voir dire* comes to the Anglo-American adversary system of jurisprudence from the Norman French, and in this sense refers to the preliminary examination of a party called as a witness in order to determine his or her competency to testify about the issues under consideration. The classic example is the case of the Nobel Prize winner in one field who was ruled incompetent to testify as an expert witness in another area. *Voir dire* also refers to the interruption permitted during the testimony of a witness in order to inquire about the source or nature of a document or some other item offered as evidence by or through the witness.

For examples from actual environmental litigation, see: Harmon Henkin, Martin J. Merta, and James Staples, *The Environment, the Establishment and the Law* (Boston: Houghton Mifflin, 1971); Victor John Yannacone, jr., "Environmental Law/Environmental Systems Science: Interaction at the Interface in Litigation and Legislation," in *Environmental Systems Science,* ed. Victor John Yannacone, jr., (Chicago: American Bar Association, 1975), pp. 191-326; Victor John Yannacone, jr., Bernard S. Cohen, and Steven G. Davison, *Environmental Rights and Remedies,* (Rochester: Lawyers Cooperative Publishing Co., 1971).

3. See: Yannacone, Cohen, and Davison, *Environmental Rights and Remedies* vol. 1, sec. 5.5; Victor John Yannacone, jr. and Steven G. Davison, "National Environmental Policy Act of 1969," 1 *Environmental Law* 8-33 (1970); Victor John Yannacone, jr., "The Origins of a National Environmental Policy," in *The Energy Crisis: Danger and Opportunity,* ed. Victor John Yannacone, jr., (St. Paul: West

Publishing Co., 1974), pp. 385-396; Yannacone, Victor John, jr., "Agricultural Lands, Fertile Soils, Popular Sovereignty, The Trust Doctrine, Environmental Impact Assessment and the Natural Law," 51 *North Dakota Law Review* 615, 637-41 (1975); Victor John Yannacone, jr., "Property and Stewardship—Private Property Plus Public Interest Equals Social Property, 23 *South Dakota Law Review* 71, 117-40 (1978).

4. Steven S. Ross, "Sorting It Out—Data vs. Information," in *Environmental Science, Technology, Information Resources,* ed. Sidney B. Tuwiner (Park Ridge, N.J.: Noyes Data Corporation, 1973), p. 35.

5. "Environmental" law and "environmental" litigation became recognized elements of our legal system in the spring of 1966 when a woman in suburban New York brought an action on behalf of all the citizens of Suffolk County, New York, not only of this generation, but of those generations yet unborn, seeking equitable relief from a toxic insult to the community ecosystem. The real defendant in that action was not the local mosquito control commission, which was still routinely using DDT in an attempt to control a mosquito population that had long since become resistant to the chemical, but the broad-spectrum, persistent, chemical biocide, 1,1,1-trichloro-2,2-bis (parachlorophenyl) ethane: DDT itself.

The New York State Supreme Court issued a temporary injunction restraining the county of Suffolk from using DDT for mosquito control on August 15, 1966, (*Carol A. Yannacone, individually and on behalf of all the People of Suffolk County, etc.* v. *Dennison, et al.,* Supreme Court: Suffolk County, NY 139050/1966) and continued this "temporary" injunction until December 6, 1967, finally holding that:

> DDT has, by its inherent chemical stability, become a continuing factor in some ecological life cycles so as to profoundly alter them and the environmental equilibrium. Thus, it is reasonably apparent that DDT is capable of and actually has to some extent caused extraordinary damage to the resources of this county. If in no other way, the chemical by its very stability has introduced an element of instability in the general ecosystem. For instance, by reducing a food source of some of the larger wildlife and so reducing the over-all larger wildlife population, lesser elements multiply more quickly. These lower forms are presumably more of a nuisance, assuming they in turn survive. Furthermore, DDT affects wildlife directly. Its ingestion, from whatever source, has the capability, it seems, to disrupt reproductive processes or even more simply act as a poison. It is fairly apparent then that the application of DDT in Suffolk County has and is continuing to have a demonstrable effect on local wildlife, reducing it slowly but surely, either directly across the board or indirectly from the top down, but reducing it nevertheless.
>
> We have a situation where plaintiff has at least minimally sustained a massive effort to validate the allegation that DDT does in fact do biological harm.
>
> *Yannacone, etc.* v. *Dennison, et al.,* 55 Misc2d 468, 285 NYS2d 476 (1967). See also, *Briefs & Record, The Suffolk County DDT Case,* reproduced and distributed by the National Audubon Society, New York City (1967).

The public interest in environmental litigation is therefore in large measure the direct result of one attorney's answer to a series of rhetorical questions posed on September 30, 1967 at the National Audubon Society Annual Convention.

> What can you do when a municipality decides that the highest and best of a mighty river is the city sewer?
>
> What can you do when government agencies seriously consider drowning the Grand Canyon or much of Central Alaska, or when a combination of government agencies and private

speculators act in concert to destroy the delicate ecological balance of the entire state of Florida?

What can you do when the United States Department of Agriculture publicly states that it does not consider the possible adverse effects of chlorinated hydrocarbon pesticides such as DDT on non-target organisms, but permits them to be sold and used even after their adverse effects become generally known?

What can you do when timber and paper companies cut down entire forests of Redwoods and other exotic species in order to "reforest" the area with faster growing pulpwood trees?

What can you do when real estate speculators insist on dredging estuaries in order to fill marshes or strip the topsoil from irreplaceable prime agricultural land in order to plant houses?

Just what can you do?

The attorney went on to say,

The time has come for you who are committed to the preservation of our environment to . . . enter the courtroom to protect our natural resources. . . .

It is time to assert your basic rights as citizens. Rights guaranteed by the Constitution and derived from Magna Carta. It is time to establish once and for all time that our natural resources are held in trust by each generation for the benefit, use and enjoyment of the next. Today, while there is still time, you must knock on the door of courthouses throughout this nation and seek equitable protection for the environment. You must assert the fundamental doctrine of equity jurisprudence—a doctrine as old as civilization, yet a doctrine as topical as today and as advanced as tomorrow: "So use your own property as not to injure that of another"—in particular that which is the common property of all mankind, the air we breathe and the water we drink. . . .

Experience has shown that litigation seems to be the only civilized way to secure immediate consideration of such basic principles of human rights. Litigation seems to be the only way to focus the attention of our legislators on these basic problems of human existence.

Conservationists! You who would make wise use of our natural resources. Look to the history of the human rights struggle in the American Courts. Look to the success of the American Labor Movement and the surprising corporate survival of General Motors, Chrysler and Ford, in spite of judicial recognition of the rights of the United Auto Workers.

The major social changes which have made the United States of America a finer place in which to live have all had their roots in fundamental constitutional litigation. . . .

Our adversary system of litigation as the means of presenting evidence to the conscience of the community has been the touchstone of Anglo-American jurisprudence since Magna Carta. That adversary system of litigation survives today as the hope of citizens seeking redress of a public wrong.

If you the citizen do not forsake your Courts, they will not forsake you in your hour of need. Thomas Becket and Thomas More are only two of the many who have given their lives that you the citizen may have your day in Court.

Although much has been directed toward serving the needs of legislators, administrative agencies and practitioners in certain areas of environmental law, environmental litigation has been largely overlooked as a primary source of environmental information.

6. In environmental planning and resource management, considerable emphasis is placed on the need to understand the system of interacting elements or component parts of the social, economic, and natural environments. For example, the total effect of siting an industrial plant or an electric generating facility cannot be determined until demographic analysis reveals the extent of associated development that will probably take place and until analysis of the environmental systems demonstrates the extent of the overall impact of the entire development process upon the

natural, social, societal, and economic systems that determine the "environment" of the region.

Environmental systems are composed of many components that interact in a variety of ways. Each biological component of the system is affected by the physical (abiotic) elements of the system, and all of the variables describing elements of environmental systems change not only with respect to time but from place to place. Discrete components interact, and each component of the system affects all of the others.

Viewing an environmental system as an interlocking complex of processes characterized by many reciprocal cause-effect pathways shows that one of the principal attributes of a system is that it can be understood only by considering it as a whole. Environmental systems analysis is a method for studying, or determining, relationships among elements of the interdependent natural, social, societal, and economic systems of a region, which taken together can be considered a set (in the mathematical sense of a collection or aggregation of objects or events) because individually they are involved in a single process or contribute to a single effect, and collectively the extent of their interactions effectively defines a region.

The principal reason for using systems analysis in ecology, economics, and, more recently, the social sciences is the complexity of environmental systems, a complexity originating from a variety of causes: number of variables, number of different types of variables, different levels of organization of systems (populations, communities, trophic levels, cycles), and the nonhomogeneous and non-uniform distribution of system elements throughout time and space. Although systems analysis had its roots in military and industrial operations research, applied mathematics, probability, statistics, computer science, engineering, econometrics, and biometrics, its central concern with optimization brought to ecology and environmental science the whole body of pure and applied mathematical theory related to the maximization and minimization of functions, the mathematics of extrema.

7. See Henkin, Merta, and Staples, *The Environment, the Establishment and the Law.*

8. *Stare decisis* is the doctrine or principle that decisions should stand as precedents for guidance in cases arising in the future, expressed in the strong judicial policy that determination of a point of law by one court will generally be followed by other courts of the same or lower rank in subsequent cases which present the same legal problem, although different parties are involved in the subsequent case. In the language of the United States Supreme Court,

> The great principle, *stare decisis,* so fundamental in our law, and so congenial to liberty, is peculiarly important in popular governments, where the influence of passions is strong, the struggles for power are violent, the fluctuations of party are frequent, and the desire of suppressing opposition, or of gratifying revenge under the forms of law and by the agency of the court, is constant and active.
>
> *Ex parte Bollman,* 4 Cranch (US) 75, 89, 2 LEd 554, 559.

However, the courts have not slavishly adhered to the doctrine no matter how often they seem to rely upon it,

> While even a single adjudication of the court, upon a question properly before it, is not to be questioned or disregarded except for the most cogent reasons, and then only in a case where

it is plain that the judgment was the result of a mistaken view of the condition of the law applicable to the question, the doctrine of *stare decisis* is not without exceptions. It does not apply where it can be shown that the law has been misunderstood or misapplied, or where the former determination is evidently contrary to reason.

Rumsey v. *New York & New England Railway Co.*, 133 NY 79, 30 NE 654.

Although legislative bodies have the power to change old rules of law, and generally American courts respect the doctrine of *stare decisis* and wait for legislative action; nevertheless, the fundamental principle of equity jurisprudence—suffer no wrong without a remedy—imposes a duty upon the courts to bring the law into accord with present-day standards of wisdom and justice. *Funk* v. *United States,* 290 U.S. 371, 382. If the rule were otherwise, we would still be burdened with many of the rules of law that were laid down during the nineteenth century.

9. Sir William Osler, *Aphorisms* from "His Bedside Teachings and Writings," (New York: Henry Schuman, 1950).

10. As recently as the nineteenth century a profession was conceived as an esoteric art practiced by a limited group of individuals, each having a personal professional relationship with a number of separate clients or patients and each collecting their own fees for services rendered. This conception of independent professionals is based on a model of what the nineteenth-century doctor and lawyer were supposed to be. Other than the English barrister and the country doctor, there are very few professionals of this sort left today since any form of group practice limits the essential autonomy of the independent professional practitioner.

In a Securities Exchange Commission report on the *Study and Investigation . . . of Protective and Reorganization Committees,* the broad problem of whether the law firm is a professional organization or a business organization was considered in the context of a study of corporate reorganizations:

. . . Corporate reorganization has long been regarded as one of the most lucrative fields of legal endeavor. . . . In the aggregate, counsel fees frequently constitute the largest single item on the list of reorganization fees.

The size of the lawyers' bill must frequently be astounding to security holders and others. This cannot be taken to mean that their compensation is always excessive. The importance of the role of lawyers in reorganization is difficult to overemphasize. . . . Nevertheless the vice of the situation remains despite persuasive arguments that particular jobs are well done. . . . Part of this unseemly tendency of the financial bar to demand huge fees may be due to the business cast of law practice of that kind. Part may be due to overspecialization in financial centers with large law offices composed of dozens of lawyers, a huge overhead, and consequent artificial standards of the worth of legal services. In other words, organization for the practice of law on the large scale of mass production has contributed to the alleged necessity of computing legal fees on an overhead rather than on a service basis. . . .

From Erwin O. Smigel, *The Wall Street Lawyer* (New York: The Free Press, 1964) p. 309, quoting Robert Aaron Gordon, *Business Leadership in the Large Corporation* (Berkeley and Los Angeles: University of California Press, in cooperation with the Brookings Institution, 1961), pp. 259-60, quoting the original report, now unavailable.

18

YAACOV CHOUEKA,
AARON M. SCHREIBER, and
MENACHEM SLAE

The Responsa Project: Computerization of Traditional Jewish Case Law*

The problems faced in reestablishing a sovereign state by a people returning to its homeland from an exile of two thousand years are unique in their nature, scope, intensity, and difficulty of solution; indeed the very phenomenon of such a return is unique in the annals of history. The challenges to the physical security of the old-new state, the problems of social integration of a polyglot community containing elements from the Orient and the Occident, the task of creating a viable economy to sustain the population in a largely arid land lacking natural resources, the difficulty of educating a heterogeneous populace in a single federal educational system, the unique program of updating the classical Hebrew language to function as a medium of communication capable of covering the many aspects of modern life—all of these are integral parts of Israel's thirty years of existence as a sovereign state. In this respect, Israel's legal system reflects faithfully (as is the case in fact with any other legal system) the nation's history, cultural setting, and spheres of common life experience.

*The Responsa Project is primarily supported by a grant from the U.S. National Endowments for the Humanities Fund (N.E.H.) to Bar-Ilan University and Yeshiva University. Parts of this report that describe the Responsa Project per se are based on a lecture given by Y. Choueka at the Third International Conference for Computing and the Humanities (ICCH/3) held at Waterloo, Canada, July 1977, an edited version of which will appear in *Computers and the Humanities.* We wish to thank Dr. Sinai Deutsch of the Faculty of Law at Bar-Ilan University, for his helpful suggestions in preparing this report.

Our aim in this chapter is to describe in broad and nontechnical terms a computerized full-text retrieval system for the Rabbinic Responsa legal (case law) literature, which has been operational in Israel since about 1967. This technological tool will be of aid in shaping a legal system that is capable of dealing with all of the complexities of a twentieth-century industrial-economic polity, yet be firmly rooted in the oldest living applied legal tradition obtaining in the Western world, Jewish law.

Jewish Law

Jewish law, which dates from the Bible, is in practice to this very day in various spheres and communities in Israel and throughout the world. The Pentateuch forms the basis of the law. A large body of oral law interpretation is, however, associated with it, eventually summarized in written form in the Talmud (the monumental compendium of Jewish religion, law, philosophy, and ethics, compiled by many generations and finally edited in the fifth century) and subsequent legal literature. The oral law includes various enactments passed by the governing bodies found throughout the thousands of years of Jewish history. Many summarizing codes and digests arose and acquired jurisdiction, each succeeding period basing its studies upon the precedent literature of the previous. This law, the *halachah*, covers all areas of human experience: religious as well as secular, monetary and criminal, philosophical as well as moral-ethical. In it are found elements of reverence of the L—d and respect of one's fellow man, the mundane and the secular, the holy and the sacred, political-social as well as individual one-to-one, I-thou-relationships, the business partnership as well as the family unit. The Jewish communities involved were (and are) Israeli as well as Diaspora, sovereign-federal, regional and city as well as internally autonomous Jewish communities embedded in a non-Jewish local government. The societies were agrarian and primitive, industrial, urban and sophisticated, Oriental and Occidental, highly educated and barely literate. In short, in the thousands of years of the Jewish folk experience, no historical, sociological, or ideological phenomenon is missed; no human life experience is lacking. The amount of life wisdom formalized in the *halachah* is quite unmatched in human history. Indeed, the Jewish law and Jewish religion are scarcely distinguishable.[1]

Modern Israeli Law

Modern Israeli law is composed historically and conceptually of various components and strata, all of which combine to form a system that is often confusing even to the expert. Historically the foundation of modern Israeli law is a body of Islamic-based law, the *Majelle*, created by the Ottoman

Turkish Empire, which governed in the then Turkish province of Palestine toward the end of the last century. The next stratum is one of British law, created by the British mandatory government and the Crown during the British mandate in Palestine (post-World War I through 1948). The last stratum is law created by legislation in the Knesset (the Parliament of Israel) and court decisions issued by the Israeli court system. In 1948, the previous body of Turkish-British law was left intact for the most part as the law of the land; subsequently, quite a few native Israeli laws were enacted. Today, perhaps a majority of substantive law is of native Israeli origin.

Jewish law obtains officially in the form of federal rabbinic courts, which have jurisdiction in matters of personal status (equivalent more or less to the realm of family law). In addition, precedents drawn from any legal system in the world, including Jewish law, can be submitted to the courts, though obviously these precedents are not binding. Traditionally Israeli courts have had a British Common-Law bias, though lately the trend is to accept arguments based upon European Continental codes or American legal materials.

Time after time the cry has been raised to replace this hodge-podge of heterogeneous and at times conflicting elements with a jurisprudence based upon Jewish law, although this argument has been opposed by some.[7] Besides casting doubts on the possibility, in principle, of using Jewish law as a basis for the legal system of a modern state, some technical difficulties are also raised. For one, Jewish law, viable for so long in the Diaspora, must be updated and written in texts comprehensible to contemporary lawyers, legislators, and judges—couched in terms and concepts obtaining in parallel legal systems. Indeed, most law students are not capable of handling the legal source materials of Jewish law. Summarizing texts are woefully lacking. Equally serious, various primary texts have no systematic indexing system.[3] The Responsa Project was initiated, in fact, to aid in solving some of these problems.

The Responsa Literature

For the past fourteen hundred years, a corpus of common law unique in character has been created by halachic jurisprudence, the Responsa literature. The basic process generating this literature is that of referring a difficult query, in writing, to a local, national, or internationally famous rabbinic court or *halachah* expert, who records his opinion, together with his reasoning and source precedents, in a written reply to the query. These responses to the referrals were collected and published, and the Responsa literature created. The resemblance between the Responsa and the British legal system is apparent; indeed the Responsa can be called the Jewish common law.

About three thousand collections of Responsa have been printed. (This number includes an adjustment for books that are only in part Responsa.) No reliable figures are available for Responsa manuscripts. Thus, it should be understood that these figures are rough estimates; a systematic and up-to-date catalog of this literature has yet to be undertaken. About one thousand authors have contributed to it. The number of Responsa documents contained in this literature (each document usually consisting of a query and the corresponding reply) is roughly estimated to be about a half-million document, but it may be closer to 750,000 documents. Assuming an average of a thousand words per responsum, we arrive at a total number of 500 million to 750 million words of running text. Multiplying these numbers by a factor of 5.6 (4.6 characters and a space per word) gives some estimate of the magnitude of this data base: between 3 billion and 4 billion characters.

The earliest Responsa can be traced to the beginning of the Gaonic period in Babylonia (around the sixth century) soon after the completion of the Talmud, and the latest Responsa book may well be only a few days old. During these fourteen hundred years, Responsa books were almost continuously written, and this activity will certainly continue to accompany the Jewish people in the future.

These texts were penned everywhere in the world that possessed a functioning Jewish community centered around an autonomous, semiautonomous, or advisory rabbinic court or a well-known *halachah* expert. These cases and legal opinions are of unique scholarly value to any researcher working in history, sociology, folklore, or linguistics of the Hebrew language (or of the various vernaculars, such as Yiddish or Ladino, that are found naturally embedded in the Responsa). But obviously the ultimate value of the literature is for students and practitioners of Jewish law.

Rich and interesting as this literature is, it does not have any global index or any manual retrieval system associated with it, or even with any significant part of it. (There do exist, however, a few highly specialized indexes that either refer to a small number of collections, or deal with narrow, clearly defined topics.) Moreover, the printed texts (some of them printed in the sixteenth and seventeenth centuries and never reprinted) are scattered throughout the world, many unavailable to interested scholars.[4] The lack of adequate indexing for this huge body of literature has long rendered their free access impossible to all but the possessor of the most phenomenal memory. What is then desired is a computerized information storage and retrieval system for this rich storehouse of legal materials.

The Responsa Project

The Responsa Project was established to solve this information problem. Our principal aim was to provide professional users with a tool to enable them to retrieve rapidly, easily, and exhaustively all documents relevant to a specific topic of interest without limitations as to the topic of investigation. From the very beginning we followed a full-text storage and retrieval concept. The advantages (and drawbacks) of full-text systems, as against indexing systems, for legal material have been dealt with in the literature. Some of the points are particularly relevant in this context to the Responsa literature. First, the richness and importance of this literature would call for a very exhaustive and diversified indexing that would satisfy the needs of various people—historians, linguists, law scholars, and rabbis, among others—an almost impossible mission. Also, the complexity of the literature, the scarcity of experts that can process it, and the subjective interpretation associated with its understanding, make the indexing process extremely slow and dubious. Finally, furnishing users with a handy printed copy of the retrieval documents would be much welcomed, taking into account the difficulty scholars encounter in finding copies of some of the oldest Responsa volumes and gathering the required documents from so many different sources in one file.

The overall design of the system was guided by a few principles. The first was to build a working retrieval system specially tailored to this unique literature. This aim implies the readiness to deal with all of the intricacies and technical difficulties of the data base. The second was to seek an optimal division of tasks between users and the machine, assigning to each the function that is optimally performed by each. The third was to put emphasis on in-depth research and serious professional use of the system, putting aside ornamental aspects designed to satisfy the layman or the casual user. The final was to strike a right balance between users' service on the one hand and research and development on the other hand—using the operational system as a vehicle for testing the soundness and efficiency of experimental research ideas in this domain.

Actually, the Responsa Project has developed a storage system of converting the full text of Hebrew language books, without any prior indexing, to computerized media—tapes and disks—and a retrieval system of Hebrew language literature searches, based upon the key-words-in-combinations concept.

The first general thoughts about the project began to crystallize in 1965 and 1966, when Professor Aviezri Fraenkel—the founder of the project and its leading figure—set up a committee for mechanization in the research of Hebrew law to discuss the possible implementation of Professor J. Horty's concepts of full-text legal retrieval systems for the Responsa case law.[5] Concrete steps were taken in 1967 when M. Cohen began writing some of the necessary computer programs, and Professor Y. Choueka began investigating the linguistic problems related to the implementation of the full-text concepts to Hebrew data bases. The project was then launched in 1967 as a joint endeavor of the Weizmann Institute of Science (Rehovot) and Bar-Ilan University (Ramat-Gan), both in Israel. During the following years, the project's activities gradually were transferred to Bar-Ilan University. Since 1974 the project has been formally housed at the university's Institute for Information Retrieval and Computational Linguistics (IRCOL), though some of the research in information retrieval techniques is still carried on jointly with the Weizmann Institute.

The project was funded during its early stages by the National Bureau of Standards (U.S.A.) and the Institute for Research in Jewish Law of the Hebrew University in Jerusalem. Subsequently grants were received from the Israel National Council for Research and Development, the National Academy of Sciences (Israel), IBM (Israel), and the Research Fund of the Israeli Association of Insurance Companies. Since 1971, the project has been supported mainly by a substantial grant from the U.S. National Endowments for the Humanities.

For hardware, since 1970 the project has used Bar-Ilan University's computer facilities. They consisted originally of an IBM 360/50 computer with 256K bytes of memory, and since 1974, a large IBM 370/168 computer with 2000K bytes of memory.

Operational Status: Data Base and Queries

In 1968 the data base consisted of one collection of Responsa: the Responsa of Rivash (an acronym of *R*abbi *I*saac *b*ar *S*heshet Perfet, one of the greatest Jewish authorities of the fourteenth century in Spain and Algiers), containing 518 documents and about a half-million words. It took about one year to place this book on the computer. Subsequently, however, the data base grew considerably during a rather short period of time (subject, of course, to budget limitations). By spring 1979 the data base consisted of 128 books, containing 31,000 documents, 28 million words of running text, and about 140 million characters. These break down by period and area as follows:

1. Twelfth to sixteenth century: texts from Provence, Spain, Algeria, France, Germany, Austria, and Italy.
2. Sixteenth century: texts from Egypt, Israel, Turkey, Poland and Italy.
3. Seventeenth through nineteenth century: texts from Israel, Russia, Germany, Hungary, Poland, Lithuania, Galicia (Poland), and Israel.
4. Twentieth century: texts from Israel, Germany, the United States, Switzerland, and Egypt.

The computerized collection thus spans eight hundred years and covers the most varied cultural and socioeconomical conditions. The oldest collection on the computer is that of Ravad (*R*abbi *A*vraham *b*en *D*avid from

Posquiers, Provence, c. 1125-1198), and the latest one is by Rabbi Ovadia Yossef (the present Chief Rabbi of Israel), which appeared in print in 1976.

Enlarging the data base goes on simultaneously with the search program. Hopefully, as of summer 1980, the data base will contain about 150 collections containing some 46,000 documents, numbering c. 42 million words.

More than eight hundred queries have been run on this data base. This number might seem surprisingly low, especially relative to similar full-text legal information projects. However, these queries usually represent an in-depth scholarly research task. The breadth and scope of the data base, both in time and geographical horizons, are such that analyzing the search's output is usually for the purpose of writing a professional publication utilizing the research finds. The very specialized nature of the data base also limits a priori the spectrum of its potential users. Most of the queries have been submitted by university scholars, usually experts (or students) in law, history, or linguistics (and occasionally in other fields, including sociology, psychology, and economics); by rabbis and rabbinical courts (both in Israel and abroad); by libraries, information centers, encyclopedia staffs; and by graduate students doing research in Judaica. Lately queries by lawyers and judges are a constant feature (examples of which appear in a later section).

Testing the System

As soon as the first version of the mechanized retrieval system became operative, an experiment was conducted for testing its basic approach and evaluating its actual performance. A carefully chosen group of queries was run on the system and simultaneously was independently processed manually by a group of outside experts. The results were subsequently analyzed in depth. Some highlights of the experiment deserve special mention and are described below.

The test consisted of some one hundred queries (as opposed to the usual range of twenty to forty, which is quite typical in such experiments), run on an experimental data base of five collections (twenty-five hundred documents, one million three hundred thousand words). Most of the queries were in Hebrew law, a few in history, and almost all were concerned with specific, well-defined topics. The queries were submitted and precisely formulated by outside experts (most of them from the Institute for Research in Jewish Law at the Hebrew University, Jerusalem). The exact scopes of the queries were very clearly delineated beforehand. The issues were clarified in a series of meetings between the query-submitting team and the project's staff, who were familiar with this literature and could foresee—and decide about—possible marginal topics of relevance. Finally, the project's team was banned from the use of the data base Responsa books. The control group of experts who was to search manually for these queries was allowed free use of all available tools and techniques, including the full reading of the data base, which they did. These conditions work against the mechanized system and do not reflect the usual working conditions of the search, since a given scholar will never read entire books of Responsa in order to retrieve relevant documents (certainly not the present data base of 128 books) and since running the query on the computer usually does include a preliminary phase of browsing in appropriate reference books and in the Responsa collections themselves for identifying relevant keywords and expressions, citations, quotations, and references. Some examples of the test queries are as follows: Can a widow marry the very same witness who testified to her husband's death? Is the claim of a woman that her husband is incapable of consummating the marriage sufficient grounds for forcing her husband to divorce her? Is a lessee entitled to sublet the leased property (no stipulation has been made in the contract)? Does a workers' union have the right to strike, when an arbitration apparatus exists to which they refuse to submit, and the goods involved are liable to perish? Could historical sociological material on indigenous Jewish communities in Algeria in the fifteenth century be found by the computer?

The computerized search gave an average recall of 98 percent of all available relevant material; the manual group retrieved only 78 percent of the relevant material. The fact that experts' reading of the entire data base retrieved only 78 percent of the relevant material seems rather surprising. The reason is that theorizing in this subject tends to conceptualize an ideal human researcher, indefatigable, consistent, always alert, and with unlimited patience and understanding. But the reality is, unfortunately, often the opposite.

General Description of the System

The Responsa Project was envisaged from inception as a batch processing system acting in a user's service center. The user submits a query in a natural language form, without restrictions. The query is analyzed by the project's search staff (experts in Judaica and the Responsa literature who have a good working knowledge of the overall design of the computer programming system), ideally and most frequently with the active cooperation of the user. The query is then framed and submitted to the computer in an appropriate technical format. In order to define a search for a certain topic adequately, one should have at the very least some basic knowledge in the field. The more knowledgeable one is in a given search topic, the better the search frame, and in general, the better the quality of the search results. The results, then, are a product of man-machine interaction, a partnership where each contributes his unique capabilities: the user's—his knowledge and the machine's—its data-processing abilities.

The Responsa Project's system, based upon a no-indexing full-text concept, passes the full brunt of the data location to the search rather than using prior manual editing of the material before computerizing it in the data base. A search on a nonindexed, full-text data base requires a characterization of a given search topic by various single words and multiword combinations that are likely to be used by the author in a passage relevant to the given search topic. For example, were we to search for information on income tax on property belonging to charitable organizations, we might ask the computer to list all documents containing all or part of the following: *income tax, charitable organizations, property, real estate,* and *buildings.* A truly comprehensive list might also include *religious organizations, orphanages, taxation,* and others. Phrases and idioms can also be searched.

This mechanical keyword system allows searching for citation references—*Federal Statutes 14:33:2,* for example, as well as text quotations and legal principles—*the common good* and *possession is nine-tenths of the law,* for example. Computer commands, commonly called *operators,* are used in the search for the creation of the keyword phrases. These are both metrical (distance) and Boolean (logical) conditions, imposed to locate the co-occurrence of some of the expressions in a given document. Thus one might require that expression A (perhaps *charitable organization*) co-occur with expression B (*property*) in the same sentence (or paragraph or document), or that expression C occur within *n* words (or sentences or paragraphs) before (or after) expression D. Also one might stipulate that the document be retrieved only if at least *k* (for example, 3 out of 5) of the previously defined conditions are satisfied, and so on.

Since the mechanism of full-text retrieval systems is by now quite well-known, herein we will concentrate on some of the more distinctive features of the Responsa system. (For more information on these and related topics, see the Annotated Bibliography.)

Unlike some of the similar ongoing systems in the United States and elsewhere, the project's natural sentence and paragraph units in the original texts have been maintained (with a few minor exceptions) in the computerized data-base file for retrieval purposes, not merely for display purposes. This, together with a particularly rich repertoire of operators, allows users to frame queries in a form closely resembling the presumed natural language structure of the topic in the literature.

Because Hebrew is a language rich in inflection and derivation patterns the number of grammatical variants of a single keyword can easily reach the thousands; conjugating some verbs can generate up to twenty thousand legitimate grammatical variants, all of which can potentially occur in the data base. This state of affairs called for a unique automatic linguistic program, capable of supplying users with all grammatical variants associated with the given keywords that actually occur in the text, once a standard form of these keywords has been submitted to the computer. Such a tool has been created and incorporated as a standard part of the operational search procedure. (The Bibliography provides further references on this topic.)

Some special tools are available to help users avoid ambiguous keywords or nonrelevant expressions or to bring to their attention some recurrent expressions that might help in framing the query. For example, a user can ask for a list of all different two-word expressions that contain a specific keyword, with relevant statistics.

Some local feedback techniques have been successfully tried to enhance the system's performance. In this type of search system, an initial search is run, the searcher audits the output, labels the relevant documents returned, and feeds this information back to the system. The computer automatically examines the search relevant-return and suggests new single keywords and keyword expressions that the user might have been missed initially. This option is used for especially complex and ill-defined topics.

The output is given to users in a variety of different formats in order to enable them to locate the relevant document quickly and easily. The most useful of these is the KWIC (Key-Words-In-Context) printout. In this printout format, all of the documents containing the keyword combinations are listed, together with a series of short lines-of-quote, that is the immediate context of material surrounding the keyword to its left and to its right in the text. For our example of "income tax on charitable institutions," we might receive a printout as shown in Table 6. This list shows that numbers 1 and 4 are not relevant, 2 and 3 are clearly relevant, and 5 is indeterminate though interesting (reference to the full text is necessary). A quick, vertical scanning of the printout usually furnishes the user with a document list of sources of interest.

The KWIC printout is conditional; not all of the keywords' occurrences in the retrieved documents are printed (with their context), but only those text occurrences that satisfy the imposed conditions. The KWIC can be sorted chronologically (by author or volume, for example), alphabetically (by keyword), or by decreasing document weight (the number of different conditions satisfied by the document). Together with the KWIC printout, several compact lists of all retrieved documents, sorted by the number of conditions or the type of condition satisfied by the documents, are given. By skimming through the KWIC and cross-checking with these lists, the user can usually ascertain quickly the relevance of the retrieved documents.

Although immediate response is not a basic requirement of the system, and most users would be quite satisfied with one or (at most) a few days delay, an online facility can nevertheless greatly enhance the system's performance by allowing the user to browse through the data base and to frame a query in a conversational mode and by a trial-and-error process.

TABLE 6 Example of KWIC Printout

Document #		
1. 143:3:7	As the income	TAX on private income is to be.....
2. 23:1:3	No income	TAX is to be laid on denominational hospitals ....
3. 37:1:4	Release from income	TAX on houses of worship.........
4. 144:3:3	Income	TAX on public officials ....
5. 203:3:7	Release from income	TAX is to be considered ....

The prime obstacle to an online mode was the fact that the system's linguistic component was not easily convertible to online processing because of its demands of large amounts of computer memory and time. New software tools had to be created for this. In spring 1977, we began building the online version of the system, so that at present this version is still in its infancy; nevertheless it is quite impressive to users, and experience has shown that the system becomes desirable and usable for large circles of users, when even simple online components are employed. Basically three features are already operational:

1. Library: The user asks for the display of any document (or any part thereof, such as a paragraph or a sentence) while supplying the request (for author or volume, for example), in a more-or-less natural language form in Hebrew. The response is immediate (less than a second), and the user can randomly skip from author to author, from one document or paragraph to another, and so forth.
2. Dictionary: The user receives a display of a page of the dictionary of the data base (with statistics) that begins with the letter combination specified by the user. At will, the user can get a dictionary page of all of the words in the data base that end with a given letter combination. This method is especially useful for Hebrew because of the possibility of adding prepositional prefixes (such as *and, the, for,*) to the word.
3. Expression search: The user gives an expression and receives as display a full KWIC of the occurrences of this expression in the data base (with or without references). If the number of occurrences is too large, the user can ask for a specified number of randomly chosen samples, sampled over the whole data base. Upon pressing on a KWIC line with a light pen, the user can get a specified context of this line (two sentences before and two sentences after, or the whole paragraph), and from this can switch back to the original KWIC display or to the library or dictionary function. Alternatively the user can ask for a KWIC of sentences rather than a line KWIC. A hard-copy print option is available.

Part of the new linguistic component is also operative, allowing morphological and statistical analysis of keyword variants.

A Sample Search Frame*

The topic is *recovery of expenditures in breach of promise:* Is one who breaches a promise to marry liable for the expenditures made by the fiancé(e)? Two distinct types of recoveries are considered: gifts of property from one party to the other and purely monetary expenses incurred in the performance of those acts demanded by custom, such as festive meals, monetary gifts to servants, contributions to charity, and travel expenses for visiting. The legal question dealt with in the first category is usually ownership of the property (return of the gift), whereas the second, since it deals with repayment of funds spent, is part of the law of torts—more precisely, indirect damage, because the defendant committed no direct physical act of injury. Indeed the damage was committed by the injured party upon himself. In the relevant legal literature, as in life, both problems are usually intertwined.

The primary source for the legal discussion of the expenses' topic is a case found in the well-known *Code of Maimonides* (eleventh century; *Zechiah U'Matanah* 6:24), where the groom-to-be made the customary party for his friends and distributed gifts, and the bride-to-be then broke the engagement. Maimonides, following precedent, finds against the bride in such cases and requires repayment of all expenses. Ravad, Maimonides' arch critic, disagrees, basing his stance upon a Talmudic decision wherein one who sells defective seed is liable only for the cost of the seed, but not for the expenses incurred by the buyer in unsuccessfully planting such seed. Thus we see—maintains Ravad—that if the immediate act of injury is performed by the plaintiff himself, but not by the original causer of the loss, the indirect act of damage involved cannot generate liability. The commentators to Maimonides' Code explain Maimonides' position as one differentiating between an act of business, such as the seed transaction, and an act dictated by local custom, as in the case of engagement. In the latter, one is liable even for what would normally be considered an indirect cause of damages. The later codes side with Maimonides, and such is the accepted practice in the courts (see *Shulchan Aruch, Even HaEzer,* section 50, paragraph 3, and *Aruch HaShulchan, loc. cit.*)[6]

The list of keywords and keyphrases (translated into English) in Table 7 can be used in the mechanized search. Thus, a search frame created for the specific search topic under study is capable of including all accepted means of data location—source citations, legal concepts and maxims, and keywords—in one search frame.

*Adapted from Y. Choueka, M. Cohen, J. Dueck, A. S. Fraenkel, and M. Slae, "Full-text Document Retrieval: Hebrew Legal Texts," in *Proceedings of the Association of Computing Machinery Symposium on Information Storage and Retrieval,* eds., J. Minker and S. Rosenfeld (College Park: University of Maryland, April 1971).

TABLE 7 List of Keywords and Keyphrases for Search

Keyword Combination	*Explanation*
1. (Tractate) *Baba Batra,* (Folio #) 92	Talmudic source germane to our topic
2. (vegetable) seeds	Subject of discussion in the text of the above Talmudic cite
3. *Code of Maimonides, Zechiah U'Matanah,* chapter 6.	Reference to code dealing with the problem
4. (Prevalent) custom, feast, breach, cause (of damage)	Terms used by Maimonides
5. *Even HaEzer* (Sect.) 50	Reference to later code
6. (Marriage) agreement, gifts, expenditures, indirect cause	Other terms germane to the topic, taken from the literature

Source: Adapted from Y. Choueka, M. Cohen, J. Dueck, A. S. Fraenkel, and M. Slae, "Full-text Document Retrieval: Hebrew Legal Texts," in *Proceedings of the Association of Computing Machinery Symposium on Information Storage and Retrieval,* eds., J. Minker and S. Rosenfeld (College Park: University of Maryland, April 1971), p. 74. Reprinted in Y. Choueka, M. Slae, S. Spero, "The Responsa Project—Revisited," in *Proceedings of the Association of Orthodox Jewish Scientists* (A.O.J.S.), no. 5 (Jerusalem and New York: Feldheim Publishing, 1978).

Examples of Legal Search Topics

During its existence, the project staff has searched for hundreds of legal topics of interest, many included in a new program started at the beginning of 1978 when a service for lawyers and court judges was inaugurated, in cooperation with and subsidized by the Israel Bar Association. We will illustrate some of the legal topics searched and some of the subsequent relevant documents retrieved.

Majority Rule

Does a communal minority have the right to refuse to accept a priori a communal enactment passed by the majority? A much-debated question in the philosophy of government throughout the ages is the right of the minority to refuse to submit to the rule of the majority when it is against the interests of the minority. Indeed, the American Civil War was fought over such an issue. The Jewish community faced this problem often, and numerous decisions, the results of appeals to the outstanding rabbinic authorities of the generation to put an end to communal majority-minority discord, are recorded. Usually, but not always, these stemmed from the taxation policies of the community. Their decisions, though not of an official nature, were usually accepted as binding on the parties and would resolve the disputes and bring communal harmony, if not good feelings. The remarkable power wielded by the *gedolei ha-dor,* the outstanding rabbinic authorities in each generation, usually operating without a formal investment of powers of appellate judicial jurisdiction in communal litigation, was a prime factor in the successful community life found in the Jewish Diapora and, of course, created the Responsa literature. Note that the membership in the Jewish community and its attendant duties was usually volitional.

A sample responsum is found in the collection of Rashba (an acronym of *R*abbi *Sh*lomo *b*en *A*dret, a thirteenth-century halachic authority of Barcelona, Spain; vol. 5, number 242). The community enacted a prohibition against concubinage. Reuben (John Doe) is living with a former non-Jewish concubine, whom he converted to Judaism. He claims that he had formally proclaimed in front of witnesses, before the communal enactment, that he would not be a party to such an enactment; it would not be binding upon him. Is such a disclaimer valid? No. Rashba found that majority rule is a time-honored halachic principle. Commenting on the verse in Malachi (3:9), "You are cursed with the curse, yet you rob Me—the whole nation," (after the J.P.S. translation), the Talmud (*Avodah Zara* 36b) takes this verse to refer to communal enactments enacted with the curse of the ban, promulgated by the "whole nation" (that is, a majority according to Rashi *loc. cit.*). Thus, rules Rashba, even if Reuben has issued a disclaimer, the community has the right to pass and enforce legislation against the will of the minority. Reuben must either marry his concubine or remove her from his domicile.

Primarily, the operatives that guided the decisions were as follows:

1. The majority has no legal right to commit an act of theft upon an individual(s) through legislative enactments. Any law that is clearly against the tenets of justice as codified in Jewish law sources or is against common sense is not binding on the minority, who could appeal the given law to the *gedolei ha-dor,* who could cancel it.
2. On the other hand, practice in communal legislation granted the community the right to legislate, even against the interests of the minority.

Does not the second point contradict the first? No, says Rabbi Moseh Isserles (Rema, Poland, sixteenth century), famed codifier of Ashkenazic Jewry. In his responsa collection (number 73), he formulated the resolution of the apparent contradiction. Certain basic rights and legal norms are prescribed by Jewish law for the community in order to regulate the various facets of economic and social life. Those norms and powers, expressly laid down in the Talmud and codes, are standard. Under nonstandard local conditions, the community can enact special legislation that deviates from the legal norms of Talmudic law (*hora'at sha'ah*), even for a long-term period. In any such deviation, minority rights must be respected, and in such a case if a minority feels wronged, they may appeal for abolition of legislation. Thus, for example, any deviation from the taxation practice found in the Talmud requires the assent of the minority present at time of enactment (the problem of a newcomer to the community is of a different consideration). Indeed, many decisions in the Responsa run in both veins.[7]

Insurance

In a study commissioned by the Israeli Association of Insurance Companies, the laws and history of insurance as found in *halachah* sources were compiled. The history of insurance dates from the Talmud, and hundreds of interesting and topical court decisions were retrieved, many dating from the sixteenth century. A typical case was decided in the sixteenth century by Maharashdam (an acronym of *R*abbi *Sh*muel *D*e *M*edina), a rabbi in Salonika, Greece, then part of Turkey (sec. *Choshen Mishpat*, 220). Reuben offered maritime insurance to Shimon (Frank Doe) in Italy for a sea shipment of goods from Italy to Turkey, the two rival and often hostile superpowers of the era. The insurance contract stipulated that the goods were insured against loss at sea or piracy. While at sea, a storm arose, and the boat was in danger of sinking. The captain and crew, in order to lighten the vessel, broke off parts of the vessel itself, including the main mast, and threw them overboard. Upon regaining the shore, the boat owner sued the shippers for the damages he ensued in transport. The shippers paid. Are these losses covered by the insurance contract or not?

Maharashdam finds against the shipper, Shimon. First, the insurer never included such an act of self-destruction in his policy; indeed the collection of such damages by the ship owner is almost to be construed as an act of theft. Second, there is no evidence that the ship would have sunk, if the act of self-destruct would have not been perpetrated.

Reuben, the insurer, is thus to be freed of his responsibilities.[8]

Abortion

Is an abortion permitted to be performed on a pregnant woman who had come in contact with a disease, such as rubella, capable of generating defects in the fetus? This question was posed to Rabbi Y. Y. Weinberg, a deceased contemporary rabbi in Montreux, Switzerland, formerly Rector of the Hildesheimer Rabbinical Seminary of Berlin. His decision was that it may be performed during the first forty days of pregnancy because at this stage the fetus is to be considered "plain water." Afterward, only in case of danger to the mother's life can an abortion be considered; *danger* includes a psychological hazard to the mother's health. Nevertheless, even in such a case he raises doubts as to the permissibility of such an operation (*Seridei Esh* III:127).[9]

Wife Beating

Should an order be issued by the court for the removal of the husband from the home, upon the claim of the wife that he has assaulted her, although this occurred only once?

A number of relevant responsa were retrieved. In general, the sources do not deal with the problem of the husband's leaving because the home usually belonged to the husband. Most of the sources dealt with the severity of wife beating and wife baiting. If the phenomenon is repeated, it becomes grounds for coercing the husband to grant a bill of divorce. On the other hand, a one-time occurrence is definitely not grounds for divorce; an "appeasement program" (such as marriage counseling), is usually in order.

Rashba (IV: 168) finds that a wife has the right to refuse to live with her mother-in-law if the mother-in-law bears her ill will. His reasoning is that even the husband is not allowed to discomfort his wife, and certainly his mother is not allowed to.

In another responsum (VII: 477) Rashba finds that a husband is forbidden to strike his wife, and it is her right in such circumstances to leave the domicile: "No one can live in a cage with a snake" (after *Ketubot* 72a). The court is bid to rebuke the husband, fine him, and warn him that if this practice continues, he will be coerced into granting a bill of divorce. Note that divorce was the last resort.

Tashbetz (an acronymn for the Responsa of R. *Sh*imon *b*en *Tz*emach Duran, Algiers, fourteenth-fifteenth century; II: 8) decides along similar lines: a husband who torments his wife beyond her bearing is forced by the court into granting a bill of divorce and paying alimony (*ketubah*).

Payment

Rates of payment for certain services may be poorly or not at all defined at the time of agreement. How are these figures to be ascertained?[10]

An interesting decision is found in Rashba (IV:125). One who has brought clients to a given store is entitled to a fee, if such is the custom in vogue among storekeepers in general. The right to payment for services derives from the benefit accrued to the storekeeper rather than from agreement.

In another decision (*Meyuchasot* 70), Rashba considered the following case: Reuben hired a skilled worker, such as a jeweler or dyer, for a given period but then refused to consummate the contract. The worker now claims payment for breach of contract. The judgment is in favor of the worker. How do we estimate his payment?

The worker is to receive the going rate paid in the given profession for an equivalent worker, minus a small amount of money based upon the fact that he did not actually work. This adjustment is to be defined according to the criterion of how much of his salary a given worker would be willing to forego in order not to have to perform the work involved.

Commenting on the above decision, Tashbetz (I:64) remarks that this decision propounding adjustment does not apply to a teacher of religion because a principled worker would never agree to sit idle rather than work.

Maharashdam (II: Pt. 1, 335) finds that if an artisan's pay has not been fixed by contract, he is to be paid at the going rate of the profession—but at the bottom of the pay scale for a similar worker rather than at the top.

Placement of Children[11]

In the Responsa of Radvaz (an acronymn of *R*abbi *D*avid *b*en *Z*imra, Cairo and Israel, sixteenth century; I:263) we find the following case. In the wake of a divorce, the court dealt with the following situation: A minor daughter had been placed with the mother. The mother has committed an act of harlotry and has even given birth to an illegitimate child. The father claims his daughter, now aged seven, on the grounds that he does not want her to learn the licentious ways of his ex-spouse. The *halachah* usually favors placing a minor daughter with the mother in a broken home situation because the mother is the natural teacher for the daughter "of the ways of women," which includes modest behavior. In this case, however, the court is to act in the best interest of the child by awarding her to the father; or, in the event that there is no father, to other relatives, or, if there are no relatives, to a foster home.

In another Responsum (I:123), the following case was dealt with by Radvaz: Reuben's wife died, leaving a sickly infant. Reuben goes to work and leaves the child with neighbors. His wife's mother demands custody of the child, for the good of the child. The verdict is that although in general a minor son, over the age of six, is to be placed with the father rather than the mother, the best interest of the child is to guide the court. In this case, the grandmother is awarded custody.

The Right to Strike

One of the all-too-recurrent economic problems of modern life is unrest in labor-employer relations. The ethical, social, and legal problems involved are obviously numerous and complex. We searched the Responsa sources for the decisions rendered in the following typical question: Does a worker under contract have the right to refuse to continue to work under his original contract conditions when the goods involved are perishable?

The computer search turned up the following principle, originating in the Mishnah (*Baba Metziah* 75b), which was well documented in many different decisions: while no one can physically force a worker to work—this would be equivalent to slavery—nevertheless, should he breach his contract and the said goods perish, the worker would be legally liable for the damage. Alternatively, the employer can hire other workers to complete the contracted task at the expense of the breaching group.[12]

The Rights, Responsibilities and Duties of Policemen

During the period of Jewish internal autonomous rule, the community was governed by a three-part form of government, which approximated the present-day legislative, judicial and executive branches of the governing body in most democratic societies. The rabbinic court (*bet din*) was the judicial, the communal board of governors (*parnassim*) was the legislative, and the agent of the court—the policeman (*shleach bet din*)—carried out the orders of the court and the board of governors. Among the main tasks assigned to policemen was the collection of debts and communal taxes.

Rabbi Eliyahu ben Chaim, rabbi in Constantinople during the second half of the sixteenth century, was asked to find in a given case of policemen's privileges (Responsa number 111). His written verdict defined the basic rights of policemen. The circumstances were that Reuben, a constable acting in his capacity as such, claimed from Shimon the taxes owed by Shimon to the community. When Shimon failed to respond, sharp words were exchanged during the heat of the moment. Shimon accused Reuben of pocketing part of the collections and similarly cast aspersions on the honor of the constable's ancestors. The constable actually was the initiator, commenting upon the honor of Shimon's family. This unfortunate exchange took place before a large crowd. The case was referred to Rabbi ben Chaim and his court.

The verdict was that a constable is allowed to use force in performance of his duties, if necessary, with no personal obligation encumbent for such use of force if injury has incurred. Certainly then no judgment can be brought against him for defamation of character, slander or insult. Nevertheless, this privilege is restricted to the absolutely necessary for fulfillment of the constable's appointed task. In the given situation, Reuben has overstepped this area; personal enmity is detected in his words. On the other hand, Shimon has insulted an agent of the court (and the community), which is equivalent to contempt of court, an infraction of a Biblical injunction (see Exod. 22:27). He is liable to the ban for such contempt. Even if the policeman were to waive his case, such a waiver is invalid: the honor of the court and the entire community has been insulted. However, it does appear that the constable was not within his jurisdiction; it was he who started the exchange, needlessly. Thus both are in the wrong. The policeman must apologize for the slurs cast on Shimon and his family; Shimon is to be fined but not placed under the ban (that is, a lightened punishment is to be meted out).[13]

Punishment for Assaulting a Policeman or Judge

Commenting upon a cowardly nighttime attack (from hiding) upon a judge, Rabbi Yehudah ben Asher (ben HaRosh), a rabbi in Toledo, Spain, at the beginning of the fourteenth century, suggests that the punishment scale should in general be severe for such acts, graded as follows: a plain citizen, a servant of the community (policeman) and a judge. The respect due to a judge, upon whom rests the responsibility for regulating society and its common good—"without the judge, the strong would swallow up the weak . . . because of the judges, the world functions in peace"—is encumbent even during the periods when he is not acting in his official capacity (the policeman also?; Resp. Zichron Yehudah 79).[14]

Jewish Law Service

A service for lawyers and court judges was inaugurated at the beginning of 1978. After a series of workshops for these potential users, an agreement was entered into with the Israeli Bar Association whereby a lawyer could order Jewish law materials from the Responsa Project for use in court cases. The service is subsidized by the Bar Association. Three problems faced the project in this program: lack of demand, because Jewish law is binding in Israel only for the realm of family law; user awareness and education as to the nature and capabilities of the computer service; and use of the materials, because most Israeli jurists were not trained in the use of Responsa or the intricacies of Jewish law. Although introductory courses in Jewish law are standard and required in law schools, as are courses in family law (where Jewish law and rabbinic courts have jurisdiction), use of primary sources is usually beyond the capabilities of the average lawyer.

As for the first problem, popularization of the materials will, we hope, expedite the use of Jewish law by the profession. Possibly the Knesset would also make use of such materials standard. To solve the problem of user awareness and education, the project presented a series of workshops and demonstrations for the legal public. Additionally, a column dealing with topical questions and their answers in Jewish law was inaugurated in the journal of the Bar Association, *Heidei Din.* As for the third problem, a faculty member of the Bar-Ilan University's Law School was added to the Project's staff to process the legal queries, primarily to summarize the yield of a given computer search in terms meaningful to a lawyer, in a form fitting for submission before the court. Full-text printouts of the relevant documents, together with position-paper summaries of the decisions, are the standard materials presented to the lawyer.

As of May 1979, about one hundred and thirty search requests had been received by the project, almost half of them in the realm of family law. Thus the service has slowly caught on with the advocates; hundreds of searches in legal topics have been run successfully prior to the service for students, scholars and research institutions.

Some Planned Developments

Being a university-promoted project, many of the ongoing activities and of the planned developments in the Responsa Project are centered around research, both in computer science and in Judaica. In the former, for example, new ideas for data compression and file handling are being sought, local feedback techniques for enhancing the system's performance will be further pursued, and topics in Hebrew computational linguistics (such as mechanical compilation of concordances, mechanical resolution of lexical ambiguity, syntactical analysis by computers) will be investigated. In Judaica, special topics (such as insurance) will be selected for in-depth study, various citation indexes for Talmudic scholars will be prepared, and experiments for using full-text systems for literary analysis of contemporary Hebrew prose will be conducted.

Following is a list of planned developments that are of direct interest to the general reader of this report.

Developing the Online Version

The online version of the Responsa retrieval system is still in its infancy, and one of the major endeavors for the near future is its perfection. Ultimately this mode will have about the same appearance as the LEXIS or JURIS online programs, but with a few distinctive features.

- A strong linguistic component that automatically gives the user all of the linguistic variants of the submitted keywords and expressions, as well as hints about possible semantically or topically related keywords that have been missed by the user.
- A rich and varied repertoire of metrical and logical operators, including the sentence and paragraph operators.
- A variety of display formats for the search yield, including KWIC lists, text excerpts, and others, sorted by appropriate keys, and including free passage from one display format to the other.

As it appears now, the online version will not make the batch obsolete. Rather, both will be used side by side but with different goals. Simple, narrow or rapid searches will be run to completion on the online versions.

For more complex or general topics, one would usually use the conversational mode for browsing in the data base, trying various keywords or citations, looking at some of the retrieved documents, and after setting up the search policy, running a complete batch search to study in depth the wealth of printed output retrieved.

Enlarging the Responsa Data Base and Building Alternate Data Bases

Enlarging the Responsa data base is a continuing process, subject to availability of funds. Again, by the summer of 1980, it is expected that the data base will consist of 150 volumes, containing some 46,000 documents. Our original goal was set for about 300 volumes, since this was considered by most experts as the "critical mass" that will give the project its full impetus. A tentative (but almost final) list of these books has been already drawn up by a committee of experts.

The feasibility of using the project's program for other Hebrew-language data bases is under study. Some of the possibilities are Israeli Supreme Court decisions, State Comptroller's reports, Supreme Rabbinic Court decisions, and the Knesset (Israeli Parliament) minutes.

Overseas Service

At present, all overseas users are serviced by the mails. In development is the installation of a copy of the data base and of the online programs at a central computer installation in New York City and hooking up terminals located at various Jewish institutions of learning or schools of law at different campuses in the United States to this computer. Also under study is the possibility of sending queries (by Telex) directly to the project center in Israel for processing and transmitting the output in an extremely compressed form through telephone lines directly to the computer in New York, where it will be decompressed, printed and transmitted to the sender. Ultimately duplication of the entire system (programs and data bases) and its installation somewhere in the United States (probably at Yeshiva University in New York) will be considered.

Notes

1. See introduction to Rabbi Dr. Isaac Herzog, *The Main Institutions of Jewish Law,* 2d ed. (London: Soncino Press, 1965), vol. 1, and, especially, M. Elon, *The Principles of Jewish Law* (Jerusalem: Keter Publishing House Jerusalem, 1973), introduction, chap. 1, and bibliography. Elon is the main reference for the background material presented here on the various Jewish law topics. See the Annotated Bibliography, appended to this chapter.

2. See, for example, Izhak Englard, *Religious Law in Israeli Legal System* (Jerusalem: Hebrew University, 1975).

3. See Elon, *The Principles of Jewish Law* especially 39 and f.

4. See Solomon Freehoff, *The Responsa Literature* (Philadelphia: Jewish Publication Society, 1959), and his *A Treasury of Responsa* (Philadelphia: Jewish Publication Society, 1963).

5. See J. F. Horty, "Searching Statutory Law by Computer," Interim Report No. 2 (Health Law Center, University of Pittsburgh, Pittsburgh, Pennsylvania, May 1962).

6. See Elon, *The Principles of Jewish Law,* art. Betrothal, 353.

7. On communal enactments, see Elton, ibid., art. *Takkanot. HaKahal,* 654. Even if Reuben were to refuse to answer "amen" to the communal enactment or even to swear that he would not accept the legislation, he is bound to it. See Rashba *Meyuchasot* 280 and 288, among others.

For communal enactment subject to rabbinic review and objective laws of justice, see, for example Rashba V:178: "The community does not have the power to steal the money of [the individual], to take it for themselves." See also Elon, *The Principles of Jewish Law.*

8. On insurance, see Passamaneck, *Insurance in Rabbinic Law* (Edinburgh: University of Edinburgh Press, 1974). See also M. Slae's book review in *Dine Israel* 6, 1975, p. cxxxi-cxxxix. Slae is currently preparing a major work on insurance in *halachah* sources.

9. See Elon, *The Principles of Jewish Law,* Abortion, 482.

10. Ibid., Labor Law, 309.

11. Ibid., Parent and Child, 427.

12. Ibid., Labor Law, 309.

13. Ibid., Slander, 513, Police Offenses, 519, Contempt of Court, 518.

14. Ibid., Contempt of Court, 518.

Annotated Bibliography

In the framework of this survey, the treatment of the various computer, legal, and Judaic points was necessarily brief. For the benefit of readers interested in further pursuing some of the areas dealt with, we list a selected bibliography of publications relevant to the various spheres encountered in the chapter. Though many of the primary sources are in Hebrew, we mention only English-language materials here. Some of the Responsa Project's own publications are still available upon request (address: Responsa Project, Computer Science Building, Bar-Ilan University, Ramat-Gan, Israel).

Jewish Law

The amount of English-language materials available on Jewish Law is lamentably sparse. For English-language readers who are unfamiliar with the basics of Jewish law, for years the only text available was the brilliant work of the former Chief Rabbi of Israel: Rabbi Dr. Isaac Herzog, *The Main Institutions of Jewish Law,* 2d ed. (London and New York: Soncino Press, 1965). A planned five-volume set, only two volumes were published: *The Law of Property* (vol. 1) and the *Law of Obligations* (vol. II). In these volumes Rabbi Herzog compares the Jewish legal system to the ancient Roman and to the modern (that is, modern as of the 1930's—

the first edition was published in 1936) British Common Law. Due to the burdens of his post as Chief Rabbi of Israel, during the Holocaust Period and that of the establishment of the state, Rabbi Herzog was never able to finish the set.

A relatively new, important source for readings in Jewish law is *Encyclopedia Judaica* (Jerusalem: Keter Pub. Co., 1972). M. Elon, Professor of Jewish Law at the Hebrew University and Supreme Court judge, long active in furthering Jewish law in legislation, court decisions, and legal education, acted as Section Editor for the Jewish law division in the *Judaica,* contributed many articles to it, and was responsible for organizing the various topics in it.

A handy compilation of the articles on Jewish law in the *Judaica* is: *The Principles of Jewish Law* (Jerusalem: Keter, 1975, edited by Professor Elon). This is in fact "the sum total of the Jewish Law articles in the Encyclopedia [*Judaica;* these] form a complete unit which offers the reader a true and methodical description of the principles and the institutions of Jewish law in all its areas" (from the preface). This text, by definition encyclopedic in nature and containing an extensive multilingual bibliography for each article, is our basic reference.

A list of the articles on Jewish Law in the *Judaica,* grouped by the various categories of legal study, is found in *Dine Israel,* ed. Z. Falk and A. Kirschenbaum, Faculty of Law, Tel-Aviv University, Tel-Aviv, vol. 4 (1973). The *Dine Israel* annual series also contains an English-language section of research and survey articles devoted to Jewish law, including a review of decisions rendered by Isareli courts involving Jewish law.

For a selected, annotated bibliographical survey of primary Jewish legal sources see John Townsend, "Rabbinic Sources," in *The Study of Judaism: Bibliographical Essays* (New York: Ktav, 1972), pp. 35-80.

On Jewish law in general, see also George Horwitz, *The Spirit of Jewish Law* (New York: Central, 1953).

On the place of Jewish law in the Israeli legal system, see Izhak Englard, *Religious Law in Israeli Legal System* (Jerusalem: Hebrew University, 1975). On the place of Jewish law in the American court system, see B. J. Mieslin, "Jewish Law of Marriage in American Courts," *Journal of Family Law* 2 (1971): 271, and "Enforceability of Religious Law in Secular Courts: It's Kosher but Is It Constitutional?" *Michigan Law Review* 71 (1973): 1641.

An excellent book on the position and the laws of the woman in *halachah* is M. Meiselman, *Jewish Woman in Jewish Law* (New York: Ktav Publishing Co. and Yeshiva University Press, 1978).

The topic of Jewish law is usually found in the American indexing literature.

The Responsa Literature

A number of good basic descriptions of the Responsa literature are available in English. In particular, two volumes by Solomon Freehoff are excellent introductions to the literature: *The Responsa Literature* (Philadelphia: Jewish Publication Society, 1959), and *A Treasury of Responsa* (Philadelphia: Jewish Publication Society, 1963).

Good survey articles can be found in the following encyclopedia articles: Jacob Lauterbach, "She'elot U'teshuvot," *The Jewish Encyclopedia* (London and New York: Funk and Wagnalls, 1901), 11: 240-251; Chaim Rabin, "Hebrew Literature: Halaka," *Encyclopedia Britannica* (1970): 11: 286; and Shlomo Tal, "Responsa,"

Encyclopedia Judaica (Jerusalem: Keter Pub. Co., 1972), 14: 83-95; Menachem Slae, "Responsa," *Encyclopedia Judaica, Supplementary Volume* (Jerusalem: Keter Pub. Co.).

The standard English work on *halachic* (indeed on Jewish) literature in general is by Meyer Waxman: *A History of Jewish Literature* (New York: Bloch, 1933). Although much new material has been subsequently produced, it is still an excellent text. A long section on the Responsa in volumes 2 and 3 traces the development of the literature through the various eras and areas.

R. D. Barnett has inaugurated a series of volumes dealing with Sephardic Jews. To date, one volume has appeared, and in it, the former head of Jews College, H. Zimmels, has contributed a survey article on Spanish Jewish responsa: Hirsh Zimmels, in *The Sephardi Heritage,* ed. R. D. Barnett (London: Vallentine, Mitchell, 1971), 1: 367-401.

On the use of the Responsa in the wake of the reestablishment of the State of Israel and the need for indexing systems, see the brief introductory remarks of Isaac Halevi Herzog, in his (English) foreword to *Otzar HaPoskim,* by Otzar HaPoskim, 3d ed. (Jerusalem, 1962), and Menachem Elon, in his (English) introduction to the *Indices to the Responsa of Jewish Law, the Responsa of R. Asher b. Yehiel,* Hebrew University, Jerusalem, 1965.

The Legal System of Israel

The following are somewhat outdated introductions to the Israeli legal system: Y. Freudenheim, *Government in Israel* (Dobbs-Ferry, N.Y.: Ocean, 1967), and H. E. Baker, *Legal System of Israel* (Jerusalem: Israel University Press, 1968); and a bibliographical reference: Wegner, *A Bibliography of Israel Law in English and Other European Languages* (Jerusalem: Hebrew University, 1972).

The latest bibliographical introduction to the Israeli legal system is: Snyder, "Guide to Israeli Legal Bibliography: Primary Sources," *Law Library Journal,* American Association of Law Libraries, Chicago, Vol. 70, 1977, p. 14-19.

The Responsa Project

DESCRIPTION

A first publication describing the project and aimed at the Jewish general reader is A. S. Fraenkel, "A Retrieval System for the Responsa," *Proceedings of the Association of Orthodox Jewish Scientists* (A.O.J.S.), no. 2 (1968): 3-42. An update of this article is Y. Choueka, M. Slae, and S. Spero, "A Computerized Retrieval System for the Responsa Literature—Revisited," *Proceedings of A.O.J.S.,* no. 5 (New York: Feldheim Publishing, 1978).

A paper describing the Responsa system to law students and scholars is A. M. Schreiber, "Computerized Storage and Retrieval of Case Law without Indexing: The Hebrew Responsa Project," *Law and Computer Technology* 2 (November 1969): 14-22.

The first formal, complete description of the project is given in Y. Choueka, M. Cohen, J. Dueck, A. S. Fraenkel, and M. Slae, "Full-text Document Retrieval: Hebrew Legal Texts," in *Proceedings of the Association of Computing Machinery Symposium on Information Storage and Retrieval,* eds. J. Minker and S. Rosenfeld

(College Park: University of Maryland, April 1971), pp. 61-69. A much enlarged version of this paper (by the same authors) emphasizing the linguistic problems and their solution is *Full-text Case Law Retrieval: The Responsa Project,* Working Papers on Legal Information Processing Series, Pamphlet No. 3 (Berlin: Schweitzer Verlag, 1972).

An updated short review of the Project, emphasizing the local feedback techniques, is A. S. Fraenkel, "The Responsa Project—An Overview (Everything you always wanted to know about the Responsa Project but were afraid to ask)." Expanded summary (*Proc. Third Symp. on Legal Data Processing in Europe,* Oslo, 1975, Council of Europe, Strasbourg, 1976, pp. 131-141), also in *Jurimetrics J.* 16 (1976): 149-156, and *Informatica e Diritto II* (September 1976): 362-370.

The following report contains some bibliographical data on the project as of summer 1976 (a short overview of the research activities, a list of the books forming the data base and short biographies of their authors, a list of search topics run on the system, and a list of publications): Y. Choueka, *The Responsa Project: A Status Report,* Technical Report No. 11 (IRCOL, Bar-Ilan University, 1976).

A nontechnical but comprehensive description of the Project's activities, emphasizing the use of full-text systems for research in the humanities, is Y. Choueka, *Computerized Full-text Retrieval Systems and Research in the Humanities,* invited address to the Third International Conference on Computing in the Humanities (ICCH/3), Waterloo, 1977. To appear in *Computer and the Humanities Journal.*

APPLICATIONS IN THE HUMANITIES AND IN LEGAL STUDIES

Most of the publications in this topic are in Hebrew (a list is available upon request). Among the English publications are M. Slae, *References to Marranos in the Responsa of Rabbi Isaac Ber Sheshet, Information Retrieval by Computer,* Bar-Ilan University Yearbook, ed. H. Hirshberg and M. Beer (1969), vol. 7-8, pp. 47-64, and M. Slae, "Glass in the Responsa Literature: A Study by Computer," *Niv-Hamidrashia* II (1974): 110-119.

TECHNICAL ASPECTS

The following provide information on the linguistic problems: R. Attar, Y. Choueka, N. Dershowitz, and A. S. Fraenkel, "KEDMA—Linguistic Tools for Retrieval Systems," *Journal of the Association for Computing Machinery* (January 1978): 52-66, A. S. Frankel and E. Spitz, *Automatic Construction of Hebrew Concordances with Ramifications to English Concordances,* Technical Report No. 1 (IRCOL, Bar-Ilan University); Y. Choueka and F. Dreizin, "Mechanical Resolution of Lexical Ambiguity in a Coherent Text: Algorithms and Experimental Results," in *Proceedings of the Second International Conference on Computational Linguistics* (Ottawa, Canada, 1976).

On the local feedback techniques, see R. Attar, A. S. Fraenkel, and J. Stein, *Local Feedback in Full-text English and Hebrew Retrieval Systems,* Technical Report No. 5 (IRCOL, Bar-Ilan University), and R. Attar and A. S. Fraenkel, "Local Feedback in Full-text Retrieval System," *Journal of the Association for Computing Machinery* 24 (1977), pp. 394-417.

Index

About the Contributors

John A. Banks, Jr. is the Director of the Division of Legislative Services of the Commonwealth of Virginia, Richmond, Virginia.

Lawrence H. Berul (JD), formerly the Senior Vice President of Aspen Systems Corporation, is the President of Berul Associates, LTD., an information management consulting firm in Rockville, Maryland.

Jane Bortnick is an Analyst in Information Sciences for the Congressional Research Service, Library of Congress, Washington, D.C. and is the co-author with Mr. Chartrand of the book *State Legislature Use of Information Technology.*

Robert L. Chartrand is a Senior Specialist in Information Policy and Technology for the Congressional Research Service, Library of Congress, Washington, D.C. and a prominent author in the field of legislative information processing.

Yaacov Choueka is Professor, Department of Mathematics and Computer Science and Director, Institute for Information Retrieval and Computational Linguistics (IRCOL) at Bar-Ilan University, Ramat Gan, Israel, and is also head of the Responsa Project.

Patricia Coss is the Editor of the TECS Newsletter of the U.S. Customs Service, Department of the Treasury, Washington, D.C.

Stanley O. Croydon, Jr. has been with the Department of Justice since 1974 and is currently an attorney/adviser with their Systems Design and Development Staff, Justice Management Division. Previously, he worked on various legal and scientific computer projects with the U.S. House of Representatives, IBM, and McDonnell-Douglas Corporation.

Gordon K. Davidson (JD) is an associate in the law firm of Fenwick, Stone, Davis, & West, Palo Alto, California, and Associate Editor of *Jurimetrics Journal.*

Joseph L. Ebersole is the Deputy Director of the Federal Judicial Center, Washington, D.C. He is a graduate of the University of Southern California Law Center and a member of the California State Bar, the District of Columbia Bar, and the American Bar Association.

William Fenwick (LLB) is a partner in the firm of Fenwick, Stone, Davis & West, and the former Chairperson of the Committee on Law Relating to Computers of the American Bar Association Section of Science and Technology.

Robert Fitchett is the Deputy Administrator of the Legislative Evaluation and Accountability Program for the State of Washington, Olympia, Washington.

Neal Gregory is the Information Policy Liaison for the Computer Subcommittee of the U.S. House of Representatives Committee on House Administration, Washington, D.C., and an author in the field of legislative information processing.

Theodor Herman is an editor on the staff of West Publishing Company, St. Paul, Minnesota.

Dozier Johnson is the Director of the System and Data Processing Division of the Florida Legislature, Tallahassee, Florida.

James Keane (JD), formerly of Aspen Systems Corporation, is Manager, Litigation Support Services, Coopers & Lybrand, Certified Public Accountants, Los Angeles, California.

Robert S. McCormick (JD) is Director of Legal Systems for Informatics, Rockville, Maryland.

Edward C. Miller is the Staff Data Processing Coordinator for the State of Washington, Olympia, Washington.

Bruce F. Norton is Associate Professor of Government and Public Administration, School of Government and Public Administration, College of Public and International Affairs, The American University and Senior Staff Member, Advanced Study Program, The Brookings Institution. From 1969 to 1970, Dr. Norton was a member of the Working Group on Computers for Congress.

Larry P. Polansky, Esquire, formerly Deputy Court Administrator for the Supreme Court of Pennsylvania, is currently the Executive Officer of the District of Columbia Courts. Mr. Polansky is a member of the Pennsylvania and District of Columbia Bars and has written extensively in the area of information systems in the courts.

Steven E. Rosen (J.D.), formerly of Informatics, Inc., is Vice President for Data Management Services, Information Handling Services Corporation.

Aaron M. Schreiber is Professor of Law at Temple University School of Law, Philadelphia, Pennsylvania, Principal Investigator of the Responsa Project, and supervisor of its activities in the United States and the western hemisphere.

Menachem Slae (Rabbi) of the Institute for Information Retrieval and Computational Linguistics (IRCOL), Ramat Gan, Israel, manages the Judaica Research Group of the Responsa Project.

Karlyn D. Stanley, formerly the Director of Communications for Mead Data Central, Inc., is the Assistant to the Director, Office of Economic Crime Enforcement, Criminal Division, Department of Justice, Washington, D.C.

Michael Stern (LLB) is Regional Manager for Aspen Systems Corporation, Rockville, Maryland.

Richard O. White is the retired Code Revisor for the State of Washington, Olympia, Washington.

Victor John Yannacone, jr., an ardent advocate for environmental protection, is a partner in the law firm of Yannacone & Yannacone, Patchogue, N.Y.

ABOUT THE EDITOR

Beth Krevitt Eres, recently a consultant to the Weizmann Institute of Science in Rehovot, Israel, is completing a doctorate and teaching at the School of Library and Information Science, Drexel University, Philadelphia, Pennsylvania. She is the author of various articles and technical reports in the field of information science.